a cook's encyclopedia of

sauces

a cook's encyclopedia of sauces

transform your cooking with over 200 step-by-step great recipes for classic sauces, toppings, dips, dressings, marinades, relishes, condiments and accompaniments

consultant editor christine france

This edition is published by Hermes House, an imprint of Anness Publishing Ltd, Hermes House, 88–89 Blackfriars Road, London SE1 8HA; tel. 020 7401 2077; fax 020 7633 9499

www.hermeshouse.com; www.annesspublishing.com

If you like the images in this book and would like to investigate using them for publishing, promotions or advertising, please visit our website www.practicalpictures.com for more information.

Publisher: Joanna Lorenz
Project Editor: Simona Hill
Designer: Simon Wilder
Production Controller: Wendy Lawson

ETHICAL TRADING POLICY

Because of our ongoing ecological investment programme, you, as our customer, can have the pleasure and reassurance of knowing that a tree is being cultivated on your behalf to naturally replace the materials used to make the book you are holding. For further information about this scheme, go to www.annesspublishing.com/trees

Previously published as *The Complete Book of Sauces, Salsas, Dips, Relishes and Marinades.*

PUBLISHER'S NOTE

Although the advice and information in this book are believed to be accurate and true at the time of going to press, neither the authors nor the publisher can accept any legal responsibility or liability for any errors or omissions that may have been made nor for any inaccuracies nor for any loss, harm or injury that comes about from following instructions or advice in this book.

NOTES

For all recipes, quantities are given in both metric and imperial measures and, where appropriate, measures are also given in standard cups and spoons. Follow one set, but not a mixture because they are not interchangeable.
Standard spoon and cup measures are level.
1 tsp = 5ml, 1 tbsp = 15ml, 1 cup = 250ml/8fl oz
Australian standard tablespoons are 20ml. Australian readers should use 3 tsp in place of 1 tbsp for measuring small quantities of salt etc.
Medium eggs are used unless otherwise stated.

Contents

Introduction

Sauce-making has gained itself a reputation for being a difficult art, but in fact, most sauces are simplicity itself and can be made in a matter of minutes. True, there are some classic sauces whose preparation takes a little time and a degree of skill, but the skills are easily learned and you don't have to be a fully trained chef to achieve success.

Once you've mastered a few basic methods and simple techniques, you'll find the myth is dispelled and you'll have a collection of sauce recipes always to hand, ready to add a touch of individuality to your cooking, whether for everyday family meals or the most sophisticated dinner parties. Even if you lack the time or skills to cook elaborate dishes, sauces will add originality to your cooking, and transform even the plainest foods into something special.

Sauces can play many different roles in cookery, covering a variety of dishes and almost every occasion. A sauce may be used to complement a dish, adding a touch of piquancy, balancing flavours, or simply enhancing the appearance. Others are used to tenderize or moisten foods before and during cooking, or to bind ingredients together. Served in the form of a tasty dip or relish, they can give an added dimension to endless snacks or party dishes.

This book collects together a comprehensive collection of sauces, salsas, dips, relishes, marinades and dressings from traditional classics to modern ideas, which build to make an invaluable reference and source of creative ideas in your kitchen.

General Reference

Whether you are a novice cook who wants to add interest and new flavours to weekday meals, or an expert who would like to broaden your culinary repertoire, understanding the basics of sauce-making will provide a firm foundation for a lifetime of creative cooking. Many sauce-making ingredients such as flour and fat are basics in every kitchen. But adding just a few other well-chosen ingredients will provide you with a store cupboard from which to make a whole range of interesting and flavourful accompaniments to meals.

Sauce-making doesn't require any specialist equipment, and much of what you already own will be sufficient – a selection of pans, bowls, whisks, ladles, sieves, weighing scales and measuring jugs will ensure the correct equipment is always to hand.

The following pages provide a brief explanation of the science behind a successful sauce – which flours to use for a smooth texture, which fats add the best flavour, how much and what type of liquid to use and how to infuse flavours. All the basic methods of sauce-making are included from a classic white sauce to a rich roux and there are plenty of hints and tips to help you produce the best results.

Flours

There is a wide range of flours and thickening agents on the market. It is important to select the right product, since the choice of flour used for a sauce will determine not only the cooking method used, but the final texture and flavour of the finished sauce. These general guidelines should help remove any mystique involved.

PLAIN WHITE FLOUR

Also known as all-purpose flour, this is the standard choice for making roux-based sauces and gravies. Its fine, smooth texture combines easily with melted fat for a sauce with a roux base, so that when heated, the starch grains burst and cook, thickening the sauce liquid.

White flour usually contains 70–75 per cent of the wheatgrain. Most of the bran and wheatgerm have been removed during milling, leaving it almost white, so it is excellent for thickening white sauces. White flour is chemically bleached, making it pale in colour and therefore more suitable for white sauces than unbleached, stone-ground flours.

Below from left to right: Brown flour, wholemeal flour

Below: Sauce flour

SELF-RAISING, STRONG AND SOFT FLOURS

These are flours designed for specific baking uses, not for sauces, but could be used in an emergency if you run out of plain flour. Self-raising flour has chemical agents added during milling which react with heat to make cake mixtures rise during cooking. Strong flour has a higher proportion of gluten, making it most suitable for bread making. Soft flours have a lower gluten content, and are designed for cakes and pastries, but they also make a good thickener for smooth sauces.

Below: Plain flour

WHOLEMEAL, WHEATMEAL AND BROWN FLOURS

All of these flours contain more of the bran and wheatgerm, between 80 and 90 per cent of the grain, which gives them a nutty flavour and coarse texture, and a darker colour than plain white flour. Because of this, they are not usually chosen for making sauces, but if you don't mind the texture and colour, there's no reason why any of these flours should not be used for thickening sauces. The bonus is that they will add a little extra dietary fibre and nutrients to the dish.

SAUCE FLOUR

This flour has been recently introduced, and has a lower protein level than ordinary wheat flour, so that sauces made with it are less likely to go lumpy. It is designed specifically for making cooked white sauces and gravies. It is also a good choice for making healthier sauces, since it is suitable for those made by the all-in-one or blending method, in which no fat is used.

Below, clockwise from top left: Cornflour, custard powder, potato flour, arrowroot

CORNFLOUR

This fine ground maize flour is a gluten-free starch. It is light and smooth-textured, producing smooth, velvety-textured, lump-free sauces, usually made by the blending method. When first added to a clear liquid it gives a cloudy appearance, but on heating, the sauce becomes almost clear. Because of this, it is a popular choice for Chinese sauces, and its smooth texture makes it particularly suitable for using in sweet white sauces or those that are to be used for coating foods.

POTATO FLOUR

Also known as farine de fécule, potato flour is made from pure potato starch. It is very fine and smooth and is bright white in colour. It makes a light, clear thickener for sauces without affecting the flavour. You will need to use slightly less potato flour than ordinary plain flour for thickening. It is most suited to the blending method of sauce making, and is often used as a thickener in Chinese and Asian dishes and stir-fry sauces, so it is easily available from Oriental stores.

ARROWROOT

This is a finely ground powder made from the root of a tropical tree, which is grown in Central America. It is used in the same way as cornflour, for sauces made by the blending method, and gives a very smooth, clear, translucent appearance to sweet or savoury sauces without affecting either the colour or the flavour.

CUSTARD POWDER

A useful store-cupboard thickener for quick custard sauces, this is simply a coloured cornflour-based flour. For a quick custard, a similar result can be achieved by using a small amount of cornflour with a few drops of yellow food colouring and vanilla essence. Make into a sauce with milk by the blending method, and sweeten to taste.

STORING FLOUR

Store flour in a cool, dark, dry, airy place, away from steam or damp. Place the flour into a clean tin or a storage jar with a close-fitting lid, and always make sure you wash and dry the container thoroughly before refilling it. Check the "use by" dates, and use up the flour within the recommended pack date, or replace it. Don't add new flour to old in a storage jar – it is always best to use up the older flour first.

Once opened, plain white flour can be stored under the right conditions for up to six months, but wholemeal and brown flours have a higher fat content so these are best used within two months. Like all food, flour is best used while fresh. Make sure it is stored in dark, cool conditions; buy it in small quantities and plan to use it quickly rather than storing it indefinitely.

Fats

Fats make sauces palatable, and improve the flavour and texture. The ones usually used in sauces are "yellow" fats such as butter or margarine, or oils. Many are added to cooked sauces as a base with flour, as in a roux, or in beurre manié where the fat and flour are heated together to cook the starch grains for thickening. The classic emulsified sauces, such as hollandaise or mayonnaise, use either melted butter or liquid oils, beaten with eggs to enrich and thicken to a thick emulsion. The same principle is used in reduced sauces such as beurre blanc, or in oil-based salad dressings such as vinaigrette, where the fat is whisked into a reduced or well-flavoured liquid base to make a smooth emulsion. In salsas and purées, oil is added for flavour, being stirred or drizzled on to the ingredients.

TYPES OF FAT

Saturated fats are solid at room temperature, and are the ones that can raise cholesterol levels in the blood. Polyunsaturated fats can help lower cholesterol levels; mono-unsaturated fats, which are beneficial in regulating cholesterol levels, are liquid but can be made solid by a process known as hydrogenation. This is the process used to make margarines and spreads.

Clockwise from top left: Ghee, clarifed butter, concentrated butter

BUTTER

A natural product made by churning cream, butter has an 80 per cent fat content, which is saturated fat. Butter is made in two basic types, sweetcream and lactic, and both are available salted, lightly salted or unsalted. The choice will depend largely on flavour, according to whether you are making a sweet or savoury sauce.

Clarified butter, ghee or concentrated butters will withstand higher temperatures than untreated butter, and will not burn as easily.

MARGARINE

Soft (tub) margarines, made from a blend of vegetable oils and/or animal oils, have a soft, spreadable texture. Hard (packet) margarines have a firmer texture and are made from animal and vegetable fats. Both types have the same fat content as butter, and can be used as a direct substitute for butter in making sweet and savoury sauces. As the flavour is inferior to butter, margarines are best chosen for more robustly flavoured sauces where their own flavour will not be as noticeable.

Left: Lactic unsalted butter (left), sweetcream salted butter

Above, from left: Polyunsaturated, olive, dairy, and reduced-fat spreads

SPREADS

The wide choice of different spreads on the market is confusing to say the least, but as a rough guide, unless they are labelled "low-fat", or "very low-fat", they are generally suitable for sauce-making. After that, choice is very much a matter of personal preference.

Polyunsaturated vegetable oil spreads: Products described in this way are made either from a single vegetable oil or sunflower oil alone, or from a blend of different vegetable oils. They vary in fat content from 61 to 79 per cent.

Monounsaturated vegetable oil spreads: Made from olive oil or rapeseed oil, these vary in fat content from 60 to 75 per cent.

Dairy spreads: These contain cream or buttermilk to retain a buttery flavour and smooth texture, while providing a lower-fat alternative to butter. The fat content varies between 61 and 75 per cent.

Reduced fat spreads: These products are either made from vegetable oils alone or may also contain some dairy or animal fat. Their fat content is between 50 and 60 per cent.

Low-fat spreads and very low-fat spreads: These spreads, popular with the weight-conscious, contain less than 40 per cent fat, and are often as low as 25 per cent. They are not recommended for cooking, although they can be added to all-in-one method sauces.

STORING FAT

All solid fats should be stored in the fridge, below 4°C/39°F. They should be covered or closely wrapped to protect them from light and air. Keep them away from strong-smelling foods as they can absorb other flavours easily. (The butter storage compartment in most fridges is in the door, and is not quite so cold as other parts, so the butter should not become too hard.) Oils tend to solidify at low temperatures, so these are best kept in a cool store cupboard with a temperature of 4–12°C/39–54°F, but keep them away from light, which will cause them to deteriorate more quickly.

Above: Margarine tub (left) and block

Right: Very low-fat (left) and low-fat spreads

OILS

These are fats that are liquid at room temperature, and are used in emulsion sauces such as mayonnaise or in salad dressings, usually balanced with vinegar or other acids such as citrus juices. However, they can also be used as a direct replacement for butter or hard fats in roux or other flour-thickened sauces, with good results. With the exception of coconut oil and palm oil, they are mostly rich in unsaturated fat, which helps reduce cholesterol levels. The choice of individual oils for a particular sauce depends largely on flavour and personal taste.

Groundnut oil: Made from peanuts, this is usually used where a mild flavour is required.

Sesame seed oil: Usually used for flavouring Oriental sauces at the end of cooking, as it has an intense, rich flavour and burns easily when heated. However it can be heated with care, or mixed half and half with another oil, such as groundnut, if necessary.

Soya oil: A mild flavoured oil which will withstand high temperatures, this keeps well and is economical to use.

Sunflower oil: A little more expensive to use than soya oil, this versatile, light-flavoured oil is good for sauces or dressings, as it does not mask other flavours.

Nut oils: Walnut and hazelnut oils are the most commonly used nut oils for dressings, lending their rich, distinctive flavours to salads. Use in moderation, perhaps combined with a milder oil, as the flavours can be strong.

OLIVE OILS

The characteristics and quality of olive oils vary and depend on variety, growing region and method of production. Many are blended, but the best quality oils are produced on individual estates. For most sauces, including mayonnaise, it's best to choose virgin or pure olive oil, and keep the more expensive extra virgin ones for salad dressings, or for drizzling directly over foods. It is more economical to buy olive oils in larger quantities.

Extra virgin first pressed or cold pressed olive oils: These oils are made from what is literally the first pressing of the olives, with no additional treatment such as heat or blending. By law, these oils never have more than 1 per cent acidity, ensuring a fine flavour. They have a very distinctive flavour, as well as a pungent aroma. They are usually a deep green colour and are sometimes cloudy, although both of these factors vary according to the area where the oil has been produced.

Virgin olive oil: This is also cold pressed and unrefined, but has a higher acidity content than extra virgin oil, with a maximum level of 1 to 1.5 per cent.

Pure olive oil: This comes from the third or fourth pressing of the olives, and is usually blended. It has a maximum acid content of 2 per cent. It is widely used in cooking since it is not overpowering.

Light olive oil: This is from the last pressing of the fruit and has the lightest flavour of all.

Below, from left: Groundnut oil, sunflower oil, soya oil, sesame oil, walnut oil

The Store Cupboard

A well-stocked store cupboard makes every cook's life a lot easier, and when it comes to sauce making, it really makes sense. Just by keeping a few basic ingredients in stock, you will always be able to whip up an impromptu sauce when the occasion demands, transforming a simple dish into something really special.

STOCK CUBES AND POWDERS

There is a wide choice of commercial stock cubes and powders on the market, and these vary in flavour and quality. Good-quality products make adequate substitutes for fresh stock, and certainly they are very convenient to use. However, some tend to be quite salty, so allow for this when adding other seasonings. Follow the pack directions for quantities to use. Generally speaking, it is worth paying a little more for good-quality stock cubes or powder, and it is worth choosing one that is made with natural ingredients, which should impart a more natural flavour.

Many supermarkets also now sell ready-made cartons of basic fresh stocks on the chilled foods counter, such as beef, chicken, fish and vegetable stock, and these are a good substitute for home-made if you're short of time to make your own.

Canned consommé makes an excellent substitute for a good brown stock in rich savoury sauces, so is well worth keeping handy in the store cupboard. If you need a light stock, the colour of consommé may be too dark, but brands vary.

CANNED TOMATOES AND SAUCES

Since many of the plum tomatoes we buy out of season in this country are lacking in flavour, it's a safer bet to go for good-quality canned tomatoes in recipes, either whole or chopped. The best are from Italy, so check the label carefully. *Polpa di pomodoro* are finely chopped or crushed. Avoid those with added herbs or spices, which are best added fresh.

Above: Consommé
Left: Stock cubes and powder
Below, clockwise from left: Passata, sugocasa, whole plum tomatoes, tomato purée, chopped tomatoes

Crushed or creamed tomatoes: Sold as sugocasa, polpa and passata, and usually packed in convenient jars or bottles, these are invaluable for sauces. Sugocasa and polpa have a chunky texture, and passata is sieved to a smooth purée.

Tomato purée: This is concentrated, cooked tomato pulp in a strong, thick paste, and is sold in tubes or cans. The strength of different brands varies, so use with care or the flavour can overpower a sauce. Sun-dried tomato paste is a purée of sun-dried tomatoes with olive oil. It has a sweet, rich flavour, and is milder than ordinary tomato purée.

Below, top row from left: Oyster sauce, soy sauce, Worcestershire sauce, fish sauce, hot pepper sauce. Bottom row: Red pesto, green pesto, English mustard

Cook's Tip

Chopped canned tomatoes are usually more expensive than whole ones, so you can save valuable pennies by simply chopping them yourself.

COMMERCIAL SAUCES

The huge range of commercially-made flavouring sauces now available is a boon to the creative cook. Some of the most useful ones to keep in your store cupboard are:

Hot pepper sauces: Widely used in West Indian and South American cooking, there are many versions of pepper sauce, the most famous being Tabasco. Use with caution, as they can be fiery hot. These sauces will pep up the flavour of almost any savoury sauce, marinade or dressing.

Mustards: Ready-made mustards are a blend of ground mustard seeds with flour and salt, often with wine, herbs and other spices. Dijon is often used for classic French sauces and for dressings such as vinaigrette and mayonnaise – it also helps to stabilize the emulsion. Yellow English mustard is a good choice to give colour and bite to cheese sauce or to flavour rich gravies for meat. Milder German mustard is good for a barbecue sauce to serve with chops or sausages. Mild, creamy American mustard is squeezed on hotdogs or burgers. Wholegrain mustard gives a pleasant texture, particularly to creamy savoury sauces and dressings.

Oyster sauce: A thicker-textured sauce made with the extract of real oysters, this adds a delicious sweet-savoury flavour to sauces for accompanying meat, fish or vegetables.

Pesto: Commercially made pesto is sold in jars, either the traditional green basil pesto, or a red pesto made from sun-dried tomatoes. Use it just as it is as a replacement for fresh pesto sauce to stir into pasta, pepped up with a little freshly grated Parmesan cheese or an extra drizzle of olive oil. You can also add it by the spoonful to enrich and enhance the flavour of tomato sauces, salsas

Coconut Milk and Cream

Coconut milk and cream are used widely in Oriental dishes, particularly those based on spicy and curried sauces. They can be used rather like dairy products, for thickening, enriching and flavouring.

Coconut milk: This is available in cans and longlife packs. It is similar in thickness to single cream.

Coconut cream: This has the thickness of double cream. Creamed coconut is solid and white; it is sold in solid blocks, so you can cut off just the amount you need and melt it into sauces.

Right, clockwise from left: Coconut cream, coconut milk, creamed coconut

and dressings. Once the jar is opened, it should be treated as fresh and stored in the fridge.

Soy sauce: Although this is traditionally used for Chinese and Japanese foods, there is no need to limit its use to Oriental dishes. Use it to flavour and colour all kinds of savoury sauces, marinades and dressings. Light soy sauce is good in light, sweet-and-sour or stir-fry sauces for fish or vegetables, and the richer, sweeter dark soy sauce is best with rich meat sauces such as satays, or for barbecue sauces.

Thai fish sauce or *nam pla*: This is a classic Thai sauce made from fermented fish. It has a pungent flavour and is best in cooked sauces. It adds a richness to sauces for both meat and fish.

Worcestershire sauce: This classic English sauce has its origins in India. Its spicy, mellowed flavour enhances savoury sauces, marinades and dressings of any type.

VINEGARS

These are made from alcoholic bases of malt, wine, beer, cider, rice wine and sugar, and most of these can be used to enhance flavour in sauces or as emulsifiers. Red and white wine vinegars and fruit vinegars are particularly useful for salad dressings, and rice vinegars add authentic flavours to Oriental sauces. When using some of the dark, long-matured sherry or balsamic vinegars, bear in mind that they often have intense, powerful flavours and you may only need a few drops.

Below, from left: Balsamic vinegar, white wine vinegar, red wine vinegar, raspberry vinegar

Herbs and Spices

Many sauce recipes call for herbs and spices to add flavour and colour, and there's no end to the variety you can buy nowadays, especially in the larger supermarkets and good Oriental grocers. Generally speaking, herbs are the leafy tops and stems of an edible plant, and spices are from the berries, seeds, bark, and roots.

CULINARY HERBS

It's worth growing a few of the more useful common herbs yourself. Some herbs grown in pots on the kitchen windowsill,will always be handy when you need to snip off a few sprigs. It is considerably cheaper, too, as supermarket fresh herbs, even the ones in pots, have a limited life and can be quite costly. A useful basic selection to grow at home would include parsley, chives, thyme, mint, oregano, sage, bay and dill.

When cooking with herbs, you don't need to be too precise. Treat the measurements quoted in recipes as a general guide, and add the herbs according to your personal preference.

Dried and Frozen Herbs

Dried herbs are useful to keep in the cupboard for emergencies, but always plump for fresh in preference if you can get them. Many of the delicate-leaved herbs, such as basil, coriander or chervil, do not dry successfully, but the ones that are worth buying dried are thyme, rosemary, parsley, mint, oregano, tarragon and dill. Store dried herbs in airtight containers in a cool place away from light, and use them quickly as their flavour is soon lost.

Frozen herbs, such as parsley, chives and coriander, retain more of the flavour of fresh herbs and can be very useful and convenient – they can be added to a sauce or dressing straight from the freezer.

Above, clockwise from top left: Chopped and frozen herbs – coriander, parsley, chives

Salt and Pepper

Good-quality sea salt has a more intense flavour than "table" or "cooking" salt. Strong black peppercorns, mild white and very mild green are all worth storing.

Below, clockwise from bowl: Tandoori curry paste, nutmeg, cinnamon sticks, vanilla pods, salt, whole coriander, cumin seeds, black, green, white peppercorns

Above, clockwise from left: Mint, bay, thyme

Above, clockwise from top: Freeze-dried mint, freeze-dried parsley, freeze-dried dill, freeze-dried tarragon, dried thyme, dried rosemary. Centre: Freeze-dried oregano

SPICES

Keep a good store of spices in the kitchen. A useful selection includes whole nutmeg, cinnamon sticks, vanilla pods, coriander seeds, cumin seeds and curry paste (curry pastes keep for much longer than powders).

Cinnamon sticks: These have a sweet, spicy flavour and are widely used in sweet sauces and chutneys. They can either be crushed or used whole and removed at the end of cooking.

Coriander: These seeds are used in chutneys and have a mild sweet flavour.

Cumin: A key ingredient in chutneys and curries, these seeds have a strong and slightly bitter taste.

Curry paste: This is sold in a range of strengths and flavours. It keeps for much longer than curry powder.

Vanilla pods: Infuse these dried pods in milk or cream for sweet sauces and custards. Store in a jar of caster sugar to make vanilla sugar.

Whole nutmeg: Freshly grated whole nutmeg is much better than the powdered variety which quickly loses its flavour.

Storing Spices

Whole spices will store for much longer than ready-ground ones and have a stronger, more intense flavour. Once ground, they begin to lose the volatile oils that give them flavour, so it is best to grind whole spices yourself, either in a pestle and mortar or with a spice mill or using an electric coffee grinder. Buy them little and often and store in airtight containers in a cool, dark, dry store cupboard. Discard any that have not been used after a year.

Essences and Flower Waters

Vanilla or other flavouring essences can be very convenient, but choose carefully, as some are inferior artificial flavourings. Check the label – it should describe the contents as pure vanilla essence or extract of vanilla, not vanilla flavouring.

Flower waters are a delightful way to flavour cold sweet sauces, syrups and creams in particular, but occasionally they are used in Middle Eastern savoury sauces. The best known are rose and orange flower water, and should be used in small amounts – the best quality flower waters are triple-distilled, so just a few drops will add a delicately exotic scent to a creamy sauce.

Right, from left: Flower essences, vanilla essence, almond essence

Dairy Products

The number of sauces based on dairy products is vast, so it is worth taking the time to understand the different products available. You may be aiming for a rich and creamy sauce, or perhaps you would prefer a lighter, healthier alternative. The following descriptions should help.

MILK

The choice of milk for sauces depends upon the richness desired – for a rich flavour and creamy texture, choose whole milk or Channel Islands milk, but if you're watching fat levels and looking for a lighter sauce, it is best to go for skimmed or semi-skimmed.

Pasteurized: Most milk sold these days has been pasteurized, i.e. heat-treated, to destroy harmful bacteria. This should keep for up to 5 days under refrigeration.

Homogenized: This has been processed to distribute the fat globules evenly throughout the milk, instead of rising to the surface as cream. It has the same keeping quality as ordinary milk.

Sterilized: This is homogenized, bottled and then heat-treated for 20 minutes, so that it keeps without refrigeration until it is opened.

UHT: This is homogenized then heat-treated to high temperatures for just 1–2 seconds. It has a slightly caramelized flavour, but is useful as a store-cupboard standby as it keeps unopened for about a year without refrigeration.

Condensed: This sweetened milk is available in cans, and has been boiled to reduce and concentrate it. It is very rich and sweet, but useful for rich dessert sauces. Lower-fat versions are available.

Evaporated: Unsweetened milk that has had some of the water removed by evaporation, this milk has a concentrated flavour and is slightly caramelized. There are also lighter-fat versions available. It is available either in cans or longlife packs.

Goat's milk: Many people who are allergic to cow's milk can tolerate goat's milk, which is now widely available and can be used as a direct substitute for ordinary milk in cooking. It has a similar flavour, although it is slightly sharper, and is more digestible.

CREAM

All kinds of creams can be used to enrich and thicken both sweet and savoury sauces, both hot and cold. The main ones are as follows:

Single cream: This cream has a fat content of just 18 per cent, which is too low for whipping. It will not withstand boiling without splitting, but can be stirred into sauces at the end of cooking to enrich the flavour.

Soured cream: In fact, this is really single cream with an added souring culture, which sharpens the flavour and thickens the texture.

Double cream: The fat content of double cream is 48 per cent. The cream almost doubles in bulk when whipped. It is especially good in hot sauces, because it can withstand boiling without separating.

Whipping cream: This has 35 per cent fat, and whips up to a light texture, or can be stirred into sauces after cooking.

Fat Levels in Milk

- Channel Islands (or breakfast milk): 5–8 per cent fat
- Whole milk: 4 per cent fat
- Semi-skimmed: 1.7 per cent fat
- Skimmed: 0.1 per cent fat

Cook's Tip

When whipping double cream, you can reduce the risk of overbeating and extend the volume by adding 15 ml/1 tbsp milk to each 150 ml/¼ pint/⅔ cup cream. Use a hand whisk instead of an electric one, so you have more control over the speed.

CRÈME FRAÎCHE

This has a mild, tangy flavour similar to that of soured cream, which makes it great for using in both sweet and savoury sauces and dressings. With a fat content of around

Below, from left: Skimmed milk, semi-skimmed milk, whole milk, Channel Islands milk, evaporated milk, condensed milk

40 per cent, it is more stable than soured cream when heated. You can also buy a half-fat version, which can be successfully added to hot sauces without curdling.

Above, clockwise from left: Single cream, double cream, crème fraîche, soured cream, whipping cream

YOGURT

Yogurt and other lower-fat dairy products such as fromage frais, make excellent lighter replacements for cream in many sweet and savoury sauces, and can be used as a direct substitute to add a lighter tang to all kinds of uncooked sauces. For cooked sauces, yogurt should be stablized first with cornflour.

Greek yogurt: This may be made from either cow's or sheep's milk. It is richer in flavour and texture than most yogurts, but still only has a fat content of around 8–10 per cent, so it makes a light substitute for cream in sauces.

Low-fat yogurt: It is the use of semi-skimmed milk that makes this yogurt low-fat. Very low-fat yogurt is made with skimmed milk. Both types have quite a sharp, tangy flavour which can be refreshing when used in light sauces, dips and dressings.

Above: Greek yogurt (left), low-fat yogurt

STABILIZING YOGURT FOR SAUCES

To prevent yogurt splitting in cooked sauces, allow 5 ml/1 tsp cornflour to each 150 ml/ ¼ pint/⅔ cup yogurt. Blend the cornflour and a little yogurt to a smooth paste before adding the rest. Add to the sauce and cook as instructed in the recipe.

Above: Eggs

EGGS

As a general rule, medium eggs are the size to use for recipes, unless the recipe states otherwise, but you may find it useful to have small eggs for using to enrich or thicken sauces.

The freshness of eggs is easier to ensure nowadays, as most are now individually marked with a date stamp on their shells. Fresh eggs should store well for 2 weeks, providing that the shell is not damaged or dirty. Egg shells are porous, so they are best stored at the bottom of the fridge away from strong smelling foods. Before use, eggs should be left at room temperature for about 30 minutes.

Safety Tip

Because of the slight risk of contamination in raw eggs, it is recommended that pregnant women, young children, elderly people or anyone weakened by chronic illness should avoid eating raw or lightly cooked eggs.

CHEESE

Many hard cheeses can be grated and melted into sauces. Strong, hard cheeses such as mature Cheddar, Gruyère and Parmesan will grate easily and melt into hot sauces. Their fine flavour complements pasta sauces or a creamy white sauce to pour over vegetables. Always grate these cheeses freshly as you need them, and never use ready-grated Parmesan, as the flavour is soon lost after grating. Once you've added cheese to a sauce, heat it gently without boiling, or the cheese will overcook and become stringy.

Soft, fresh cheeses such as ricotta or mascarpone are also used to enrich a wide range of sauces and dips, from tomato sauces to fruit purées or custards. Ricotta is light in texture and mild in flavour, and makes a good base for dips instead of yogurt, or can be melted into hot sauces. Mascarpone has a luxuriously rich texture, creamy and high in fat, and can be used in the same way as thick cream.

Below, clockwise from top: Parmesan, mascarpone, ricotta, Cheddar, Gruyère

Sauce-making Equipment

Making sauces requires very little in the way of specialist equipment, but a carefully selected set of basic equipment will help make tasks such as boiling, whisking and straining much easier. You may even find that most of these items are already in your kitchen. Shop around for those you still need, as quality varies enormously.

SAUCEPANS

The rule here is to choose the right pan for the job, which means that your saucepans do not necessarily have to be a matching set. Some pans may be suitable for more than one task, but you will need a variety of sizes and types. Look for solid, heavy-based pans which are stable when empty, and have tight-fitting lids and firmly riveted handles. Buying good-quality pans is an investment, as they will last for years, but cheap, thin pans will not only wear out quickly, but will conduct heat unevenly and cause burnt spots. A good selection would be:

- Milk pan with high sides and a lip. This may be non-stick, but is not essential.
- 3 saucepans with lids, ranging in size from about 1 litre/1¾ pints/4 cups to 7 litres/12½ pints/30 cups. They should be deep and straight-sided to minimize evaporation.
- Sauté pan with deep, straight sides.
- Double boiler – a useful pan for making delicate creams and custards, and melting ingredients such as chocolate. If you don't have one, improvise with a heatproof bowl placed over a pan of hot water.

Materials for Saucepans

Stainless steel: This is attractive and hard-wearing, and providing they have a thick base with aluminium or copper, the pans will conduct heat evenly and efficiently.

Anodized aluminium: Light and easy to clean, this conducts the heat well and does not corrode. The metal reacts when in contact with acid and alkaline, so food should not be left to stand for too long in these pans.

Copper: These pans are expensive but conduct heat very efficiently and

Top: Double boiler and heatproof bowl placed over pan
Right, clockwise from left: Enamelled, anodized aluminium and copper pans

Above, from left: Spiral sauce whisks, balloon whisk, wooden spoons

are attractive and durable. Choose pans with a stainless steel lining, which is harder-wearing than tin.

Enamelled cast iron: This is heavy, but conducts the heat well, evenly and slowly. These pans retain the heat for a long time, and are hard-wearing and durable.

WOODEN SPOONS

A good assortment of wooden spoons is essential, and it is a good idea to keep them for individual uses. For example, you might reserve one for spicy sauces, one for creams and custards, and so on; then there is no risk of flavour transfer. A good selection includes a wooden spoon, a wooden corner spoon with an edge to reach into the corners of saucepans, and a flat-edged wooden spatula, for efficient stirring without scratching.

WHISKS

Balloon whisks and spiral sauce whisks are the most efficient for blending sauce ingredients or whisking dressings, and it is useful to have two different sizes. Choose ones with a comfortable grip.

LADLES

Available in various sizes, ladles are very useful for spooning and pouring sauces over foods. Some smaller ones have a useful lip for more precise pouring. Stainless steel ladles are the best. A slotted stainless steel draining spoon is invaluable for skimming and removing small pieces of ingredients from sauces.

Bottom, from left: Draining spoon, ladles

MEASURING JUG

Choose a solid jug marked clearly with standard measurements. Heatproof glass is ideal, as it is easy to see the liquid level and can take boiling liquids, yet the handle remains cool as it is a poor conductor of heat. Stainless steel jugs are attractive and hard-wearing.

MEASURING SPOONS

A set of British Standard measuring spoons marked in imperial and metric, is essential for accurate measuring of small amounts of sauce ingredients, as ordinary kitchen spoons vary in capacity. Spoon measurements given in recipes are always level.

SIEVE AND CHINOIS

A fine-meshed stainless steel sieve is essential for sauce making, and it can also be very useful to have a chinois, a cone-shaped sieve that is used for straining and puréeing a range of ingredients.

ELECTRICAL EQUIPMENT

Although not essential for making sauces, a blender, food processor, hand blender or whisk can take much of the hard work out of many sauces and dressings. Hand-held electric blenders are perhaps more versatile and convenient than larger machines for sauces, as they can be used to blend or purée ingredients directly in a saucepan or jug, and are easy to clean by simply swishing in hot soapy water after use. A hand-held electric whisk is also invaluable for quick and easy beating and whisking.

Below, from top: Hand-held electric whisk, hand blender
Right, from top: Sieve and chinois, measuring jug and spoons

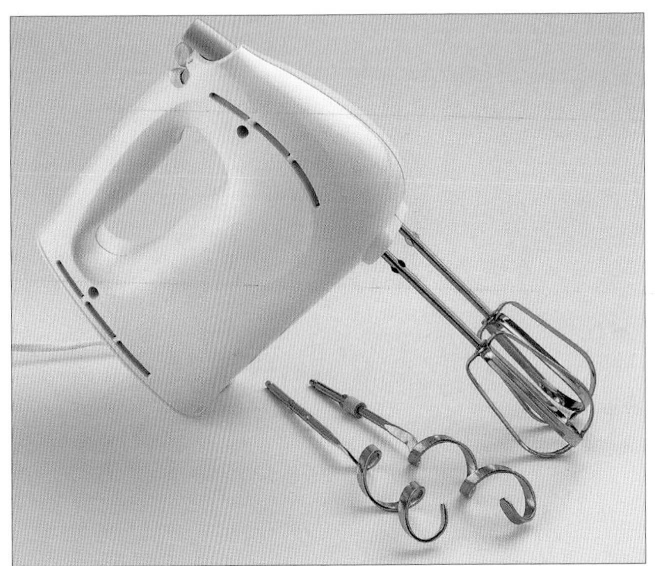

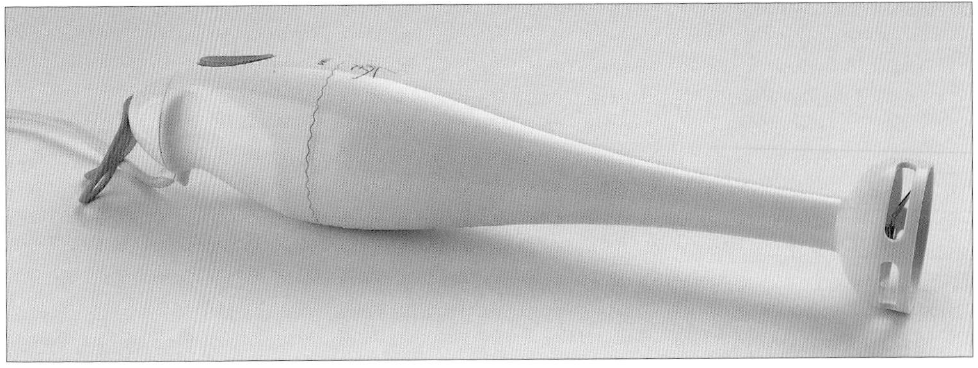

Making Basic Stocks

A good home-made stock is simple to make and adds a rich flavour to all kinds of savoury sauces.Commercial stock cubes and bouillon powder won't match the flavour of home-made stock. However, they can be very useful for enriching a stock which lacks flavour: heat it until boiling then stir in a stock cube or a teaspoonful of bouillon powder until dissolved. Each recipe below makes approximately 1 litre/1¾ pints/4 cups.

Beef Stock

INGREDIENTS

675g/1½lb shin of beef, diced
1 large onion, chopped
1 large carrot, chopped
1 celery stick, chopped
bouquet garni
6 black peppercorns
2.5ml/½ tsp sea salt
1.75 litres/3 pints/7½ cups water

1 Place all the ingredients in a large pan and slowly bring to the boil.

2 Cover the pan and simmer very gently for 4 hours, skimming occasionally to remove scum. Strain the stock and cool.

Fish Stock

INGREDIENTS

1kg/2¼lb white fish bones and trimmings
1 large onion, sliced
1 large carrot, sliced
1 celery stick, sliced
bouquet garni
6 white peppercorns
2.5ml/½ tsp sea salt
150ml/¼ pint/⅔ cup dry white wine
1 litre/1¾ pints/4 cups water

1 Place the ingredients in a pan and bring to the boil.

2 Skim any scum from the surface, cover the pan and simmer for 20 minutes. Strain and allow to cool.

Chicken Stock

INGREDIENTS

1 chicken carcass
chicken giblets
1 leek, chopped
1 celery stick, chopped
bouquet garni
5ml/1tsp white peppercorns
2.5ml/½ tsp sea salt
1.75 litres/3 pints/7½ cups water

1 Break up the carcass, place in a pan with the remaining ingredients. Bring to the boil.

2 Reduce the heat, cover and simmer gently for about 2½ hours, skimming occasionally to remove scum. Strain the stock and cool.

Vegetable Stock

INGREDIENTS

500g/1¼lb chopped mixed vegetables, e.g. onions, carrots, celery, leeks
bouquet garni
6 black peppercorns
2.5ml/½ tsp sea salt
1 litre/1¾ pints/4 cups water

1 Place all the ingredients in a large pan and slowly bring to the boil.

2 Skim any scum from the surface, then cover the pan and simmer gently for 30 minutes. Strain the stock and allow to cool.

Making a Bouquet Garni

A traditional bouquet garni usually contains a bay leaf, a sprig of thyme and a few sprigs of parsley, but this can be varied according to taste, and to suit the dish you are making. Other vegetables or herbs you may like to include are a piece of celery stick for poultry dishes; a rosemary sprig for beef or lamb; or a piece of fennel or leek, or a strip of lemon zest, to flavour fish dishes.

Tie the herbs together firmly with fine cotton string, so the bundle is easy to remove from the stock after cooking.

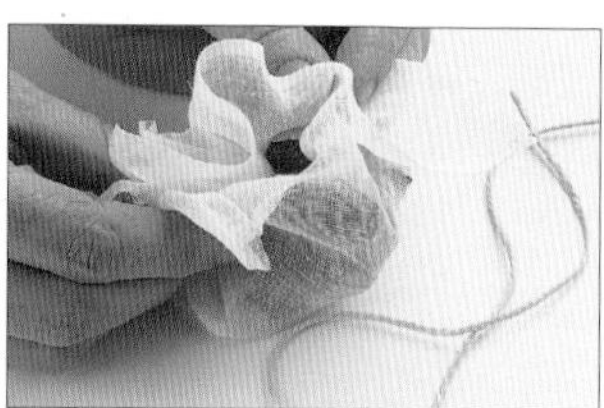

Alternatively, tie the herbs in a square of clean muslin. Leave a long length of the string to tie to the pan handle.

Keeping Stock Clear

For a clear soup it is important to keep the stock clear; avoid boiling the soup, and skim the top from time to time.

1 Trim any fat from the meat or bones before adding to the stock pan, as this can create a cloudy stock.

2 Keep the heat at a low simmer, and skim off any scum as it gathers on the surface during cooking. Most vegetables can be added to stock for flavour, but potatoes tend to break down and make the stock cloudy so it's best to avoid these.

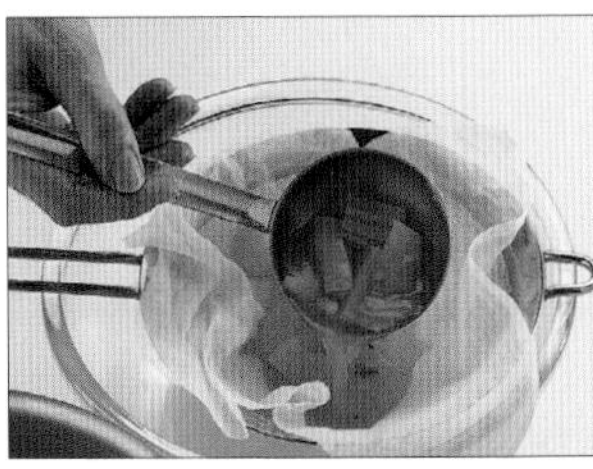

3 Strain the cooked stock through a sieve lined with muslin, and avoid pressing the solids, as this may spoil the stock's clarity.

Removing Fat from Stock

Excess fat should always be removed from the liquid to improve the look and taste of the stock; it also helps keep the stock clear.

1 Let the stock stand until the fat settles on the surface, then skim off as much fat as possible with a large, shallow spoon. To absorb even more grease, blot the surface of the soup with several layers of kitchen paper.

2 Then, drop in a few ice cubes. The fat will set around the ice so it can be simply spooned off.

3 Alternatively, allow the stock to cool on a work surface, then chill in the refrigerator until the fat layer rises to the surface and sets. Then the fat can simply be lifted off. Use a large spoon to remove the solidified fat and discard it.

How to Store Stock

Stock will keep for up to a week in the fridge, and freezes well. Reduce it first so that it takes up less room in the freezer.

1 To freeze, pour into airtight containers, allowing 2.5cm/1 inch headspace for expansion, then seal and freeze for up to 3 months.

2 To freeze stock in convenient portions to add to sauces, pour into ice cube trays for freezing.

Cook's Tip

- *Use salt sparingly at the beginning of cooking – if you are going to reduce the stock it will become much more salty.*
- *To make a brown stock from beef or veal bones, roast the bones in a hot oven for 40 minutes. Add the vegetables halfway through the roasting time. Deglaze the pan with a little water and simmer the bones and vegetables as usual.*
- *To make a stock with a concentrated flavour, simmer the stock until reduced by half. Continue to reduce the stock until it will coat the back of a spoon. At its most concentrated it will set as a solid jelly and give you a quick and easy way to add rich flavour to sauces and soups.*

Flour-based Sauces

The standard way to adjust the consistency of a sauce is to thicken it with one of the different available types of flour. There are three basic methods for this – roux, blending or all-in-one. Once you've learned the basic skills of these methods, you'll be able to tackle any flour-thickened sauce without problems.

Many of the classic white sauces are based on a "roux", which is simply a cooked mixture of flour and fat. The most basic white sauce uses milk, but by varying the liquid used other well-known white sauces can be made. For a classic béchamel sauce, the milk is flavoured first by infusing with pieces of vegetables and herbs. For velouté sauce, the milk is replaced with stock, giving the sauce a more opaque appearance, and the thickened sauce may be enriched with cream after cooking. Brown sauces or gravy are made by browning the roux, usually with onions, before adding stock or other liquid such as wine.

Basic Recipe for White Roux Sauces
Using the classic roux method, you can adjust the amount of thickening to create varying consistencies of sauces. A pouring sauce is used, as it suggests, to be poured directly over foods when serving. The slightly thicker coating sauce is used to make a smooth covering for fish or vegetables.

For a pouring consistency:
15g/½oz/1 tbsp butter
15g/½oz/2 tbsp flour
300ml/½ pint/1¼ cups liquid

For a coating consistency:
25g/1oz/2 tbsp butter
25g/1oz/¼ cup flour
300 ml/½ pint/1¼ cups liquid

Making a Roux-based White Sauce

The trick to making a roux is to stir the pan over the whole of the base, and add the liquid gradually; it is a good idea to heat the milk or stock before adding to the roux as this helps avoid lumps.

1 Melt the butter in a saucepan, then add the flour. To prevent browning, cook on a low heat and stir with a wooden spoon, for 1–2 minutes. Allow the mixture to bubble until it resembles a honeycomb in texture. It is important to cook well at this point, to allow the starch grains in the flour to swell and burst, and avoid lumps forming later.

2 Remove the pan from the heat and gradually stir in the liquid, which may be either hot or cold. Return to the heat and stir until boiling and thickened. Reduce the heat and simmer, stirring constantly, for 2 minutes, until the sauce is thickened and smooth.

Blending Method

Sauces which are thickened by the blending method are usually made with cornflour, arrowroot, potato flour or sauce flour. Cornflour and sauce flour make light, glossy, lump-free sauces, which are good for freezing as the starch does not break down. If you need a crystal-clear result for glazing, use arrowroot or potato flour. The liquid may be milk, stock, fruit juice, or syrup from canned or poached fruit. As an approximate guide, you will need 20g/¾oz/3 tbsp cornflour or sauce flour to thicken 300ml/½ pint/1¼ cups liquid to a pouring consistency. Arrowroot or potato flour are slightly stronger, so use approximately 15g/½oz to 300ml/½ pint/1¼ cups liquid to obtain the same consistency.

1 Place the flour in a bowl and add just enough liquid to make a smooth, thin paste. Heat the remaining liquid in a saucepan until almost boiling.

2 Pour a little of the liquid on to the blended mixture, stirring. Pour the blended mixture back into the pan, whisking constantly to avoid lumps. Return to the heat and stir until boiling, then simmer gently for 2 minutes, stirring until thickened and smooth.

All-in-one Method

This method uses the same ingredients and proportions as the roux method, but the liquid added must be cold.

Place the flour, butter and cold liquid in the saucepan and whisk with a sauce whisk or balloon whisk over a moderate heat until boiling. Stir over the heat for 2 minutes, until thickened and smooth.

Using an Egg Yolk Liaison

This is a simple way to lightly thicken hot milk or stock, cream or reduced poaching liquids, and is good for enriching savoury white or velouté sauces. Two egg yolks should be enough to enrich and thicken about 300ml/½ pint/1¼ cups liquid, depending on the recipe. A mixture of egg yolk and cream has the same effect, but add it when the pan is off the heat to avoid curdling.

Place two egg yolks in a small bowl and stir in 30ml/2 tbsp of the hot liquid or sauce. Stir the egg mixture into the remaining liquid or sauce and heat gently, stirring, without boiling.

Making Beurre Manié

Literally translated as "kneaded butter", this is a mixture of flour and butter, which can be stirred into a hot sauce, poaching liquid or cooked dish such as a casserole or ragout to thicken the juices. It's a convenient way to adjust the consistency of a sauce or dish at the end of cooking, and is easy to control as you can add the exact amount required, adjusting as it thickens. The butter adds flavour and a glossy sheen to the finished sauce. Any leftover beurre manié can be stored in a covered jar in the refrigerator for about two weeks, ready to use in sauces, soups, stews or casseroles.

1 Place equal amounts of butter and flour in a bowl and knead together with your fingers or a wooden spoon to make a smooth paste.

2 Drop teaspoonfuls of the beurre manié paste into the simmering sauce, whisking thoroughly to incorporate each spoonful before adding the next, until the sauce is thickened and smooth and the desired consistency is achieved.

Infusing Flavours

To infuse flavours into milk, stock or other liquids before using in sauces such as béchamel, pour the liquid into a saucepan and add thin slices or dice of onion, carrot and celery, a bouquet garni, peppercorns or a mace blade. Bring the liquid slowly to the boil, then remove the pan from the heat. Cover and leave to stand for about 10 minutes. Strain the milk to remove the flavourings before use.

Adding Flavourings to Flour-based Sauces

Once you've made your basic sauce, try some of these quick flavour additions to pep up the flavour and add variety:

- Stir 50g/2oz/½ cup grated Cheddar or other strong cheese into a basic white sauce with 5ml/1 tsp wholegrain mustard and a generous dash of Worcestershire sauce.
- Wine livens up the flavour of most stock-based sauces – boil 60ml/4 tbsp red or white wine in a saucepan until well-reduced, then stir into the finished sauce with a grating of nutmeg or black pepper.
- Parsley, or any fresh herbs will infuse and change the flavour of a white sauce. Add chopped herbs a few minutes before the end of the cooking time.

Correcting a Lumpy Sauce

If your flour-thickened sauce has gone lumpy, don't despair – it can be corrected.

1 First, try whisking the sauce hard with a light wire whisk in the saucepan to smooth out the lumps, then reheat gently, stirring.

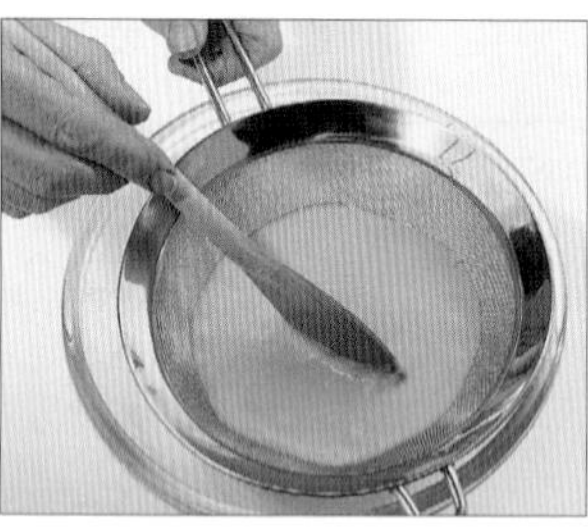

2 If the sauce is still not smooth, rub it through a fine sieve, pressing firmly with a wooden spoon. Return to the pan and reheat gently, stirring.

3 Alternatively, pour the sauce into a food processor and process until smooth. Return to the pan and reheat gently, stirring.

Keeping Sauces Hot

1 To keep sauces hot, pour into a heatproof bowl and place over a pan of very gently simmering water.

2 To prevent a skin from forming over the surface, place a sheet of lightly oiled or wetted greaseproof or non-stick baking paper directly on to the surface of the sauce. Stir before serving.

Degreasing Sauces

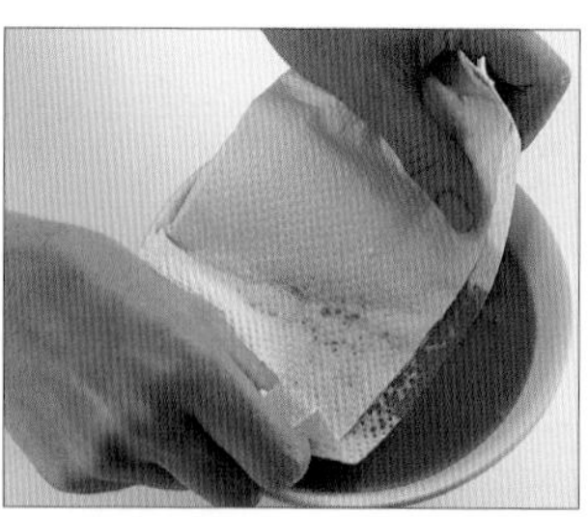

Even after skimming any surplus fat from a finished hot sauce or gravy with a flat metal spoon, final traces of fat may still remain. These can be removed by dragging the flat surface of a piece of kitchen paper over the surface to absorb traces of grease.

Making a Roux-based Brown Sauce

A brown roux is the basis of many meat dish sauces. Onions or other vegetables are usually browned in fat before flour is added. The fat can be a mixture of butter and oil, or dripping. Butter alone is unsuitable as it burns easily at high temperatures. Use about 30ml/2 tbsp oil and about 25g/1oz/¼ cup flour for the roux to about 600ml/1 pint/2½ cups reduced brown stock. At the last moment, stir in 15g/½oz/1 tbsp chilled butter to give a glossy finish.

1 Melt the fat and fry one small, finely chopped onion until softened and golden brown. Sprinkle on the flour and stir in with a wooden spoon. Stir over a low heat for 4–5 minutes, until the mixture colours to a rich brown.

2 Remove the pan from the heat and gradually stir in the liquid, which may be either hot or cold. Return to the heat and stir until boiling. Simmer gently, stirring, for a further 2 minutes, until the sauce is thick and smooth. The sauce may be strained to remove the onions at this stage if preferred.

Using a Deglazed Sauce

Deglazing means adding a small amount of liquid to the pan after roasting or pan-frying to dilute the rich concentrated juices into a simple sauce. Spoon off the excess fat, and then scrape up the sediment from the pan bottom with a spoon as you stir in the liquid.

1 Tilt the pan and spoon off excess fat from the surface of the juices.

2 Stir in a few tablespoons of wine, stock or cream.

3 Simmer over a moderate heat, stirring and scraping up the sediment as the sauce boils. Boil rapidly to reduce the juices until syrupy, then pour over the food.

Making Traditional Gravy

Good gravy should be smooth and glossy, never heavy and floury. Generally speaking, it's best to use the minimum of thickening, but this can be adjusted to your own taste. Providing the meat has been roasted to a rich brown, the meat juices will have enough colour to colour the gravy. If it is too pale, a few drops of gravy browning can be stirred in to darken it slightly.

1 To make a thickened gravy, skim off all except about 15ml/1 tbsp of the fat from the juices in the tin after roasting meat. Gradually stir in about 15ml/1 tbsp flour, scraping up the sediment and meat juices.

2 Place the tin directly over the heat and stir until bubbling. Cook, stirring constantly, for 1–2 minutes until the roux is brown and the flour cooked.

3 Gradually stir in the liquid, which may be either stock or vegetable water, until the gravy is of the thickness desired. Simmer for 2–3 minutes, stirring constantly, and adjust the seasoning to taste.

Ideas for Deglazed Sauces

Brandy and Peppercorn – deglaze the pan with brandy or sherry, stir in cream and coarsely ground black pepper. Serve with grilled or fried steaks.

Red Wine and Cranberry – deglaze the pan with red wine and stir in cranberry sauce or jelly. This recipe is good with roast game or turkey.

Sauce Bercy – deglaze with dry white wine or vermouth, stir in a finely chopped shallot and sauté gently until soft. Add cream, lemon juice and chopped parsley. Excellent with fried or poached fish.

Adding Flavourings to a Brown Sauce

A well-flavoured brown stock, which has been reduced by between one-third to a half, is the basis of a good brown sauce but it can also be enhanced by the addition of a variety of flavourings.

- A handful of chopped fresh basil, chives or flat leaf parsley, stirred into the sauce just before serving, will improve the flavour and look of a basic brown sauce.
- For game or poultry, stir a little curry paste, 2 crushed cloves of garlic and 1 finely chopped onion into the roux and cook for about 5 minutes before adding the stock. Stir in a handful of chopped fresh coriander just before serving.
- Add coarsely grated orange rind to a basic brown sauce and serve it with duck or game.

Vegetable Sauces and Salsas

Many sauces use vegetables for flavour, colour and texture, and there's no end to the healthy variations you can make with a few very simple techniques. Puréed or chopped vegetables can be used to make both cooked sauces and fresh salsas. Vegetable sauces and salsas make fresh, colourful, low-fat alternatives to more conventional sauces, and they are invariably very easy and quick to make.

Basic Tomato Sauce

For the best flavour, use plum tomatoes. If using canned make sure they are not already flavoured with herbs. Peel fresh tomatoes before using. Fresh tomatoes rather than canned tomatoes can be used. Substitute about 500g/1¼lb of tomatoes for each 400g/14oz can.

Makes about 450ml/¾ pint/ scant 2 cups

INGREDIENTS

15ml/1tbsp olive oil
15g/½oz/1 tbsp butter
1 clove garlic, finely chopped
1 small onion, finely chopped
1 stick celery, finely chopped
400g/14oz can chopped tomatoes
handful of basil leaves
salt and ground black pepper

1 Heat the oil and butter in a heavy-based saucepan.

2 When the oil starts to bubble, add the garlic, onion and celery. Sauté the ingredients gently over a low heat, stirring occasionally, for about 15–20 minutes or until the onions soften and are just beginning to colour.

3 Stir the chopped tomatoes into the sauce and bring to the boil. Cover and simmer gently for 10–15 minutes, stirring occasionally, until thick.

4 Tear or roughly chop the basil leaves and stir into the sauce. Adjust the seasoning with salt and pepper and serve hot.

Cook's Tip

A soffritto (Italian), or sofrito (Spanish), is the basis of many Mediterranean meat or tomato sauces. It's such a classic that some recipes list "soffritto" simply as an ingredient with no other explanation. A basic soffritto usually consists of onion, garlic, green pepper and celery, sometimes with a little carrot or pancetta added. The finely chopped ingredients are sautéed slowly to soften and caramelize the flavours and are used in soups and sauces.

Making Quick Salsa Crudo

This is literally a "raw sauce" of vegetables or fruits, and it's easy to create your own combinations of flavour. A good basic start for a salsa crudo is chillies, peppers, onions, and garlic. Serve with grilled chicken, pork, lamb or fish.

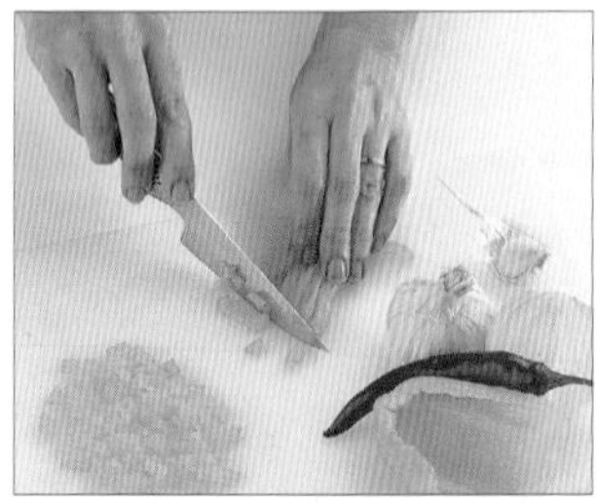

1 Peel, deseed or trim the vegetables as necessary, then use a sharp knife to cut into small, even dice. Try to combine texture and colour as well as taste, and use chillies and other very spicy ingredients sparingly. Put all the diced ingredients into a bowl.

2 Add 15–30ml/1–2 tbsp olive oil and a squeeze of lime or lemon juice and stir in finely chopped fresh basil, coriander, flat leaf parsley or mint, to enrich the flavour. Season to taste and toss well before serving.

To Peel Tomatoes

1 Cut a small cross in the skins of the tomatoes. Bring a pan of water to the boil and add the tomatoes. Turn off the heat and leave for 30 seconds, then lift out carefully with a draining spoon and place in a bowl of cold water. Using a small knife, peel off the skins.

2 Alternatively, place the tomato firmly on the prongs of a fork and hold in a gas flame until the skin blisters and splits. When the tomatoes are cool enough to handle, peel off the skins using a small knife.

Chargrilling Vegetables for Purées and Sauces

Many puréed sauces or salsas call for cooked or chargrilled vegetables. Char-grilling on a barbecue is the best way to get the finest flavour from many vegetables, such as peppers, aubergines, tomatoes, garlic or onions, retaining and caramelizing the flavourful juices and tenderizing the flesh. However, since this method is not always practical, the next best is to roast the vegetables on a baking sheet under a grill.

Roasted Vegetable Sauce

Serve roasted vegetable sauce with pork, ham, poultry or game. If you prefer a sauce with more texture, simply process for a shorter time.

Makes about 300ml/½ pint/1¼ cups

INGREDIENTS

2 red or orange peppers
1 small onion
1 small aubergine
2 tomatoes with skins removed
2 garlic cloves, unpeeled
30–45ml/2–3 tbsp olive oil
15ml/1 tbsp lemon juice
25g/1oz/½ cup fresh white breadcrumbs

1 Cut the peppers, onion and aubergine in half, leaving the skins on, and, if necessary, remove any seeds and core. Place the vegetables cut-side down on a baking sheet with the garlic cloves. Place under a very hot grill, or in a hot oven and cook until the skins are blackened and charred, and the flesh is tender.

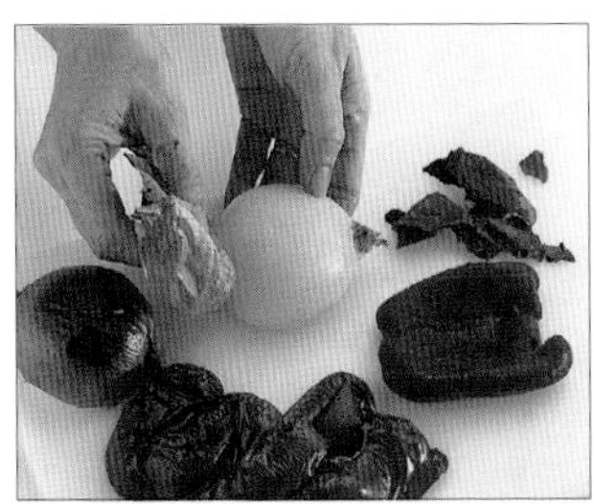

2 Remove from the heat and leave until cool enough to handle, then peel off the skins from the peppers and onions.

3 Scoop the flesh from the aubergines, and squeeze the flesh from the garlic.

4 Place all the vegetables in a blender or food processor and process to a very smooth purée, adding oil and lemon juice to taste. If you prefer a very smooth sauce, rub the purée through a fine sieve.

5 To thicken a vegetable puree, stir in a handful of fresh breadcrumbs and process for a few seconds to the desired consistency.

Savoury Butter Sauces

The simplest sauce of all is a melted butter sauce, flavoured with lemon juice or herbs – ideal to drizzle over a simply cooked piece of fish or vegetables. A more refined version of this is clarified butter sauce, which is butter with the moisture and impurities removed. Emulsions of butter with vinegar or other flavourings make deliciously rich beurre blanc or hollandaise sauce. Cold, flavoured butters are useful to add last-minute melting flavours on to hot foods, and can be shaped prettily for extra garnish.

Blender Hollandaise

Hollandaise is a wonderfully rich butter sauce, rather like a hot mayonnaise. This quick method eliminates whisking by hand and uses a blender to incorporate the ingredients to a thick, smooth emulsion where two liquids are combined by the dispersion of one in the other.

Makes 250ml/8fl oz/1 cup

INGREDIENTS

60ml/4 tbsp white wine vinegar
6 peppercorns
1 bay leaf
3 egg yolks
175g/6oz/¾ cup clarified butter
salt and ground black pepper

1 Place the wine vinegar, peppercorns and bay leaf in a small pan and heat until boiling, then simmer to reduce to about 15ml/1 tbsp. Remove from the heat and discard the flavourings.

2 Place the egg yolks in the blender goblet and start the motor. Add the reduced white wine vinegar liquid through the feeder tube and blend for 10 seconds.

3 Heat the butter until hot. With the motor running, pour the butter through the feeder tube in a thin, steady stream until thick and smooth. Adjust the seasoning to taste with salt and pepper, and serve warm with poached fish, eggs or vegetables.

Preventing Curdling

If hollandaise sauce is overheated, or if the butter is added too quickly, it may curdle and become slightly granular in texture. If this happens, remove it from the heat immediately, before the sauce separates.

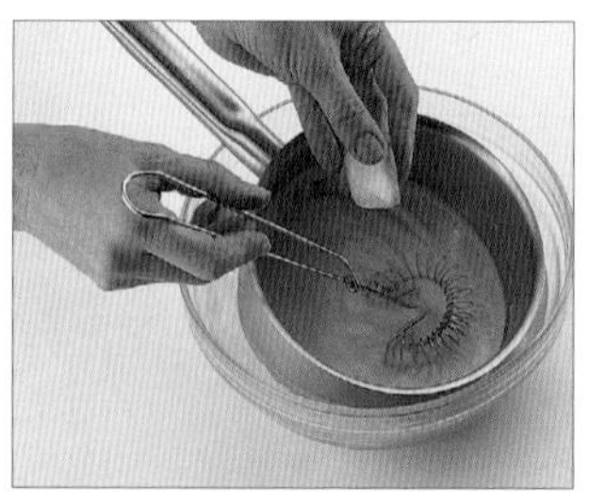

Quickly drop an ice cube into the sauce, then beat hard until the cube melts and cools the sauce. It also helps to stand the base of the pan in a bowl of iced water whilst whisking in the ice cube.

Beurre Blanc

This is one of the simplest sauces to make. White wine and vinegar are reduced in volume over a high heat to produce an intense flavour. Butter is whisked into the liquid to enrich and thicken it. It is good with poached or grilled fish or chicken.

1 Place 45ml/3 tbsp each of white wine vinegar and dry white wine in a small saucepan with a finely chopped shallot. Bring to the boil and boil until reduced to about 15ml/1 tbsp.

2 Cut 225g/8oz/1 cup chilled unsalted butter into small cubes. On a low heat, gradually whisk in the butter, piece by piece, allowing each piece to melt and be absorbed before adding the next. Season to taste and serve immediately.

How to Clarify Butter

Ideal for serving with vegetables such as asparagus or artichokes, clarified butter is butter which has been melted and has had all the salts, moisture and impurities removed, leaving it clear, with a rich, pure flavour. Clarified butter, called ghee in Indian cooking, keeps longer and can be heated to higher temperatures than ordinary butter without the risk of burning. It can be used for sautéing, and in sauces it gives a mild flavour and a high gloss. There are two main methods of clarifying:

Place the butter in a saucepan with an equal quantity of water. Heat until the butter melts. Remove the pan from the heat and leave to cool until the butter sets. Carefully lift out the fat, leaving the water and solids behind.

Alternatively, melt the butter in a small pan over a very low heat, then skim off the froth with a perforated spoon. Pour the rest through a sieve lined with fine muslin, to strain out the solids.

Making Savoury Butters

Flavoured butters can be shaped or piped decoratively to serve with grilled steaks or poached or grilled fish.

To make a herb-flavoured butter, finely chop your choice of fresh herbs. Beat the butter until softened then stir in the herbs to mix evenly.

Making Shaped Slices

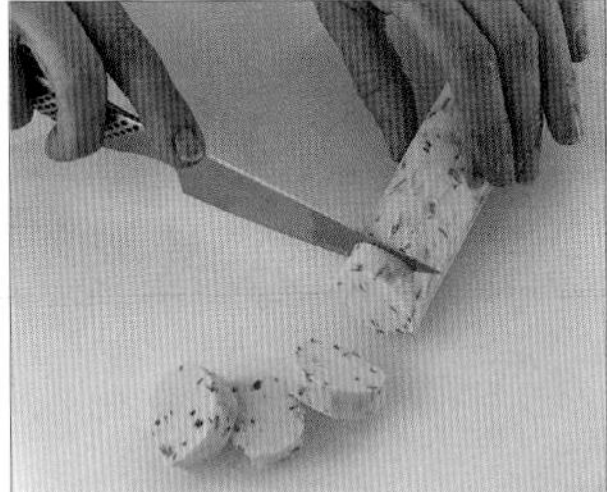

To make butter slices, chill the softened herb butter lightly. With your hands, roll the butter into a long sausage-shape and wrap in non-stick paper or clear film. Chill and cut off slices of the butter as required.

Piping Butter

Using a star nozzle, pipe softened butter on to non-stick baking paper.

Making Shaped Butters

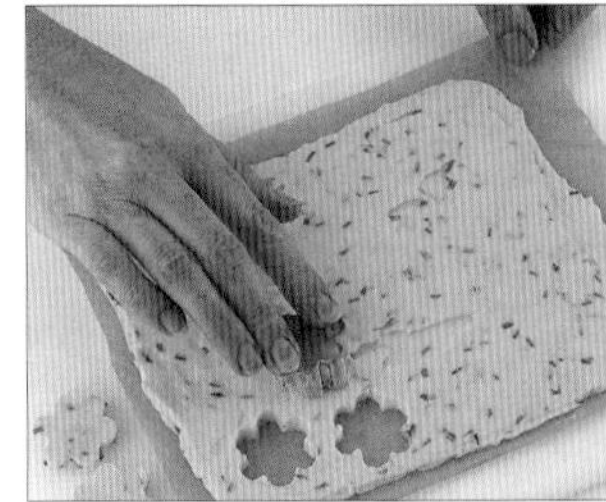

To make shaped butter pats, chill lightly, roll out the butter between two sheets of non-stick baking paper. Chill until firm, then remove the top sheet and stamp out small shapes with a cutter.

Flavourings for Savoury Butters

As well as being the traditional accompaniment to steaks, flavoured butters can be rubbed on to meat before roasting or spread over chops and cutlets before grilling or barbecuing. They can also be spread on fish that is foil-wrapped and baked in the oven or used as you would garlic butter to make deliciously flavoured breads.

- Finely chopped herbs, e.g. chives, parsley, dill, mint, thyme or rosemary. Use one herb or a combination of your choice and add as much as the butter will comfortably absorb, or to achieve the desired flavour.
- Finely grated lemon, lime or orange zest and juice.
- Finely chopped canned anchovy fillets.
- Finely chopped gherkins or capers.
- Crushed, dried chillies or finely chopped fresh chillies.
- Crushed, fresh garlic cloves, or roasted garlic purée.
- Ground coriander seeds, curry spices or paste.

Savoury Egg Sauces

The versatility of eggs comes in useful in all kinds of sauces, most commonly for thickening and enriching cooked sauces, or for holding an emulsion such as in mayonnaise. Keep spare egg yolks in the freezer, ready to enrich sauces whenever needed – stir in a pinch of salt or sugar before freezing to prevent them thickening.

Mayonnaise

The texture of a hand-whisked mayonnaise is quite unlike any other – smooth, glossy and rich, the perfect partner to delicately poached salmon or a chicken salad. The choice of oil for mayonnaise depends on personal taste, but most people would find mayonnaise made with extra virgin olive oil rather too powerful in flavour. So, it's a good idea to use either a pure olive oil, or alternatively use a mix of half pure olive oil with half sunflower oil, or another lighter-flavoured oil.

It is easier to get a good emulsion and prevent the mayonnaise curdling if all the ingredients are at room temperature.

Makes about 300ml/½ pint/1¼ cups

INGREDIENTS

2 egg yolks
15ml/1 tbsp lemon juice
5ml/1 tsp Dijon mustard
300ml/½ pint/1¼ cups light olive oil
salt and ground black pepper

1 Place the egg yolks, lemon juice, mustard, salt and pepper in a bowl and beat the egg yolk mixture until smooth and evenly combined.

2 Pouring with one hand and whisking with the other, add the oil gradually, drop by drop, making sure that each drop is whisked in before adding more.

3 Once a thick emulsion has formed, the oil can be poured faster, in a fine, steady stream, whisking until the mixture becomes smooth and thick. Adjust the seasoning to taste.

Using a Food Processor for Mayonnaise

A food processor can speed up the making of mayonnaise. Use a whole egg instead of the egg yolks.

Process the egg and flavourings for a few seconds then slowly pour in the oil through the feeder tube in a thin, steady stream with the motor running, until the mixture forms a smooth, creamy texture.

Preventing Mayonnaise Separating

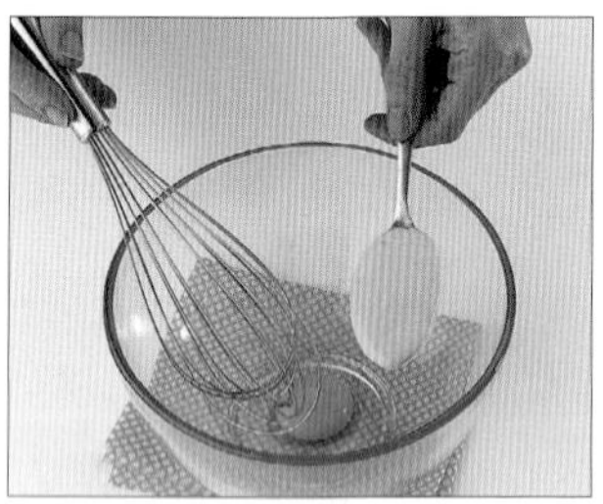

If the oil is added too quickly, the mayonnaise may separate, but this can be corrected if you work quickly.

Break a fresh egg yolk into a clean bowl. Gradually whisk in the separated mayonnaise, a small spoonful at a time, whisking constantly until it begins to thicken. Continue until all the mixture has been incorporated.

Mayonnaise Variations

- For Garlic Mayonnaise, crush 3–6 garlic cloves into the ingredients.
- For Spicy Mayonnaise, add in 15ml/1 tbsp of mustard, 7–15ml/ ½–1 tsp Worcestershire sauce and a dash of Tabasco sauce.
- for Green Mayonnaise, combine 1oz/30g each of parsley and watercress sprigs in a blender or food processor. Add 3–4 chopped spring onions and 1 garlic clove. Blend until finely chopped. Add 4fl oz/120ml mayonnaise and blend until smooth. Season to taste.
- For Blue Cheese Dressing, mix 8oz/225g crumbled Danish blue cheese into the mayonnaise.

Sweet Egg Sauces

Sweet egg sauces include many rich and creamy techniques, from classic egg-based custards to serve with winter puddings to light and fluffy sabayon which can be served on its own or as a luxurious sauce for gilded fruits, or traditional baked custard which can be served hot or cold.

Egg Custard Sauce

Crème anglaise is the traditional vanilla custard sauce made with eggs, a far cry from the quick custard powder versions so often used. As well as being served as a classic sauce, either hot or cold, *crème anglaise* is often used as the base for other sweet sauces, such as the *crème pâtissière* used to fill éclairs and profiteroles. It's frequently enriched with cream instead of milk, or flavoured with liqueurs for special desserts.

The trick here is to be patient – the egg must be cooked slowly; if it's overheated it will turn to scrambled egg.

Makes about 400ml/14fl oz/1⅔ cups

INGREDIENTS

300ml/½ pint/1¼ cups milk
1 vanilla pod
3 egg yolks
15ml/1 tbsp caster sugar

1 Heat the milk with the vanilla pod until just boiling, then remove from the heat. (To intensify the flavour split the pod lengthways.) Cover and leave to infuse for 10 minutes then strain into a clean pan. Beat the eggs and sugar together lightly in a bowl.

2 Pour the milk on to the eggs, whisking constantly.

3 Pour into the pan and stir until the custard thickens just enough to lightly coat the back of a wooden spoon. Remove from the heat and pour into a jug to prevent overcooking.

Preventing Curdling

Remove the egg custard from the heat and plunge the base of the pan into cold water. Whisk in a teaspoonful of cornflour until smooth, then reheat.

Sabayon Sauce

1 Whisk 1 egg yolk and 15ml/1 tbsp caster sugar per portion in a bowl over a pan of simmering water. Whisk in 30ml/2 tbsp sweet white wine, liqueur or full-flavoured fruit juice, for each egg yolk. Whisk the sauce over a constant heat until frothy.

2 Whisk until the sauce holds a trail on top of the mixture. Serve immediately or whisk until cool.

Baked Custard

Preheat the oven to 180°C/350°F/Gas 4. Grease an ovenproof dish. Beat together 4 large eggs, a few drops of vanilla essence and 15–30ml/1–2 tbsp caster sugar. Whisk in 600ml/1 pint/2½ cups hot milk, then strain into the prepared dish. Stand the dish in a roasting tin and pour in warm water to half fill the tin. Bake for 50–60 minutes.

Dessert Sauces

As well as the popular custards and flavoured white sauces, quick and easy dessert toppings can be made almost instantly from ready-made ingredients, and these are ideal to serve over scoops of ice cream. They could also be served with pancakes and are particularly popular with children.

How to Use Vanilla Pods

Vanilla pods are commonly used in sweet dessert sauces, but they are occasionally used to flavour delicate savoury cream sauces.

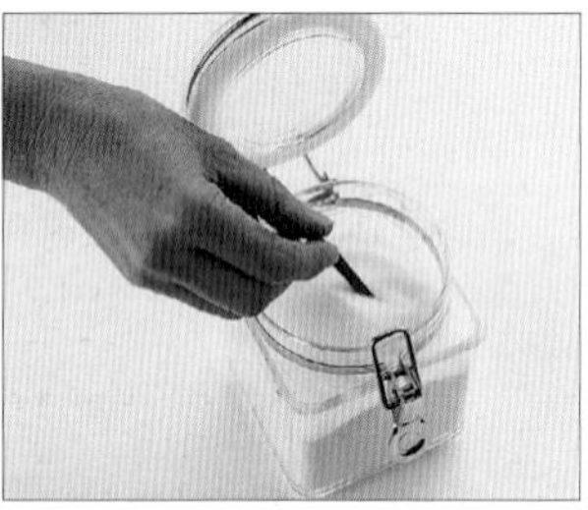

To flavour sugar, bury a vanilla pod in a jar of caster sugar. It can be used as vanilla-flavoured sugar to add to sweet sauces and desserts.

To infuse vanilla flavour into milk or cream, heat it gently with the vanilla pod over a low heat until almost boiling. Remove from the heat, cover and leave to stand for 10 minutes. Remove the pod, rinse and dry; it may be re-used several times in this way.

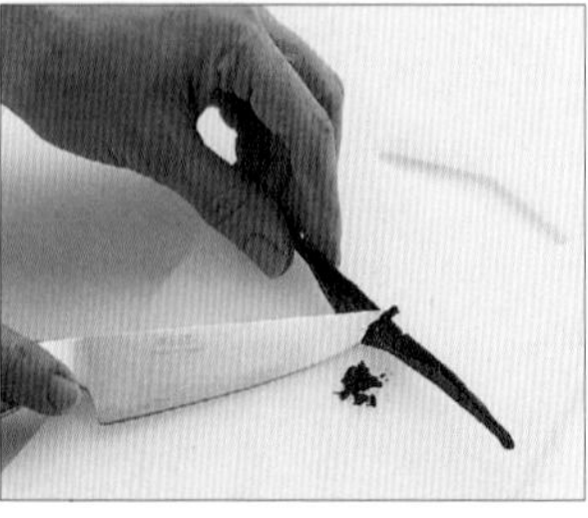

To get maximum flavour from the pod, use a sharp knife to slit the pod lengthways and open out. Use the tip of the knife to scrape out the sticky black seeds inside and add to the hot sauce.

Speedy Sauces for Topping Ice Cream

Lots of store-cupboard ingredients can be quickly transformed into irresistible sauces to spoon on top of ice cream, so you'll always have a quick dessert.

Marshmallow Melt

Melt 90g/3½ oz marshmallows with 30ml/2 tbsp milk or cream in a small pan. Add a little grated nutmeg and spoon over ice cream.

Black Forest Sauce

Drain a can of black cherries, reserving the juice. Blend a little of the juice with a little arrowroot or cornflour. Add the cornflour mixture to the remaining juice in a saucepan. Stir over a moderate heat until boiling and lightly thickened, then add the cherries and a dash of kirsch. Bubble for a few seconds, then spoon over the ice cream and top with grated chocolate.

Chocolate-toffee Sauce

Chop a Mars bar and heat very gently in a saucepan, stirring until just melted. Spoon over scoops of vanilla ice cream and sprinkle with chopped nuts.

Marmalade Whisky Sauce

Heat 60ml/4 tbsp chunky marmalade in a pan with 30ml/2 tbsp whisky, until just melted. Allow to bubble for a few seconds then spoon over ice cream.

Whisky Sauce

Measure 600ml/1 pint/2½ cups milk. Mix together 30ml/2 tbsp cornflour with 15ml/1 tbsp of the milk. Bring the remaining milk to a boil, remove from the heat and pour a little on the cornflour mixture. Return the mixture to the pan and heat gently, stirring constantly, until thickened. Simmer for 2 minutes.

Remove from the heat and stir in 30ml/2 tbsp caster sugar and 60–90ml/4–6 tbsp whisky.

Presentation Ideas

When you've made a delicious sauce for a special dessert, why not make more of it by using it for decoration on the plate, too? Try one of the following simple ideas to make your sauce into a talking point. Individual slices of desserts, cakes or tarts, or a stuffed baked peach, look especially good like this.

Marbling

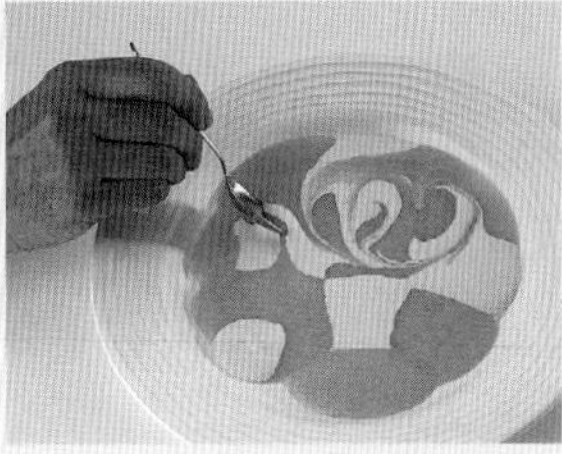

Use this technique when you have two contrasting sauces of similar thickness, such as a fruit purée with custard or cream. Spoon alternate spoonfuls of the sauces into a bowl or on to a serving plate, then stir the two sauces lightly together, swirling to create a marbled effect.

Yin-Yang Sauces

This is ideal for two contrasting colours of purée or coulis, such as a raspberry and a mango fruit coulis. Spoon one sauce on each side of a serving plate and push them together gently with a spoon, swirling one around the other, to make a yin-yang shape.

Drizzling

Pour a smooth sauce or coulis into a jug with a fine pouring lip. Drizzle the sauce in droplets or a fine wavy line on to the plate around the food.

Piping Outlines

Spoon a small amount of fruit coulis or chocolate sauce into a piping bag fitted with a plain writing nozzle. Pipe the outline of a shape on to a serving plate, then spoon in sauce to fill the inside.

Feathering Hearts

Flood the plate with a smooth sauce such as fruit purée. Add small droplets of pouring cream into it at intervals. Draw the tip of a small knife through the cream, to drag each drop into a heart.

Quick Sauces for Crêpes

Rich Butterscotch Sauce

Heat 75g/3oz/6 tbsp butter, 175g/6oz/1½ cups brown sugar and 30ml/2 tbsp golden syrup in a pan over a low heat until melted. Remove from the heat and add 75ml/5 tbsp double cream, stirring continuously, until smooth. If you like, add about 50g/2oz/½ cup chopped walnuts. Serve hot with ice cream and crêpes or waffles.

Orange Sauce

Melt 25g/1oz/2 tbsp unsalted butter in a heavy-based saucepan. Stir in 50g/2oz/¼ cup caster sugar and cook until golden brown. Add the juice of 2 oranges and ½ lemon and stir until the caramel has dissolved.

Summer Berries

Melt 25g/1oz/2 tbsp of butter in a frying pan. Add in 50g/2oz/¼ cup caster sugar and cook until golden brown. Add the juice of 2 oranges and the ring of ½ orange and cook until syrupy. Add 350g/12oz/3 cups of mixed berries and warm through. Add 45ml/3 tbsp of Grand Marnier and set alight. Spoon over the crêpes.

Fruit Sauces

From the simplest fresh fruit purée, to a cooked and thickened fruit sauce, there are hundreds of ways to add flavour to puddings, tarts and pies. The addition of a little liqueur or lemon juice can bring out the fruit flavour and prevent discoloration. Some fruit sauces, notably apple and cranberry, partner meat and poultry dishes, and fresh fruit salsas can be eaten to cool down spicy hot dishes.

Making a Fruit Coulis

A delicious fruit coulis will add a sophisticated splash of colour and flavour to desserts and ices. It can be made from either fresh or frozen fruit, in any season. Soft fruits and berries such as raspberries, blackcurrants or strawberries are ideal, and tropical fruits like mango and kiwi fruit can be quickly transformed into exotically flavoured coulis. A few drops of orange flower water or rose water will give a scented flavour, but use it with caution – too much will overpower delicate ingredients.

1 Remove any hulls, stems, peel or stones from the fruit.

2 Place the prepared fruit in a blender or food processor and process until smooth.

3 Press the purée through a fine sieve, to remove the pips or fibrous parts and leave a smooth, syrupy juice. Sweeten to taste with icing sugar, and if necessary add a squeeze of lemon juice to sharpen the flavour.

Cook's Tip

For cooked peeled fruit, mash with a potato masher for a coarser purée.

Peach Sauce

Purée a 400g/14oz can of peaches, together with their juice and 1.5ml/¼ tsp of almond essence in a blender or food processor; chill before serving with fruit tarts or cakes.

Passion Fruit Coulis

Cut 3 ripe papayas in half and scoop out the seeds. Peel them and cut the flesh into chunks. Thread the chunks on bamboo skewers.

1 Halve eight passion fruit and scoop out the flesh. Purée in a blender for a few seconds.

2 Press the pulp through a sieve and discard the seeds. Add 30ml/2 tbsp of lime juice, 30ml/2 tbsp of icing sugar and 30ml/2 tbsp of white rum. Stir well until the sugar has dissolved.

3 Spoon some of the coulis on to a serving plate. Place the skewers on top. Drizzle the remaining coulis over the skewers and garnish with a little toasted coconut, if liked.

Chocolate Sauces

Chocolate sauces are enduringly popular, from simple custards to richly indulgent versions combined with liqueur or cream. They can be served with ice cream and other frozen desserts, but are also delicious with poached pears and a wide range of puddings. Flavoured liqueurs can be chosen to echo the flavour of the dessert, and coffee, brandy and cinnamon all go especially well with chocolate.

The more cocoa solids chocolate contains, the more chocolatey the flavour will be. Plain chocolate may have between 30–70 percent of cocoa solids. Plain dark chocolate has around 75 percent, so if you're aiming at a really rich, dark sauce, this is the best choice. Milk chocolate is much sweeter, containing 20 per cent cocoa solids.

White chocolate contains no cocoa solids, so strictly speaking it is not a chocolate at all, but gets its flavour from cocoa butter.

The best method of melting chocolate is in a double boiler or in a bowl over a pan of hot water. Never allow water or steam to come into contact with the chocolate as this may cause it to stiffen. Overheating will also spoil the flavour and texture. Plain chocolate should not be heated above 49°C/120°F, and milk or white chocolate not above 43°C/110°F.

For sauce recipes where the chocolate is melted with a quantity of other liquid such as milk or cream, the chocolate may be melted with the liquid in a pan over direct heat, providing there is plenty of liquid. Heat gently, stirring until melted.

Cocoa is ground from the whole cocoa mass after most of the cocoa butter has been extracted.

Creamy Chocolate Sauce

Place 120ml/4fl oz/½ cup double cream in a saucepan and add 130g/4½oz chocolate pieces to the pan. Stir over a low heat until the chocolate has melted. Serve warm or cold.

Cook's Tip

If you run out of chocolate for a sauce recipe, you can use cocoa as an emergency substitute. Mix 45ml/3 tbsp cocoa with 15ml/1 tbsp melted butter to replace each 25g/1oz chocolate.

Chocolate Custard Sauce

1 Melt 90g/3½oz plain dark chocolate in a bowl over a pan of hot water.

2 Heat 200ml/7fl oz/scant 1 cup *crème anglaise* until hot but not boiling and stir in the melted chocolate until evenly mixed. Serve hot or cold.

Rich Chocolate Brandy Sauce

Break up 115g/4oz plain chocolate into a bowl over a pan of hot water, then heat gently until melted. Remove from the heat and add 30ml/2 tbsp brandy and 30ml/2 tbsp melted butter, then stir until smooth. Serve hot.

Making Marinades and Dressings

Marinades can be savoury or sweet, spicy, fruity, fragrant or exotic, to add a contrasting flavour to all kinds of foods. They're useful not only for adding flavour, but also for tenderizing and keeping foods moist during cooking, and can also be used to form the basis of a sauce to serve with the finished dish.

Oil-based Marinades

Choose an oil-based marinade for low-fat foods, such as lean meat, poultry or white fish, which may dry out during cooking. Oil-based marinades are especially useful for grilling and barbecuing, and at their simplest consist of oil with crushed garlic and chopped herbs. Add crushed chillies for a hot and spicy marinade. Avoid adding salt to a marinade as this draws the juices out of the meat.

1 Place the marinade ingredients in a measuring jug and beat well with a fork to mix thoroughly. Arrange the food in a single layer in a non-metallic dish and pour the marinade over.

2 Turn the food to coat evenly in the marinade. Cover and leave in the fridge to marinate from 30 minutes to several hours, depending on the recipe. Turn the food occasionally.

3 When ready to cook, remove the food from the marinade. The marinade can be poured into a small pan and simmered for several minutes until thoroughly heated, then served spooned over the cooked food.

Wine- or Vinegar-based Marinades

Wine- or vinegar-based mixtures are best with rich foods such as game or oily fish, to add flavour, and to contrast and balance richness. Use herb-flavoured vinegars for oily fish and add chopped fresh herbs, such as tarragon, parsley, coriander and thyme.

The acid in the wine or vinegar starts the tenderizing process well before cooking. For game, which can have a tendency to be tough, leave in the marinade overnight. Add lemon juice, garlic, black pepper and herbs, and even sherry, cider or orange juice according to your preference.

Yogurt is a good marinade and can be flavoured with crushed garlic, lemon juice, and handfuls of chopped mint, thyme or rosemary for grilled lamb or pork. For fish or shellfish, use a marinade based on lemon juice with a little oil and plenty of black pepper.

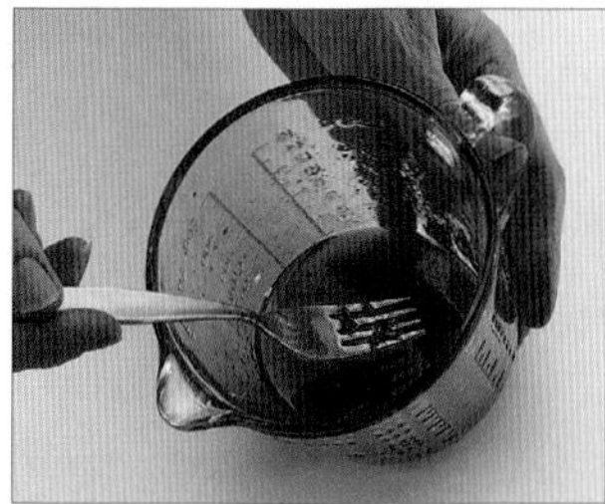

1 Measure the ingredients into a jug and beat with a fork.

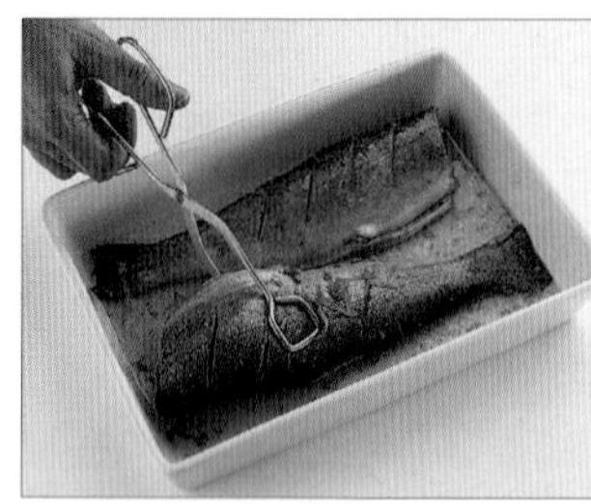

2 Arrange the food in a wide, non-metallic dish in a single layer and spoon over the marinade, turning the food to coat evenly. Cover with cling film and chill for 30 minutes up to several hours, depending on the recipe.

3 Drain the food of excess marinade before cooking. If the food is to be griddled or grilled, use the marinade to brush over the food during cooking to add extra flavour and keep it moist.

Making an Oil-based Dressing

A good vinaigrette can do more than dress a salad. It can also be used to baste meat, poultry, seafood or vegetables during cooking. Many classic dressings, such as vinaigrette or French dressing, are based on an oil and acid mixture. The basic proportions are 3 parts oil to 1 part acid beaten together to form an emulsion. This can be done by simply whisking with a fork in a jug, or the ingredients can be placed in a screw-topped jar and shaken thoroughly. The oil you choose for a dressing adds character to the flavour, and which one you use for which dressing depends upon your own taste and upon the salad ingredients. A strongly flavoured extra virgin olive oil adds personality to a simple green leaf or potato salad, but can overpower more delicate ingredients. Pure olive oil or sunflower oil adds a lighter flavour. Nut oils, such as walnut or hazelnut, are expensive, but can add a distinctive unusual flavour to a salad when used in small quantities.

The acid in a dressing may be vinegar or lemon juice, and this can define the flavour of the finished salad. Choose from wine, sherry or cider vinegars, herb, chilli or fruit vinegars, to balance or contrast with the salad ingredients and the type of oil. Matured vinegars such as balsamic can be strong in flavour. Balsamic has a distinctive flavour, because of its ageing in wooden barrels and so the basic proportions of 3 parts oil to 1 of vinegar should be amended to 5 parts oil and 2 of balsamic vinegar.

Lemon juice adds a sharper flavour, which can be useful to add a lively tang to a bland dish. Other fruit juices, such as orange or apple juice can be used instead for a sweeter, less acid flavour.

Left: Bottled dressings make pleasing kitchen ornaments and excellent gift ideas.

Variations

- *Use red.or white wine vinegar. Or use a herb-flavoured vinegar.*
- *Use lemon juice instead of vinegar.*
- *Replace 1 tablespoon of the vinegar with wine.*
- *Use olive oil, or a mixture of vegetable and olive oils.*
- *Use 4fl oz/120ml olive oil and 30ml/2 tbsp walnut or hazelnut oil.*
- *Add 15–30ml/1–2 tbsp Dijon mustard to the vinegar before whisking in the oil.*
- *Add 1 crushed garlic clove before whisking in the oil.*
- *Add 15–30ml/1–2 tbsp chopped herbs (parsley, basil, chives, thyme, etc) to the viaigrette.*

Classic Vinaigrette

To ensure the ingredients blend together in a smooth emulsion, make sure all the ingredients are at room temperature.

Put 30ml/2 tbsp vinegar in a bowl with 10ml/2 tsp Dijon mustard, salt and ground black pepper. Add 1.5ml/¼ tsp caster sugar if you like. Whisk to combine.

Slowly drizzle in 90ml/6 tbsp oil, whisking constantly, until the vinaigrette is smooth and well blended. Check the seasoning and adjust if necessary.

Creamy Orange Dressing

This tangy orange dressing is versatile enough to complement a mixed green salad with orange segments and tomatoes. It could also partner grilled chicken or smoked duck breasts, or chicken kebabs, served on a bed or rice salad.

Serves 4

45ml/3 tbsp half-fat crème fraîche
15ml/1 tbsp white wine vinegar
finely grated rind and juice of 1 small orange
salt and ground black pepper

1 Measure the crème fraîche and wine vinegar into a screw-topped jar with the orange rind and juice.

2 Shake well until evenly combined, then adjust the seasoning to taste as desired.

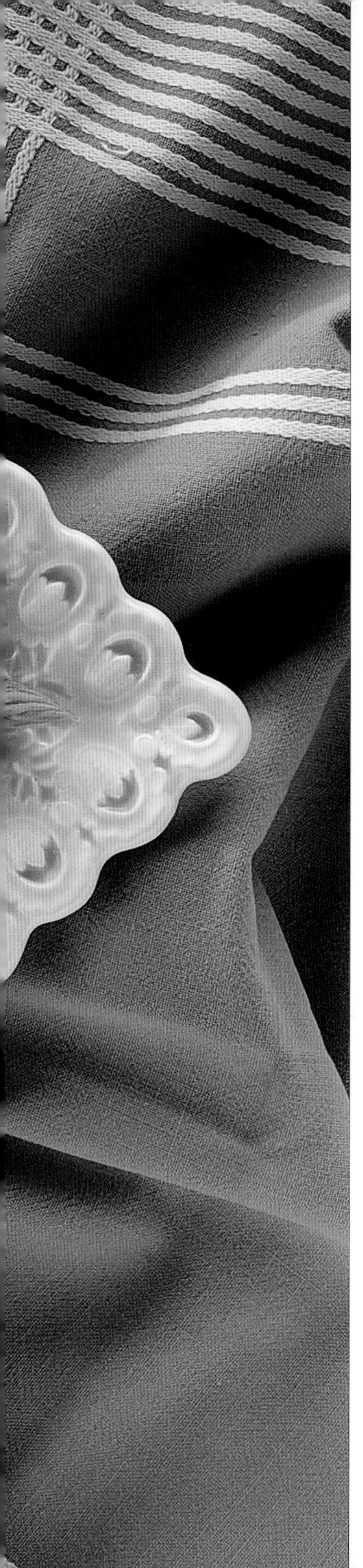

Classic Sauces

A comprehensive collection of sauce recipes must, by definition, include as its foundation the traditional, classic recipes that have been handed down through many generations of cooks.

Every country has its enduring time-honoured sauces, from French favourites, such as elegant Béchamel Sauce, and rich, brown Espagnole Sauce, to British favourites such as Horseradish or Bread Sauce; from all-American Cranberry Sauce to vibrant fresh Italian Pesto. Each has evolved from the imaginative use of local foods and has been created to enhance the flavours of the traditional cuisine of the country.

These well-tried classics form the basis of a repertoire essential to every professional cook. They encompass all of the sauce-making techniques, such as flour-thickened roux and rich emulsions, and some of them form an integral part of world-famous dishes.

In the past, the art of sauce-making required that stocks and other ingredients were prepared entirely by hand, but cooks today have electric mixers and food processors to assist them. The substitution of commercial stock can also save time and effort, and still provide the busy cook with an impressive result, complementing the flavour of both plain and rich cooking.

Béchamel Sauce

THIS IS A CREAMY white sauce with an excellent, mellow flavour, which makes it ideal for lasagne as well as a suitable base or accompaniment for many fish, egg and vegetable dishes.

Serves 4

INGREDIENTS

1 small onion
1 small carrot
1 celery stick
bouquet garni
6 black peppercorns
pinch of freshly grated nutmeg or a blade of mace
300ml/½ pint/1¼ cups milk
25g/1oz/2 tbsp butter
25g/1oz/¼ cup plain flour
30ml/2 tbsp single cream
salt and ground black pepper

1 Peel and finely chop the vegetables. Put the vegetables, flavourings and milk in a saucepan. Bring to the boil. Remove from the heat, cover and allow to infuse for 30 minutes.

2 Over a gentle heat, melt the butter in a saucepan, remove from the heat and stir in the flour. Return to the heat and cook for 1–2 minutes, stirring, to make a roux.

3 Reheat the flavoured milk until almost boiling. Strain into a jug, pressing the vegetables with the back of a spoon to extract the juices.

4 Off the heat, gradually blend the milk into the roux, stirring vigorously after each addition. Bring to the boil and stir continuously until the sauce thickens. Simmer gently for 3–4 minutes.

5 Remove the pan from the heat. Season with salt and pepper to taste and stir in the cream.

Basic White Sauce

THIS WHITE SAUCE IS wonderfully adaptable for all kinds of savoury dishes, but it can be bland so always taste and season carefully.

Serves 6

INGREDIENTS

600ml/1 pint/2½ cups milk
25g/1oz/2 tbsp butter
25g/1oz/¼ cup plain flour
salt and ground black pepper

1 Warm the milk in a saucepan over a low heat, but do not boil.

2 In a separate saucepan melt the butter, then stir in the flour and cook gently for 1–2 minutes to make a roux. Do not allow the roux to brown.

3 Remove the pan from the heat, gradually blend in the milk, stirring vigorously after each addition to prevent lumps forming.

4 Return to the heat and bring to the boil slowly, stirring continuously until the sauce thickens.

5 Simmer gently for a further 3–4 minutes until thickened and smooth. Season with salt and ground black pepper to taste.

COOK'S TIPS

- *For a thicker, coating sauce, increase the amount of flour to 50g/2oz/½ cup and the butter to 50g/2oz/¼ cup.*
- *If you aren't using a non-stick pan, use a small whisk to incorporate the flour and milk smoothly.*

VARIATIONS

- *Parsley sauce is traditionally served with bacon, fish and broad beans. Stir in 15ml/1 tbsp chopped fresh parsley just before serving.*
- *Cheese sauce makes delicious egg and vegetable gratins. Stir in 50g/2oz/½ cup finely grated mature Cheddar and 2.5ml/½ tsp prepared mustard.*

Velouté Sauce

THIS SAVOURY POURING SAUCE is named after its smooth, velvety texture. It's based on a white stock made from fish, vegetables or meat, so it can easily be adapted to the dish you are serving.

Serves 4

INGREDIENTS

600ml/1 pint/2½ cups stock
25g/1oz/2 tbsp butter
25g/1oz/¼ cup plain flour
30ml/2 tbsp single cream
salt and ground black pepper

1 Heat the stock until almost boiling, but do not boil. In another pan melt the butter and stir in the flour. Cook, stirring, over a moderate heat for 3–4 minutes, or until a pale, straw colour, stirring continuously.

2 Remove the pan from the heat and gradually blend in the hot stock. Return to the heat and bring to the boil, stirring continuously, until the sauce thickens.

3 Continue to cook at a very slow simmer, stirring occasionally, until reduced by about a quarter.

4 Skim the surface during cooking to remove any scum, or pour through a very fine strainer.

5 Just before serving, remove from the heat and stir in the cream. Season to taste.

VARIATION

For a richer flavour in a special dish, replace 30–45ml/2–3 tbsp of the stock with dry white wine or vermouth.

Lemon Sauce with Tarragon

THE SHARPNESS OF LEMON and the mild aniseed flavour of tarragon add zest to chicken, egg or steamed vegetable dishes.

Serves 4

INGREDIENTS

1 lemon
a small bunch of fresh tarragon
1 shallot, finely chopped
90ml/6 tbsp white wine
1 quantity Velouté sauce
45ml/3 tbsp double cream
30ml/2 tbsp brandy
salt and ground black pepper

1 Thinly pare the rind from the lemon, taking care not to remove any white pith. Squeeze the juice from the lemon and pour it into a saucepan. Discard the lemon.

2 Discard the coarse stalks from the tarragon. Chop the leaves and add all but 15ml/1 tbsp to the pan with the lemon rind and shallot.

3 Add the wine and simmer gently until the liquid is reduced by half. Strain into a clean saucepan.

4 Add the Velouté sauce, cream, brandy and reserved tarragon. Heat through, taste and adjust the seasoning if necessary.

COOK'S TIP

This sauce goes well with pieces of boned chicken breast, wrapped with streaky bacon rashers and grilled or pan-fried.

Espagnole Sauce

ESPAGNOLE IS A CLASSIC rich brown sauce, ideal for serving with red meat and game. It also makes a delicious, full-flavoured base for other sauces.

Serves 4–6

INGREDIENTS

25g/1oz/2 tbsp butter
50g/2oz bacon, chopped
2 shallots, unpeeled and chopped
1 carrot, chopped
1 celery stick, chopped
mushroom trimmings (if available)
25g/1oz/¼ cup plain flour
600ml/1 pint/2½ cups hot brown stock
bouquet garni
30ml/2 tbsp tomato purée
15ml/1 tbsp sherry (optional)
salt and ground black pepper

1 Melt the butter in a heavy-based saucepan and fry the bacon for 2–3 minutes. Add the shallots, carrot, celery and mushroom trimmings, if using, and cook the mixture for a further 5–6 minutes, or until golden.

2 Gradually stir in the flour and cook for 5–10 minutes over a medium heat until the roux has become a rich brown colour.

3 Remove the pan from the heat and gradually blend in the stock.

4 Slowly bring to the boil, continuing to stir until the sauce thickens. Add the bouquet garni, tomato purée, sherry, if using, and seasoning. Reduce the heat and simmer gently for one hour, stirring occasionally.

5 Strain the Espagnole sauce, and gently reheat before serving.

COOK'S TIP

This sauce can be covered and stored in the fridge for up to 4 days, or it can be frozen for up to 1 month. It's worth making double the quantity and keeping a batch in reserve.

Chasseur Sauce

THIS EXCELLENT MUSHROOM and wine sauce will transform simple pan-fried or grilled chicken, grilled or roast pork, or rabbit dishes. To give the sauce more flavour use chestnut mushrooms.

Serves 3–4

INGREDIENTS

25g/1oz/2 tbsp butter
1 shallot, finely chopped
115g/4oz/2 cups mushrooms, sliced
120ml/4fl oz/½ cup white wine
30ml/2 tbsp brandy
1 quantity Espagnole sauce
15ml/1 tbsp chopped fresh tarragon or chervil

1 Melt the butter in a medium or large saucepan over a medium heat, and fry the shallot until soft but not brown.

2 Add the mushrooms and sauté, stirring occasionally until they just begin to brown.

3 Pour in the wine and brandy, and simmer over a medium heat until reduced by half.

4 Add the Espagnole sauce and herbs and heat through, stirring occasionally. Serve hot.

Tangy Orange Sauce

KNOWN AS *SAUCE BIGARADE*, this is the perfect accompaniment for roast duckling and rich game. For a full mellow flavour it is best made with the rich roasting-pan juices.

Serves 4–6

INGREDIENTS

roasting-pan juices or 25g/1oz/ 2 tbsp butter
40g/1½oz/⅓ cup plain flour
300ml/½ pint hot stock (preferably duck)
150ml/¼ pint/⅔ cup red wine
2 Seville oranges or 2 sweet oranges plus 10ml/2 tsp lemon juice
15ml/1 tbsp orange-flavoured liqueur
30ml/2 tbsp redcurrant jelly
salt and ground black pepper

1 Carefully pour off any excess fat from the roasting pan, leaving the rich meat juices behind, or melt the butter in a small saucepan.

2 Sprinkle the flour into the juices or butter and cook, stirring continuously, for about 4 minutes, or until the mixture is lightly browned.

3 Off the heat, gradually blend in the hot stock and wine. Return to the heat and bring to the boil, stirring continuously. Lower the heat and simmer gently for 5 minutes.

4 Meanwhile, using a citrus zester, peel the rind thinly from one orange. Squeeze the juice from both of the oranges.

5 Place the rind in a small pan, cover with boiling water and bring back to the boil. Simmer for 5 minutes, then strain and add the rind to the sauce.

6 Add the orange juice to the sauce, along with the lemon juice, if using, and the liqueur and jelly. Stir until the jelly has dissolved. Season with salt and pepper to taste.

COOK'S TIP

Seville oranges have a distinctive bitter flavour, which is good for savoury dishes, but they have a short season. They can be frozen whole, or you can freeze the juice and rind separately.

Hollandaise Sauce

A RICH BUTTER SAUCE rather like a warm mayonnaise, is perfect for either steamed or grilled fish, such as salmon, or fresh vegetables such as broccoli, asparagus or new potatoes. The secret of success is patience. Slowly and thoroughly work in the butter to give a thick, glossy texture.

Serves 2–3

INGREDIENTS

30ml/2 tbsp white wine or tarragon vinegar
15ml/1 tbsp water
6 black peppercorns
1 bay leaf
115g/4oz/½ cup butter
2 egg yolks
salt and ground black pepper

1 Place the vinegar, water, peppercorns, and bay leaf in a saucepan. Simmer the liquid gently until it has reduced by half. Strain and allow to cool.

2 In a separate bowl, cream the butter until soft.

3 In a double boiler, or a heatproof bowl sitting over a saucepan of gently simmering, but not boiling, water, whisk the egg yolks and infused vinegar liquid together gently until the mixture is light and fluffy.

4 Gradually add the butter a tiny piece at a time – about the size of a hazelnut will be enough. Whisk quickly until all the butter has been absorbed before adding any more.

5 Season lightly and, if the sauce is too sharp, add a little more butter.

6 For a thinner version of the sauce, stir in 15–30ml/1–2 tbsp single cream. Serve immediately.

COOK'S TIP

Any leftover sauce can be stored in the fridge for up to a week. Reheat very gently in a bowl over simmering water, whisking continuously.

Mousseline Sauce

A TRULY LUSCIOUS SAUCE, that is subtly flavoured, rich and creamy. Try serving it as a dip for prepared artichokes or artichoke hearts, or with shellfish.

Serves 4

INGREDIENTS

2 egg yolks
15ml/1 tbsp lemon juice
75g/3oz/6 tbsp softened butter
90ml/6 tbsp double cream
extra lemon juice (optional)
salt and ground black pepper

1 To make the sauce, whisk the yolks and lemon juice in a bowl over a pan of barely simmering water, or a double boiler, until very thick and fluffy.

2 Whisk in the butter, but only a very little at a time, until it is thoroughly absorbed and the sauce has the consistency of mayonnaise.

3 In a separate bowl, whisk the cream until it forms stiff peaks. Fold into the warm sauce and adjust the seasoning. You can add a little more lemon juice for extra sharpness.

VARIATION

For a lavish accompaniment to special fish dishes such as lobster or Dover sole, stir in 30–45ml/2–3 tbsp caviar before serving as a Caviar Mousseline.

Béarnaise Sauce

FOR DEDICATED MEAT EATERS, this herby butter sauce adds a note of sophistication without swamping your grilled or pan-fried steak. It also enhances plain vegetables.

Serves 2–3

INGREDIENTS

45ml/3 tbsp white wine vinegar
30ml/2 tbsp water
1 small onion, finely chopped
a few fresh tarragon and chervil sprigs
1 bay leaf
6 crushed black peppercorns
115g/4oz/½ cup butter
2 egg yolks
15ml/1 tbsp chopped fresh herbs, such as tarragon, parsley, chervil
salt and ground black pepper

1 Place the vinegar, water, onion, herb sprigs, bay leaf and peppercorns in a saucepan. Simmer gently until the liquid is reduced by half. Strain and cool.

2 In a separate bowl, cream the butter until soft.

3 In a bowl over a saucepan of gently simmering water, or a double boiler, whisk the egg yolks and liquid until light and fluffy.

4 Gradually add the butter, half a teaspoonful at a time. Whisk until all the butter has been incorporated before adding any more.

5 Add the chopped fresh herbs and season to taste.

6 Serve warm, not hot, on the side of a grilled steak or allow a good spoonful to melt over new potatoes.

VARIATION

To make Choron sauce, which is very good with roast or grilled lamb, stir in 15ml/1 tbsp tomato purée to the sauce at the end of step 1.

Newburg Sauce

THIS CREAMY MADEIRA-FLAVOURED sauce originated in America. Its rich flavour will not mask delicate foods and it is therefore ideal for serving with shellfish. It also goes well with pan-fried chicken.

Serves 4

INGREDIENTS

15g/½oz/1 tbsp butter
1 small shallot, finely chopped
pinch of cayenne pepper
300ml/½ pint/1¼ cups double cream
60ml/4 tbsp Madeira
3 egg yolks
salt and ground black pepper

1 Melt the butter in a heatproof bowl placed over a saucepan of simmering water, or in a double boiler.

2 Add the chopped shallot to the butter and cook gently until it is soft and transparent.

3 Add the cayenne and all but 60ml/4 tbsp of the cream. Leave over the simmering water for 10 minutes to reduce slightly.

4 Stir in the Madeira. Beat the yolks with the remaining cream and stir into the hot sauce. Continue stirring the sauce over barely simmering water until thickened. Season to taste. Serve immediately.

COOK'S TIPS

- *To give the sauce a luxurious festive look, stir in 15–30ml/1–2 tbsp of pink or black lumpfish roe at the end of cooking.*
- *Spoon over seafood or chicken, reserving some for pouring, and serve immediately. Garnish the dish with fresh herbs.*

Pesto Sauce

THERE IS NOTHING MORE evocative of the warmth of Italy than a good home-made pesto. Serve in generous spoonfuls with your favourite pasta.

Serves 3–4

INGREDIENTS

50g/2oz/1 cup basil leaves
2 garlic cloves, crushed
30ml/2 tbsp pine nuts
120ml/4 fl oz/½ cup olive oil
40g/1½oz/½ cup finely grated fresh Parmesan cheese
salt and ground black pepper

1 **By hand:** Using a mortar and pestle, grind the basil, garlic, pine nuts and seasoning to a fine paste.

2 Transfer the mixture to a bowl and whisk in the oil a little at a time.

3 Add the cheese and blend well. Adjust the seasoning to taste and heat the sauce gently.

1 **Using a food processor:** place the basil, garlic, pine nuts and seasoning in the food processor and process as finely as possible.

2 With the machine running slowly add the oil in a thin stream, combining the ingredients until they have formed a smooth paste.

3 Add the cheese and pulse quickly 3–4 times. Adjust the seasoning if necessary and heat gently.

VARIATION

Pesto makes an excellent dressing for boiled new potatoes. Serve while hot or allow to cool to room temperature.

Rich Tomato Sauce

FOR A FULL TOMATO flavour and rich red colour, fresh Italian plum tomatoes are an excellent choice if they are available.

Serves 4–6

INGREDIENTS

30ml/2 tbsp olive oil
1 large onion, chopped
2 garlic cloves, crushed
1 carrot, finely chopped
1 celery stick, finely chopped
675g/1½lb tomatoes, peeled and chopped
150ml/¼ pint/⅔ cup red wine
150ml/¼ pint/⅔ cup vegetable stock
bouquet garni
2.5–5ml/½–1 tsp sugar
15ml/1 tbsp tomato purée, or to taste
salt and ground black pepper

1 Heat the oil in a saucepan, add the onion and garlic and sauté until soft and pale golden brown. Add the carrot and celery and continue to cook, stirring occasionally, until golden.

2 Stir in the tomatoes, wine, stock and bouquet garni. Season with salt and ground black pepper to taste.

3 Bring the tomato mixture to the boil, then cover and simmer gently for 45 minutes, stirring occasionally to avoid the burning. Remove the bouquet garni from the liquid, taste the sauce and adjust the seasoning, adding a pinch of sugar and tomato purée as necessary.

4 Serve the sauce as it is or, for a smoother texture, press through a sieve, or purée in a blender or food processor. This is delicious spooned over sliced courgettes or whole French beans.

Blue Cheese and Walnut Sauce

THIS IS A VERY quick but indulgently creamy sauce. The blue cheese melts easily with cream to make a simple sauce to serve with vegetables or pasta for a delicious lunch or supper.

Serves 2

INGREDIENTS

50g/2oz/¼ cup butter
50g/2oz/¾ cup button mushrooms, sliced
150g/5oz hard blue cheese, such as Gorgonzola, Stilton or Danish Blue
150ml/¼ pint/⅔ cup soured cream
25g/1oz/⅓ cup grated Pecorino cheese
50g/2oz/⅓ cup broken walnut pieces
salt and ground black pepper

1 Melt the butter in a saucepan, add the mushrooms and gently fry for 3–5 minutes, stirring occasionally until lightly browned.

2 Place the blue cheese and cream in a bowl, add seasoning to taste, and mash together well using a fork.

3 Stir the cheese mixture into the mushroom mixture and heat gently, stirring, until melted.

4 Finally, stir in the Pecorino cheese and the walnut pieces. Serve warm.

Quick Satay Sauce

THERE ARE MANY VERSIONS of this tasty peanut sauce. This one is very speedy and it tastes delicious drizzled over grilled or barbecued skewers of chicken. For parties, spear chunks of chicken with cocktail sticks and arrange around a bowl of warm sauce.

Serves 4

INGREDIENTS

200ml/7fl oz/scant 1 cup coconut cream
60ml/4 tbsp crunchy peanut butter
1 tsp Worcestershire sauce
Tabasco sauce, to taste
fresh coconut, to garnish (optional)

1 Pour the coconut cream into a small saucepan and heat it gently over a low heat for about 2 minutes.

2 Add the peanut butter and stir vigorously until it is blended into the coconut cream. Continue to heat until the mixture is warm but not boiling hot.

3 Add the Worcestershire sauce and a dash of Tabasco to taste. Pour into a serving bowl.

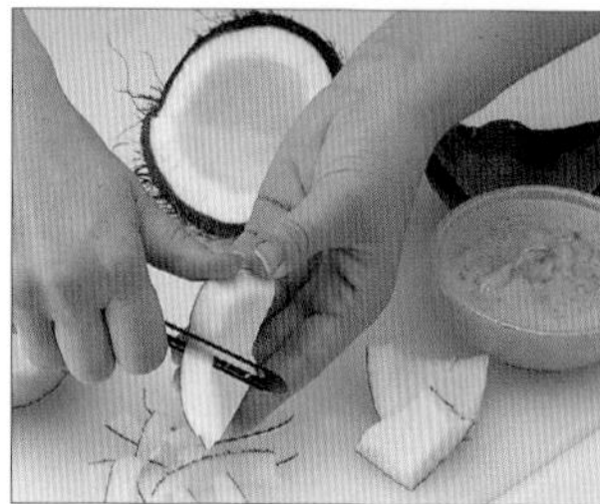

4 Use a potato peeler to shave thin curls from a piece of fresh coconut, if using. Scatter the coconut over the dish of your choice and serve immediately with the sauce.

COOK'S TIP

Thick coconut milk can be substituted for coconut cream, but take care to buy an unsweetened variety for this recipe.

Green Peppercorn Sauce

THIS SAUCE IS EXCELLENT with pasta, pork steaks or grilled chicken. The green peppercorns in brine are a better choice than the dry-packed type because they tend to give a more rounded flavour.

Serves 3–4

INGREDIENTS

15ml/1 tbsp green peppercorns in brine, drained
1 small onion, finely chopped
25g/1oz/2 tbsp butter
300ml/½ pint/1¼ cups light stock
juice of ½ lemon
15ml/1 tbsp beurre manié
45ml/3 tbsp double cream
5ml/1 tsp Dijon mustard
salt and ground black pepper

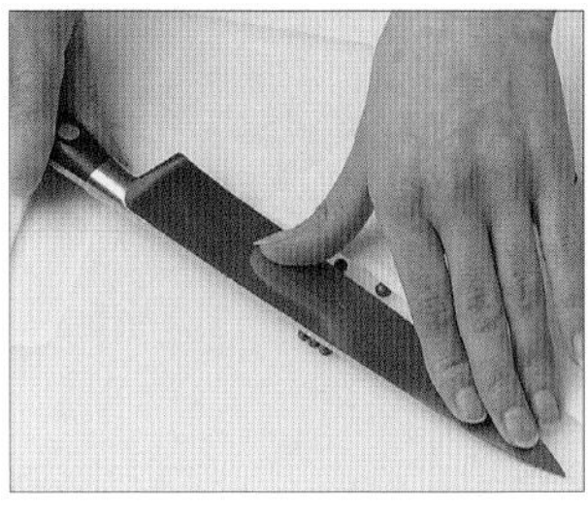

1 Dry the peppercorns on absorbent kitchen paper, then crush lightly under the blade of a heavy-duty knife or use a mortar and pestle.

2 Soften the onion in the butter, add the stock and lemon juice and simmer for 15 minutes.

3 Whisk in the beurre manié a little at a time and continue to cook, stirring, until the sauce thickens.

VARIATION

For a lighter, less rich sauce, use crème fraîche instead of the double cream.

4 Reduce the heat and stir in the peppercorns, cream and mustard. Heat until boiling then season to taste. Serve hot with buttered pasta or the dish of your choice.

COOK'S TIP

For beurre manié, knead together equal quantities of butter and flour.

Barbecue Sauce

BRUSH THIS SAUCE OVER chops, kebabs or chicken drumsticks before cooking on the barbecue, or serve as a hot or cold accompaniment to hot dogs and burgers.

Serves 4

INGREDIENTS

30ml/2 tbsp vegetable oil
1 large onion, chopped
2 garlic cloves, crushed
400g/14oz can tomatoes
30ml/2 tbsp Worcestershire sauce
15ml/1 tbsp white wine vinegar
45ml/3 tbsp honey
5ml/1 tsp mustard powder
2.5ml/½ tsp chilli seasoning or mild chilli powder
salt and ground black pepper

1 In a saucepan, heat the oil and fry the onion and garlic until soft.

2 Stir in the remaining ingredients and bring to the boil. Simmer, uncovered, for 15–20 minutes, stirring occasionally. Cool slightly.

3 Pour into a food processor or blender and process until smooth.

4 Press the sauce through a sieve if you prefer a smoother result, and adjust the seasoning with salt and pepper to taste before serving.

VARIATION

For a really rich, spicy chilli flavour, omit the chilli seasoning and add instead a small red chilli, seeded and chopped. Leave the seeds in if you like it really hot.

Apple Sauce

REALLY MORE OF A condiment than a sauce, this tart purée is usually served cold or warm, rather than hot. It's typically served with rice, roast pork or duck, but is also good with cold meats and savoury pies.

Serves 6

INGREDIENTS

225g/8oz tart cooking apples
30ml/2 tbsp water
thin strip of lemon rind
15ml/1 tbsp butter
15–30ml/1–2 tbsp caster sugar

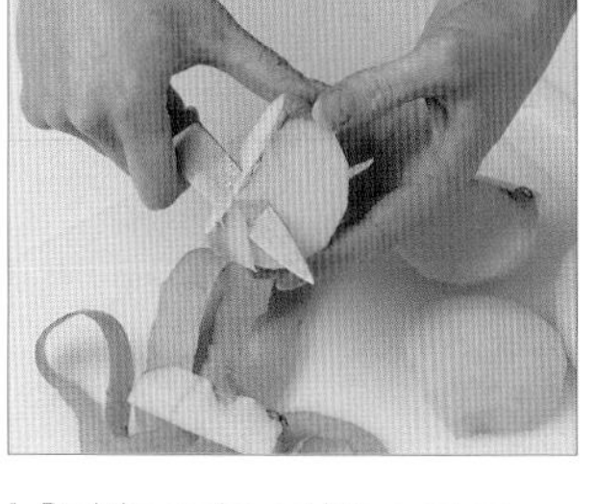

1 Peel the apples, cut into quarters and remove the core. Cut into thin, even slices.

2 Place the apples in a saucepan with the water and lemon rind. Cook, uncovered, over a low heat until very soft, stirring occasionally.

3 Remove the lemon rind from the pan and discard. Beat the apples to a pulp with a spoon, or press through a sieve.

4 Stir the butter into the apple sauce and then add sugar to taste.

VARIATIONS

- *To make a Normandy Apple Sauce, try stirring in 15ml/1 tbsp Calvados with the butter and sugar at step 4.*
- *To make a creamy savoury Apple Sauce, stir in 30ml/2 tbsp soured cream or crème fraîche at step 4.*

Mint Sauce

TART, YET SWEET, this simple sauce is the perfect foil to rich meat. It's best served, of course, with the new season's tender roast lamb, but it is also wonderful with grilled lamb chops or pan-fried duck.

Serves 6

INGREDIENTS

small bunch of mint
15ml/1 tbsp sugar
30ml/2 tbsp boiling water
45ml/3 tbsp white wine vinegar

1 Strip the mint leaves from the stalks and finely chop the leaves.

2 Place in a bowl with the sugar and pour on the boiling water. Stir well and allow the mixture to stand for 5–10 minutes.

3 Add the vinegar and leave to stand for 1–2 hours before serving.

COOK'S TIP

This sauce also makes a refreshing dressing to enhance the summery flavour of fresh peas or new potatoes.

Cranberry Sauce

THIS IS THE TRADITIONAL sauce for roast turkey, but don't keep it just for festive occasions. The vibrant colour and tart taste are a perfect partner to any white roast meat, and it makes a great addition to a chicken or Brie sandwich.

Serves 6

INGREDIENTS

1 orange
225g/8oz/2 cups cranberries
250g/9oz/1¼ cups caster sugar
150ml/¼ pint/⅔ cup water

1 Pare the rind thinly from the orange using a swivel-bladed vegetable peeler, taking care not to remove any white pith. Squeeze the juice.

2 Place in a saucepan with the cranberries, sugar and water.

3 Bring to a boil, stirring until the sugar has dissolved, then allow to simmer gently for 10–15 minutes or until the berries burst.

4 Remove the orange rind and allow to cool before serving.

COOK'S TIP

Fresh or frozen cranberries may be used in this sauce, depending on the season. Use fresh as a first choice.

Horseradish Sauce

THIS LIGHT, CREAMY SAUCE has a peppery flavour that's spiced with just a hint of mustard. It is the classic accompaniment to roast beef, but is perfect, too, with herby sausages and grilled fish, especially oily fish such as mackerel.

Serves 6

INGREDIENTS

7.5cm/3in piece fresh horseradish
15ml/1 tbsp lemon juice
10ml/2 tsp sugar
2.5ml/½ tsp English mustard powder
150ml/¼ pint/⅔ cup double cream

1 Scrub and peel the piece of fresh horseradish, and then grate it as finely as possible.

2 In a bowl, mix together the grated horseradish, lemon juice, sugar and mustard powder.

3 Whip the cream until it stands in soft peaks, then gently fold in the horseradish mixture.

VARIATION

For a change of flavour, replace the lemon juice with tarragon vinegar.

Bread Sauce

SMOOTH AND SURPRISINGLY DELICATE, this old-fashioned sauce dates back to medieval times. It's traditionally served with roast chicken, turkey and game birds.

Serves 6

INGREDIENTS

1 small onion
4 cloves
bay leaf
300ml/½ pint/1¼ cups milk
90g/3½oz/scant 2 cups fresh white breadcrumbs
15ml/1 tbsp butter
15ml/1 tbsp single cream
salt and ground black pepper

1 Peel the onion and stick the cloves into it. Put it into a saucepan with the bay leaf and pour in the milk.

2 Bring to the boil, then remove from the heat and allow to infuse for 15–20 minutes. Remove the bay leaf and onion from the milk.

3 Return to the heat and stir in the breadcrumbs. Simmer for 4–5 minutes, or until thick and creamy.

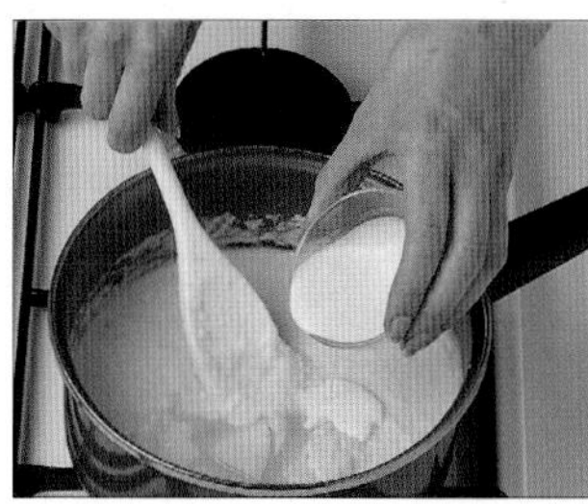

4 Stir in the butter and cream, then season to taste.

COOK'S TIP

If you would prefer a less strong flavour, reduce the number of cloves in the onion to one or two and add a little freshly grated nutmeg to the milk instead.

Sauces for Pasta Dishes

There's a wealth of sauce recipes for all types of pasta, and not surprisingly they are often Italian in origin. Endlessly varied in style, they may be delicate, buttery herb mixtures or rich cream sauces, hearty meat ragús or chunky vegetable sauces. Many are based on tomatoes from southern Italy, and make the very best use of those other Mediterranean flavours – olive oil, garlic and basil – all classic partners for pasta.

Most pasta sauces are refreshingly simple and foolproof, and do not need hours of preparation. Most are cooked in a matter of minutes, retaining all the natural flavours of fresh ingredients, with the exception of long-simmered rich meat and tomato ragús, which by tradition are simmered at length on a low flame for a more concentrated, mature flavour.

Many of these sauces are designed to match particular types or shapes of pasta, but there are no hard and fast rules. Many of the sauces work well with other types of pasta, so try experimenting with your favourites.

It's rare for a pasta sauce to be flour-thickened, but many are enriched or thickened with eggs, such as Carbonara. Those that are simmered over long periods, such as Bolognese Sauce, reach a thicker consistency as they are reduced and become more concentrated. Many form an integral part of the dish, and may be as simple as olive oil with Parmesan cheese and herbs. The choice is yours.

Making Pasta Dough

Home-made pasta has a wonderfully light, almost silky texture – quite different from the so-called fresh pasta that you buy in the shops. If you use egg in the mixture, which is recommended if you are making pasta at home, the dough is easy to make and the initial process is not that different from making bread.

Pasta with Eggs

INGREDIENTS

300g/11oz/2¾ cups flour
3 eggs
5ml/1 tsp salt

COOK'S TIP

Don't skimp on the kneading time or the finished pasta will not be light and silky.

1 Mound the flour on a clean surface and make a large, deep well in the centre with your hands. Keep the sides of the well so that when the eggs are added they will stay in the well.

2 Crack the eggs into the well and add the salt. With a table knife, mix the eggs and salt together, then gradually incorporate the flour from the sides of the well.

3 As soon as the mixture is no longer liquid, dip your fingers in the flour and work the ingredients into a rough and sticky dough. If the dough is too dry, add a few drops of cold water; if it is too moist, sprinkle a little flour over it.

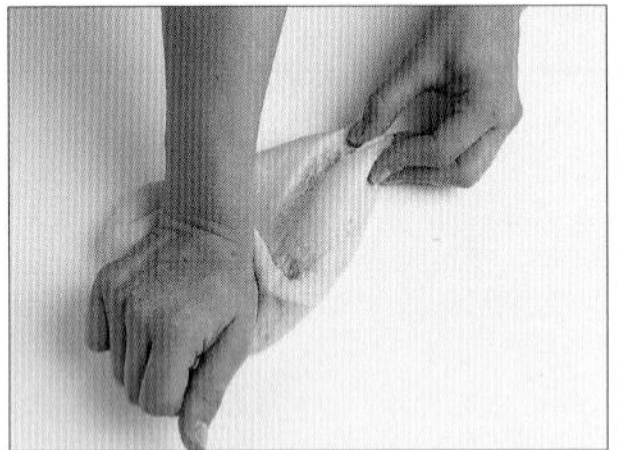

4 Press the dough into a rough ball and knead it as you would bread. Push it away from you with the heel of your hand, then fold the dough back on itself so that it faces towards you and push it out again.

5 Continue folding the dough back a little further each time and pushing it out until you have folded it back all the way towards you and all the dough has been kneaded. Give the dough a quarter turn anti-clockwise, then continue kneading, folding and turning for 10 minutes. The dough should be very smooth and elastic.

6 Wrap the dough in clear film and leave to rest for 15–20 minutes at room temperature. It will then be ready to roll.

Making Pasta Shapes

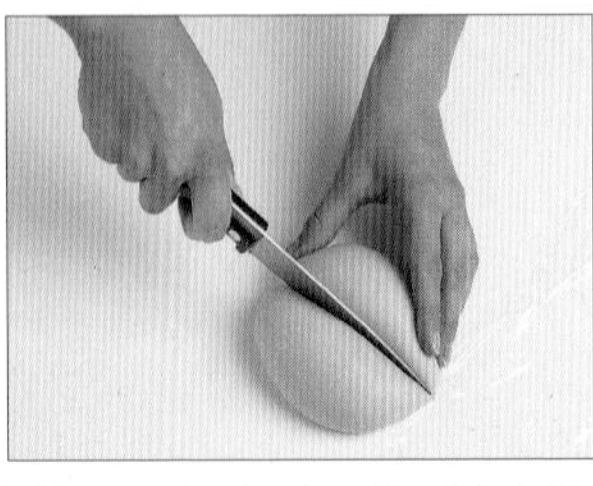

1 Unwrap the dough and cut it in half. Work on half at once.

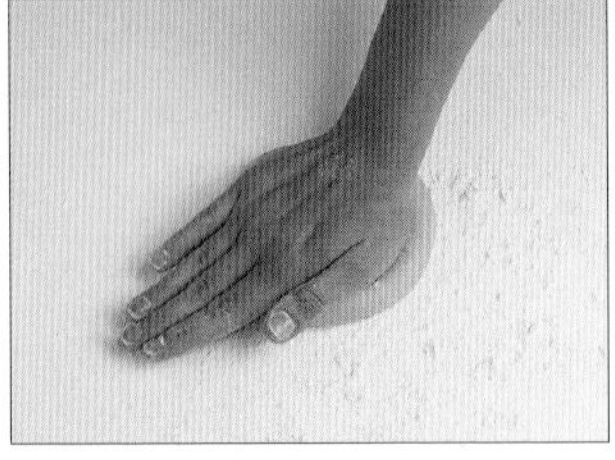

2 Sprinkle flour on the work surface, add the dough and flatten it.

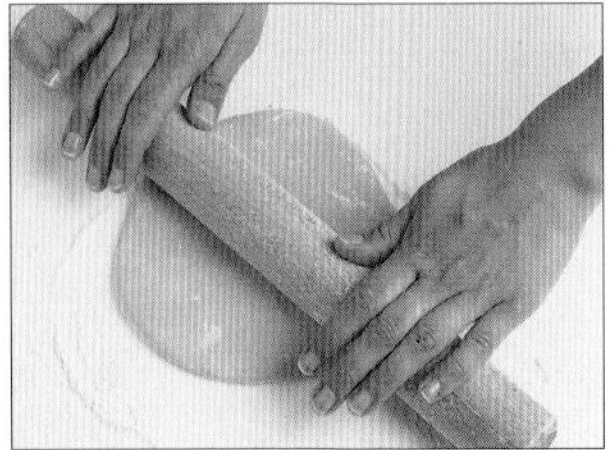

3 Roll out the dough, turning it as you work until it is 3mm/⅛in thick.

Italian Plum Tomato Sauce with Cheese and Ham Ravioli

THIS TASTY SAUCE USES store-cupboard ingredients, which is time saving if you have an elaborate pasta to make. It can also be served with meat or fish.

Serves 4–6

INGREDIENTS

500g/1¼lb fresh pasta dough with eggs
60ml/4 tbsp grated fresh Pecorino cheese, plus extra to serve

For the filling

175g/6oz ricotta cheese
30ml/2 tbsp grated fresh Parmesan cheese
115g/4oz prosciutto, finely chopped
150g/5oz fresh mozzarella cheese, drained and finely chopped
1 small egg
15ml/1 tbsp chopped fresh flat leaf parsley, plus extra to garnish

For the Italian plum tomato sauce

30ml/2 tbsp olive oil
1 onion, finely chopped
400g/14oz can chopped plum tomatoes
15ml/1 tbsp sun-dried tomato paste
5–10ml/1–2 tsp dried oregano
salt and ground black pepper

1 To make the sauce, heat the oil in a saucepan, add the onion and cook, stirring frequently, until softened.

2 Add the tomatoes. Fill the empty can with water, pour it into the pan, then stir in the tomato paste, oregano and seasoning to taste. Bring to the boil and stir well, then cover the pan and simmer for 30 minutes, stirring occasionally and adding more water if the sauce becomes too thick.

3 Put the filling ingredients in a bowl and season to taste. Mix with a fork, breaking up the ricotta.

4 Using a pasta machine, roll out one-quarter of the pasta into a 90–100cm/36–40in strip. Cut the strip into two 45–50cm/18–20in lengths.

5 Using two teaspoons, put little mounds of the filling, 10–12 in total, along one side of one of the pasta strips, spacing them evenly. The filling will be quite moist. Brush a little water around each mound, then fold the plain side of the pasta strip over.

6 Starting from the folded edge, press down gently with your fingertips around each mound, pushing the air out at the unfolded edge.

7 Sprinkle lightly with flour. With a fluted pasta wheel, cut along each long side, then in between each mound, to make small square shapes.

8 Put the ravioli on floured dish towels; sprinkle lightly with flour. Allow to dry while repeating the process with the remaining pasta, to give you 80–96 ravioli altogether.

9 Drop the ravioli into a large pan of boiling, lightly salted water, bring the water back to the boil and boil for 4–5 minutes. Drain well. Spoon about a third of the ravioli into a warmed serving bowl. Sprinkle with 15ml/1 tbsp grated Pecorino and pour over a third of the tomato sauce.

10 Repeat the layers twice, then top with the remaining grated Pecorino. Serve immediately, garnished with chopped parsley.

Tomato and Chilli Sauce with Pasta

THIS IS A SPECIALITY OF LAZIO in Italy – the Italian name for the sauce, *al arrabbiata*, means rabid or angry, and describes the heat that comes from the chilli.

Serves 4

INGREDIENTS

300g/11oz dried penne or tortiglioni

For the tomato and chilli sauce

500g/1¼lb sugocasa
2 garlic cloves, crushed
150ml/¼ pint/⅔ cup dry white wine
15ml/1 tbsp sun-dried tomato paste
1 fresh red chilli
30ml/2 tbsp finely chopped fresh flat leaf parsley, plus extra to garnish
salt and ground black pepper
grated fresh Pecorino cheese, to serve

1 Put the sugocasa, garlic, wine, tomato paste and whole chilli in a saucepan and bring to the boil. Cover and simmer gently.

2 Drop the pasta into a large saucepan of rapidly boiling salted water and cook for 10–12 minutes, or until *al dente*.

3 Remove the chilli from the sauce and add the parsley. Taste for seasoning. If you prefer a hotter taste, chop some or all of the chilli and return it to the sauce.

4 Drain the pasta and tip into a warmed large bowl. Pour the sauce over the pasta and toss to mix. Serve at once, sprinkled with parsley and grated Pecorino.

COOK'S TIPS

• *If you prefer the flavour to be slightly less hot, remove the seeds from the chilli before using. Split the chilli down its length and scrape out the fiery seeds with the tip of a knife.*

• *Sugocasa literally means "house sauce" and consists of tomatoes, crushed coarsely so that they have a chunky texture.*

Sun-dried Tomato and Radicchio Sauce with Paglia e Fieno

THIS IS A LIGHT, MODERN pasta dish of the kind served in fashionable restaurants. It is the presentation that sets it apart. It is very quick and easy to prepare.

Serves 4

INGREDIENTS

45ml/3 tbsp pine nuts
350g/12oz paglia e fieno pasta
30ml/2 tbsp extra virgin olive oil
4–6 spring onions, thinly sliced into rings

For the sun-dried tomato and radicchio sauce

15ml/1 tbsp extra virgin olive oil
30ml/2 tbsp sun-dried tomato paste
40g/1½oz radicchio leaves, finely shredded
salt and ground black pepper

1 Put the pine nuts in a heavy-based frying pan and toss over a medium heat for 1–2 minutes until they are lightly toasted and golden brown. Remove and set aside.

2 Cook the pasta according to the packet instructions, keeping the colours separate by using two pans.

3 To make the sauce, heat the oil in a medium frying pan or saucepan. Add the sun-dried tomato paste, then stir in two ladlefuls of pasta cooking water. Simmer until the sauce is slightly reduced, stirring constantly.

4 Stir in the shredded radicchio, then taste and season. Keep on a low heat. Drain the pasta, keeping the colours separate, and return them to the pans in which they were cooked. Add 15ml/1 tbsp of oil to each pan and toss over a medium to high heat until the pasta is glistening.

5 Arrange a portion of green and white pasta in each of four warmed bowls, then spoon the sun-dried tomato and radicchio sauce in the centre. Sprinkle the spring onions and toasted pine nuts decoratively over the top and serve immediately. Before eating, each diner should toss the sauce with the pasta to mix well.

COOK'S TIP

If you find the presentation too fussy, you can toss the sun-dried tomato and radicchio mixture with the pasta in one large warmed bowl before serving, then sprinkle with spring onions and pine nuts.

Cannelloni with Two Sauces

THE COMBINATION OF THE full-flavoured tomato sauce and the creamy white sauce makes this cannelloni dish a success. For a special occasion, make it in advance to the baking stage. Add the white sauce and bake on the day.

Serves 6

INGREDIENTS

15ml/1 tbsp olive oil
1 small onion, finely chopped
450g/1lb minced beef
1 garlic clove, finely chopped
5ml/1 tsp dried mixed herbs
120ml/4fl oz/½ cup beef stock
1 egg
75g/3oz cooked ham or Mortadella sausage, finely chopped
45ml/3 tbsp fine fresh white breadcrumbs
115g/4oz/1¼ cups freshly grated Parmesan cheese
18 precooked cannelloni tubes
salt and ground black pepper

For the tomato sauce
30ml/2 tbsp olive oil
1 small onion, finely chopped
½ carrot, finely chopped
1 celery stalk, finely chopped
1 garlic clove, crushed
400g/14oz can chopped plum tomatoes
a few sprigs of fresh basil
2.5ml/½ tsp dried oregano

For the white sauce
50g/2oz/¼ cup butter
50g/2oz/½ cup plain flour
900ml/1½ pints/3¾ cups milk
fresh nutmeg

1 Heat the olive oil in a saucepan and cook the chopped onion over a gentle heat, stirring occasionally, for about 5 minutes, until softened.

2 Add the minced beef and garlic and cook for 10 minutes, stirring and breaking up any lumps with a wooden spoon.

3 Add the herbs, and season to taste, then moisten with half the stock. Cover the pan and allow to simmer for 25 minutes, stirring occasionally and adding more stock as it reduces. Spoon into a bowl and allow to cool.

4 To make the tomato sauce, heat the olive oil in a saucepan, add the vegetables and garlic and cook over a medium heat, stirring frequently, for 10 minutes. Add the tomatoes. Fill the empty can with water, pour it into the pan, then add the herbs, and season to taste. Bring to a boil, lower the heat, cover and simmer for 25–30 minutes, stirring occasionally. Purée the tomato sauce in a blender or food processor.

5 To the meat, add the egg, ham or mortadella, breadcrumbs and 90ml/6 tbsp of the grated Parmesan, and stir well to mix. Taste for seasoning.

6 Spread a little of the tomato sauce over the bottom of a rectangular baking dish. Using a teaspoon, fill the cannelloni with the meat mixture.

7 Place the cannelloni in a single layer on top of the sauce. Pour the remaining tomato sauce over the top.

8 Preheat the oven to 190°C/375°F/Gas 5. For the white sauce, melt the butter in pan, add the flour and cook for 1–2 minutes. Remove from the heat and blend in the milk.

9 Return to the heat, bring to the boil and stir until smooth and thick. Grate in fresh nutmeg, and season.

10 Pour over the cannelloni, then sprinkle with Parmesan. Bake for 40–45 minutes. Leave to stand for 10 minutes before serving.

Tomato and Courgette Sauce with Tagliatelle

THE TOMATO AND COURGETTE sauce goes well with a variety of pastas and only takes minutes to prepare.

Serves 3–4

INGREDIENTS

225g/8oz wholewheat tagliatelle

For the tomato and courgette sauce

5–6 ripe plum tomatoes
30ml/2 tbsp olive oil
1 onion, chopped
2 celery sticks, chopped
1 garlic clove, crushed
2 courgettes, halved lengthways and sliced
30ml/2 tbsp sun-dried tomato paste
salt and ground black pepper

To serve

50g/2oz/½ cup flaked almonds, toasted

1 To make the sauce, place the tomatoes in a bowl of boiling water for 30 seconds to loosen the skins. Peel, then chop.

2 Bring a large pan of lightly salted water to the boil, add the pasta and cook for about 12 minutes, or according to the instructions on the packet, until *al dente*.

3 Meanwhile, heat the oil in another pan and add the chopped onion, celery, garlic and courgettes.

4 Sauté over a gentle heat for 3–4 minutes, until the onions have become lightly browned.

5 Stir in the tomatoes and sun-dried tomato paste. Cook gently for a further 5 minutes, then add salt and pepper to taste.

6 Drain the pasta, return it to the pan and add the sauce. Toss well. Place in a serving dish and scatter the toasted almonds over the top to serve.

COOK'S TIP

If using fresh pasta, you'll need double the quantity, i.e. 450g/1lb tagliatelle for 3–4 hearty appetites. Fresh tagliatelle takes only 3–4 minutes to cook.

Tomato, Pepper and Chilli Sauce

A MELLOW SAUCE, ideal for serving with pasta. For a more extravagant dish, add sliced chorizo sausage.

Serves 3–4

INGREDIENTS

350g/12oz filled pasta, such as tortelloni

For the tomato, pepper and chilli sauce

30ml/2 tbsp olive oil
1 onion, chopped
1 garlic clove, crushed
2 large red or orange peppers, seeded and finely chopped
5ml/1 tsp chilli seasoning
15ml/1 tbsp paprika
2.5ml/½ tsp dried thyme
225g/8oz can chopped tomatoes
300ml/½ pint/1¼ cups vegetable stock
2.5ml/½ tsp sugar
30ml/2 tbsp sun-dried tomatoes in oil, drained and chopped
salt and ground black pepper

1 Heat the oil and sauté the onion, garlic and peppers for 4–5 minutes until softened.

2 Add the chilli, paprika and thyme and cook for a further minute, stirring constantly.

3 Stir in the tomatoes, vegetable stock, sugar and seasoning, and bring to the boil. Cover and allow to simmer for 30 minutes or until soft, adding more stock if necessary.

4 About 10 minutes before the end of cooking, add the sun-dried tomatoes and stir in.

5 Cook the pasta in salted boiling water according to the packet instructions. Drain and serve with the hot sauce.

COOK'S TIP

If you can't get sun-dried tomatoes in oil, use sun-dried tomatoes from a pack.

Tomato and Aubergine Sauce with Pasta

FULL OF FLAVOUR, THIS sauce goes well with any short pasta shapes. It can be layered with sheets of pasta and cheese sauce to make lasagne.

Serves 4–6

INGREDIENTS

350g/12oz dried short pasta shapes

For the tomato and aubergine sauce

30ml/2 tbsp olive oil
1 small fresh red chilli
2 garlic cloves
2 handfuls fresh flat leaf parsley, coarsely chopped, plus extra to serve
450g/1lb aubergine, chopped
200ml/7fl oz/scant 1 cup water
1 vegetable stock cube
1 handful fresh basil leaves
8 plum tomatoes, peeled and chopped
60ml/4 tbsp red wine
5ml/1 tsp sugar
1 envelope saffron powder
2.5ml/½ tsp ground paprika
salt and ground black pepper

1 Heat the oil in a large frying pan and add the whole chilli, whole garlic cloves and one handful of chopped parsley. Smash the garlic cloves with a wooden spoon to release their juice, then cover the pan and cook the mixture over a low to medium heat for about 10 minutes, stirring occasionally.

2 Remove and discard the chilli. Add the aubergine to the pan. Pour in half the water. Crumble in the stock cube and stir until it is dissolved, then cover and cook, stirring frequently, for about 10 minutes.

3 Add the tomatoes, wine, sugar, saffron and paprika with another handful of parsley, the basil and seasoning. Pour in the remaining water. Stir well, replace the lid and cook for 30–40 minutes, stirring occasionally.

4 About 10 minutes before the sauce is ready, cook the pasta in boiling salted water according to the instructions on the packet until *al dente*.

5 Check the sauce for seasoning, then toss with the drained pasta in warmed bowls. Garnish with extra chopped parsley.

Carbonara Sauce with Spaghetti

AN ALL-TIME FAVOURITE sauce that is perfect for spaghetti or tagliatelle. This version has plenty of pancetta or bacon and is not too creamy, but you can vary the amounts.

Serves 4

INGREDIENTS

350g/12oz fresh or dried spaghetti

For the carbonara sauce

30ml/2 tbsp olive oil
1 small onion, finely chopped
8 pancetta or lean bacon strips, cut into 1cm/½in strips
4 eggs
60ml/4 tbsp crème fraîche
60ml/4 tbsp freshly grated Parmesan cheese, plus extra to serve
salt and ground black pepper

1 Heat the oil in a frying pan, add the onion and cook, stirring, over a low heat, for 5 minutes until softened.

2 Add the strips of pancetta or bacon to the onion in the pan and cook for about 10 minutes, stirring almost all the time.

3 Meanwhile, cook the pasta in a pan of salted boiling water according to the instructions on the packet, until *al dente*.

4 Put the eggs, crème fraîche and grated Parmesan in a bowl. Grind in plenty of pepper, then beat the mixture together well.

5 Drain the pasta, turn it into the pan with the pancetta or bacon and toss well to mix.

6 Turn the heat off under the pan. Immediately add the egg mixture and toss vigorously so that it cooks lightly and coats the pasta.

7 Quickly taste for seasoning, then divide among four warmed bowls and sprinkle with black pepper. Serve immediately, with extra grated Parmesan offered separately.

Gorgonzola Sauce with Gnocchi

THIS CHEESE SAUCE has a strong flavour and so is ideal with potato dumplings or a plain pasta like macaroni. Either way, it makes a filling dish ideal for a winter supper.

Serves 4

INGREDIENTS

450g/1lb potatoes, unpeeled
1 large egg
115g/4oz/1 cup plain flour
salt and ground black pepper
fresh thyme sprigs, to garnish
60ml/4 tbsp freshly grated Parmesan cheese, to serve

For the Gorgonzola sauce

115g/4oz Gorgonzola cheese
60ml/4 tbsp double cream
15ml/1 tbsp chopped fresh thyme

1 Cook the potatoes in boiling salted water for about 20 minutes until they are tender. Drain and, when cool enough to handle, remove the skins.

2 Press the potatoes through a sieve, using the back of a spoon, into a mixing bowl. Season, then beat in the egg. Add the flour a little at a time, stirring well with a wooden spoon after each addition until you have a smooth dough. (You may not need all the flour.)

3 Turn the dough out on to a floured surface and knead it for about 3 minutes, adding more flour if you need to, until it is smooth and soft and not sticky to the touch.

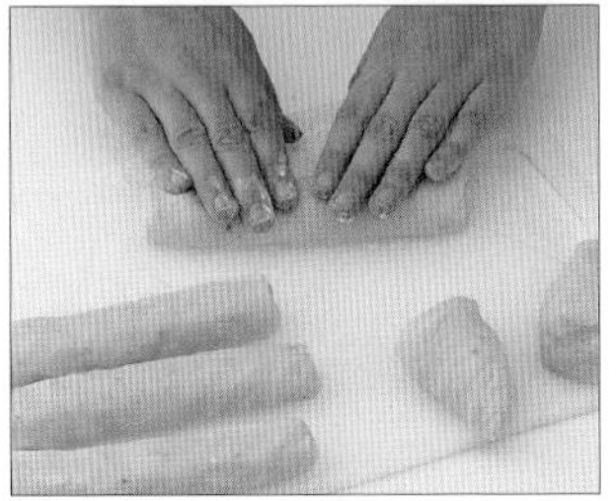

4 Divide the dough into six equal pieces. Flour your hands and gently roll each piece on a board into a log shape measuring 15–20cm/6–8in long and 2.5cm/1in diameter. Cut each log into six to eight pieces, each about 2.5cm/1in long, then gently roll each piece in the flour. Form into gnocchi by gently pressing each piece on to the floured surface with the tines of a fork to form ridges.

5 To cook, drop the gnocchi into a pan of boiling water about 12 at a time. Once they rise to the surface, after about 2 minutes, cook them for 4–5 minutes more, then drain.

6 To make the sauce, place the Gorgonzola, cream and thyme in a large frying pan and heat gently until the cheese melts to form a thick, creamy consistency, then heat through.

7 Add the drained gnocchi to the sauce and toss well to combine. Serve with Parmesan and garnish with thyme.

VARIATION

The Gorgonzola sauce could also be used in a fondue, with croûtons or vegetable pieces to dip.

Cream and Parmesan Sauce with Spinach and Ricotta Ravioli

THIS CREAMY PARMESAN SAUCE is a perfect accompaniment to home-made spinach and ricotta ravioli but would be just as delicious on store-bought tortelloni or any other fresh pasta with a stuffing to give flavour.

Serves 8

INGREDIENTS

500g/1¼lb fresh pasta dough
grated fresh Parmesan cheese, to serve
salt and ground black pepper

For the filling

45ml/3 tbsp butter
175g/6oz fresh spinach leaves, trimmed, washed and shredded
200g/7oz/scant 1 cup ricotta cheese
25g/1oz/⅓ cup freshly grated Parmesan cheese
freshly grated nutmeg
1 small egg

For the cream and Parmesan sauce

50g/2oz/¼ cup butter
120ml/4fl oz/½ cup double cream
50g/2oz/⅔ cup freshly grated Parmesan cheese

1 To make the filling, melt the butter in a saucepan, add the spinach and salt and pepper to taste and cook over a medium heat for 5–8 minutes, stirring frequently, until the spinach is wilted and tender. Increase the heat to high. Stir until the water boils off and the spinach is quite dry.

2 Tip the spinach into a bowl and set aside until cold, then add the ricotta, grated Parmesan and freshly grated nutmeg to taste. Beat well to mix, taste for seasoning, then add the egg and beat well again.

3 Using a pasta machine, roll out one-quarter of the pasta into a 90–100cm/36–40in strip. Cut the strip with a sharp knife into two 45–50cm/18–20in lengths (you can do this during rolling if the strip gets too long to manage).

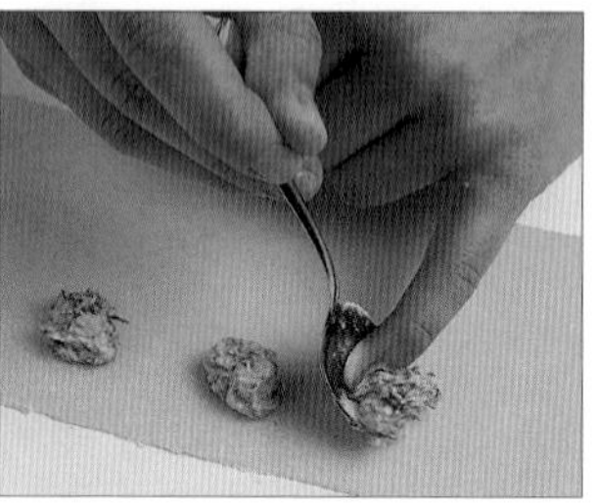

4 Using a teaspoon, put 10–12 little mounds of the filling along one side of one of the pasta strips, spacing them evenly. Brush a little water around each mound, then fold the plain side of the pasta strip over the filling.

5 Starting from the folded edge, press down gently with your finger-tips around each mound of filling, pushing the air out at the unfolded edge. Sprinkle lightly with flour.

6 With a fluted pasta wheel, cut along each long side, then in between each mound to make small square shapes.

7 Put the ravioli on floured dish towels, sprinkle lightly with flour and allow to dry while repeating the process with the remaining pasta, to give you 80–96 ravioli altogether.

8 Drop the ravioli into a large pan of boiling salted water, bring back to the boil and boil for 4–5 minutes.

9 Meanwhile, make the sauce. Gently heat the butter, cream and Parmesan in a medium saucepan until the butter and Parmesan have melted.

10 Increase the heat and simmer for a minute or two until the sauce is slightly reduced, then add salt and pepper to taste.

11 Drain the ravioli and divide them equally among eight warmed large bowls. Drizzle the sauce over them and serve sprinkled with Parmesan and ground pepper.

VARIATION

This cheese sauce would also work well with a baked pasta dish such as macaroni. Sprinkle the top generously with grated parmesan before baking.

Butter and Herb Sauce with Chitarra Spaghetti

YOU CAN USE JUST one favourite herb or several for this recipe. The result is the simplest way to dress up pasta but also one of the tastiest.

Serves 4

INGREDIENTS

400g/14oz fresh or dried spaghetti alla chitarra

freshly grated Parmesan cheese, to serve

For the butter and herb sauce

2 good handfuls mixed fresh herbs, plus extra herb leaves and flowers to garnish

115g/4oz/½ cup butter

salt and ground black pepper

1 Cook the pasta in boiling, lightly salted water according to the packet instructions, until almost *al dente*.

2 To make the sauce, chop the herbs coarsely or finely, as you prefer.

3 When the pasta is almost *al dente*, melt the butter in a large frying pan or saucepan. As soon as it sizzles, drain the pasta and add it to the pan, then sprinkle in the herbs with salt and pepper to taste.

4 Toss over a medium heat until the pasta is coated in butter and herbs. Serve immediately in warmed bowls, sprinkled with extra herb leaves and flowers. Pass round some extra grated Parmesan separately.

VARIATION

If you like the flavour of garlic with herbs, add 1–2 crushed garlic cloves when melting the butter.

Bolognese Sauce with Ravioli

PERHAPS ONE OF THE most famous pasta sauces outside Italy, Bolognese sauce is a rich ragù from the city of Bologna in Emilia-Romagna, an area famous for fine foods.

Serves 6

INGREDIENTS

225g/8oz cottage cheese
30ml/2 tbsp freshly grated Parmesan cheese, plus extra for serving
1 egg white, beaten, including extra for brushing
1.5ml/¼ tsp ground nutmeg
300g/11oz fresh pasta dough
flour, for dusting
salt and ground black pepper

For the Bolognese sauce

1 medium onion, finely chopped
1 garlic clove, crushed
150ml/¼ pint/⅔ cup beef stock
350g/12oz minced extra-lean beef
120ml/4fl oz/½ cup red wine
30ml/2 tbsp concentrated tomato purée
400g/14oz can chopped plum tomatoes
2.5ml/½ tsp chopped fresh rosemary
1.5ml/¼ tsp ground allspice

1 To make the filling, mix the cottage cheese, grated Parmesan cheese, egg white, seasoning and nutmeg together thoroughly.

2 Roll the pasta into thin sheets, then place small amounts of filling along the pasta in rows, leaving a gap of 5cm/2in between them. Moisten round the filling with beaten egg white.

3 Place a second sheet of pasta lightly over the top. Press between each pocket to remove air, and seal.

4 Cut into rounds with a fluted ravioli or pastry cutter. Transfer to a floured dish towel and leave to rest for at least 30 minutes before cooking.

5 To make the Bolognese sauce, cook the onion and garlic in the stock for 5 minutes or until all the stock has reduced. Add the beef and cook quickly to brown, breaking up the meat with a fork.

VARIATION

Stir in a handful of chopped chicken livers with the minced beef to add a more meaty richness to the sauce.

6 Add the wine, tomato purée, chopped tomatoes, rosemary and allspice. Bring to the boil and simmer for 1 hour. Season to taste.

7 Cook the ravioli in a large pan of boiling, salted water for 4–5 minutes. (Cook in batches to stop them sticking together.) Drain thoroughly. Serve topped with the Bolognese sauce. Serve grated Parmesan cheese separately.

Cream and Walnut Sauce on Pansotti

THIS WALNUT AND CREAM pesto is a simplified version of the one traditionally served with pansotti in Liguria. It would go equally well with any pasta stuffed with ricotta or spinach, or for a less rich alternative serve it with plain pasta shells.

Serves 6–8

INGREDIENTS

500g/1¼lb herb-flavoured pasta dough with eggs
50g/2oz/¼ cup butter
freshly grated Parmesan cheese, to serve
salt and ground black pepper

For the filling

250g/9oz/generous 1 cup ricotta cheese
115g/4oz/1¼ cups freshly grated Parmesan cheese
1 large handful fresh basil leaves, finely chopped
1 large handful fresh flat leaf parsley, finely chopped
a few sprigs of fresh marjoram or oregano, leaves removed and finely chopped
1 garlic clove, crushed
1 small egg

For the cream and walnut sauce

90g/3½oz/1 cup shelled walnuts
1 garlic clove
60ml/4 tbsp extra virgin olive oil
120ml/4fl oz/½ cup double cream

1 To make the filling, put the ricotta cheese, Parmesan cheese, basil, parsley, marjoram or oregano, garlic and egg in a bowl. Season with salt and ground black pepper to taste, and beat well to mix.

2 To make the sauce, put the walnuts, garlic clove and oil in a food processor and process to a paste, adding up to 120ml/4fl oz/½ cup warm water, through the feeder tube, to thin down the paste.

3 Spoon the mixture into a bowl and add the cream. Beat well to mix, then season to taste.

4 Using a pasta machine, roll out one-quarter of the pasta into a 90–100cm/36–40in strip. Cut the strip with a sharp knife into two 45–50cm/18–20in lengths (you can do this during rolling if the strip gets too long to manage).

5 Using a 5cm/2in square ravioli cutter, cut eight to ten squares from one of the pasta strips.

6 Using a teaspoon, put a mound of filling in the centre of each square.

7 Brush a little water around the edge of each square, then fold the square diagonally in half over the filling to make a triangle. Press gently to seal.

8 Spread out the pansotti on clean floured dish towels, sprinkle lightly with flour and set aside to dry, while repeating the process with the remaining dough, to make a total of 64–80 pansotti.

9 Cook the pansotti in a large pan of boiling salted water for 4–5 minutes.

10 Meanwhile, put the walnut sauce in a large, warmed bowl and add a ladleful of the pasta cooking water to thin it down. Melt the butter in a small saucepan until sizzling.

11 Drain the pansotti and tip them into the bowl of walnut sauce. Drizzle the butter over them, toss well, then sprinkle with grated Parmesan. Alternatively, toss the pansotti in the melted butter, spoon into warmed individual bowls and drizzle over the sauce. Serve the dish immediately, with extra Parmesan handed round separately.

COOK'S TIP

Take care not to overfill the pansotti, or they will burst open during cooking.

Spinach Sauce with Seafood Pasta Shells

SOFT CHEESE AND SPINACH complements all kinds of pasta. This sauce would be perfect with any filled fresh pasta.

Serves 4

INGREDIENTS

32 large dried pasta shells
salt and ground black pepper

For the filling

15g/½oz/1 tbsp butter or margarine
8 spring onions, finely sliced
6 tomatoes
225g/8 oz cooked peeled prawns
175g/6 oz can white crab meat, drained and flaked

For the spinach sauce

225g/8 oz/1 cup soft cheese
90ml/6 tbsp milk
pinch of freshly grated nutmeg
115g/4oz frozen chopped spinach, thawed and drained
salt and ground black pepper

1 Preheat the oven to 150°C/300°F/Gas 2. Melt the butter or margarine in a saucepan and cook the spring onions for 3–4 minutes, or until soft.

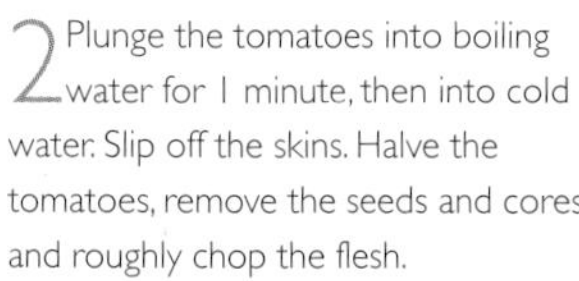

2 Plunge the tomatoes into boiling water for 1 minute, then into cold water. Slip off the skins. Halve the tomatoes, remove the seeds and cores and roughly chop the flesh.

3 Cook the pasta shells in lightly salted boiling water for about 10 minutes, or until *al dente*. Drain.

4 To make the sauce, put the soft cheese and milk into a saucepan and heat gently, stirring until blended. Season with salt, ground black pepper and a pinch of nutmeg.

5 Measure 30ml/2 tbsp of cheese mixture into a bowl. Add the onions, tomatoes, prawns, and crab meat. Mix well. Spoon the filling into the shells and place in a single layer in a shallow ovenproof dish. Cover with foil and cook for 10 minutes.

6 Stir the spinach into the remaining sauce. Bring to the boil and simmer gently for 1 minute, stirring all the time. Drizzle over the pasta and serve hot.

Smoked Haddock and Parsley Sauce for Pasta

THIS HEARTY SAUCE made with smoked haddock makes any hollow pasta shape into a healthy lunch or supper. Shell-shaped pasta is ideal to hold the sauce, but corkscrew and tube shapes work just as well.

Serves 4

INGREDIENTS

225g/8oz pasta shells
15g/½oz toasted flaked almonds, to serve

For the smoked haddock and parsley sauce

450g/1lb smoked haddock fillet
1 small leek or onion, thickly sliced
300ml/½ pint/1¼ cups milk
bouquet garni (bay leaf, thyme and parsley stalks)
25g/1oz/2 tbsp butter or margarine
25g/1oz/¼ cup plain flour
30ml/2 tbsp chopped fresh parsley
salt and ground black pepper

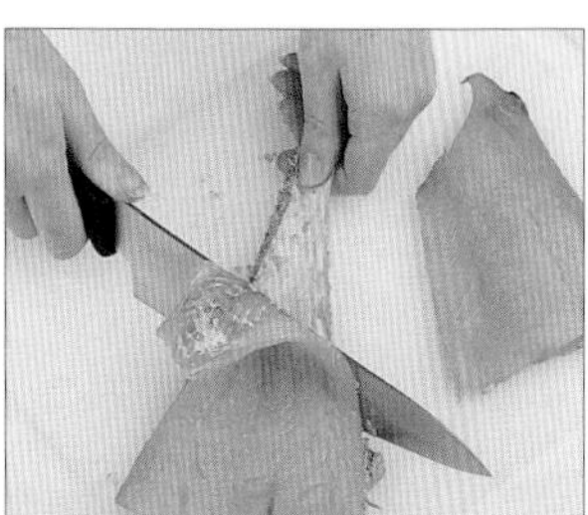

1 Remove all the skin and any bones from the haddock and discard. Put the fish into a pan with the leek or onion, milk and bouquet garni. Bring to the boil, cover and simmer gently for 8–10 minutes, or until the fish flakes easily.

2 Strain, reserving the milk for making the sauce, and discard the bouquet garni.

3 Put the butter or margarine, flour and reserved milk into a pan. Bring to the boil and whisk until smooth. Season and add the fish and leek or onion.

4 Cook the pasta in a large pan of boiling salted water until *al dente*. Drain thoroughly and stir into the sauce with the chopped parsley. Serve immediately, scattered with toasted flaked almonds.

Squid Sauce with Black Pasta

WHAT BETTER PARTNER FOR a delicious squid sauce than squid ink tagliatelle? The tastes blend perfectly, but the sauce will enhance any plain pasta.

Serves 4

INGREDIENTS

450g/1lb squid ink tagliatelle

For the squid sauce

105ml/7 tbsp olive oil
2 shallots, chopped
3 garlic cloves, crushed
45ml/3 tbsp chopped fresh parsley
675g/1½lb cleaned squid, cut into rings and rinsed
150ml/¼ pint/⅔ cup dry white wine
400g/14oz can chopped plum tomatoes
2.5ml/½ tsp dried chilli flakes or powder
salt and ground black pepper

1 Heat the oil in a pan and add the shallots. Cook until pale golden, then add the garlic.

2 When the garlic colours a little, add 30ml/2 tbsp of the parsley, stir, then add the squid and stir again. Cook for 3–4 minutes, then add the wine.

3 Simmer for a few seconds, then add the tomatoes and chilli.

4 Season the mixture with salt and pepper. Cover and simmer gently for about 1 hour, until the squid is tender. Add more water if necessary.

5 Cook the pasta in plenty of boiling, salted water, according to the instructions on the packet, until *al dente*. Drain and return the tagliatelle to the pan. Add the squid sauce and mix well.

6 Serve at once, sprinkled with the remaining chopped parsley.

COOK'S TIP

Take care to simmer the squid very gently, as it can become tough if overheated. Baby squid may need a shorter cooking time.

Clam and Tomato Sauce with Vermicelli

CLAM AND TOMATO SAUCE is a regular dish in Neopolitan restaurants, and is often served with vermicelli or spaghetti. Fresh mussels could be substituted for the clams.

Serves 4

INGREDIENTS

350g/12oz vermicelli

For the clam and tomato sauce

1kg/2¼lb fresh hard-shell clams
250ml/8fl oz/1 cup dry white wine
2 garlic cloves, bruised
1 large handful fresh flat leaf parsley
30ml/2 tbsp olive oil
1 small onion, finely chopped
8 ripe plum tomatoes, peeled, deseeded and finely chopped
½–1 fresh red chilli, deseeded and finely chopped
salt and ground black pepper

1 Scrub the clams thoroughly under cold running water and discard any that are open and that do not close when they are sharply tapped against the work surface.

2 Pour the wine into a large saucepan, add the garlic cloves and half the parsley, then the clams. Cover tightly with the lid and bring to the boil over a high heat. Cook for about 5 minutes, shaking the pan frequently, until the clams have opened.

3 Tip the clams into a large colander set over a bowl and let the liquid drain through. Set aside the clams until cool enough to handle, then remove about two-thirds of them from their shells, pouring the clam liquid into the bowl of cooking liquid. Discard any clams that have failed to open. Set both shelled and unshelled clams aside, keeping the unshelled clams warm in a bowl covered with a lid.

4 Heat the oil in a saucepan, add the onion and cook gently, stirring frequently, for about 5 minutes until softened and lightly coloured. Add the tomatoes, then strain in the clam cooking liquid. Add the chilli and salt and pepper to taste. Chop the remaining parsley finely and set aside.

5 Bring to the boil, half-cover the pan and allow to simmer gently for 15–20 minutes.

6 Meanwhile, cook the pasta according to the instructions on the packet, until it is *al dente*.

7 Add the shelled clams to the tomato sauce, stir well and heat through very gently for 2–3 minutes.

8 Drain the cooked pasta well and tip it into a warmed bowl. Taste the sauce for seasoning, then pour the sauce over the pasta and toss everything together well. Serve garnished with the reserved clams and sprinkled with parsley.

Prawn and Vodka Sauce with Pasta

THE COMBINATION OF PRAWNS, vodka and pasta may seem unusual, but has become a modern classic in Italy. Here it is served with two-coloured pasta, but the sauce goes equally well with short shapes such as penne, rigatoni and farfalle.

Serves 4

INGREDIENTS

350g/12oz fresh or dried paglia e fieno

For the prawn and vodka sauce

30ml/2 tbsp olive oil
¼ large onion, finely chopped
1 garlic clove, crushed
15–30ml/1–2 tbsp sun-dried tomato paste
200ml/7fl oz/scant 1 cup double cream
12 large raw prawns, peeled and chopped
30ml/2 tbsp vodka
salt and ground black pepper

1 Heat the oil in a medium saucepan, add the onion and garlic and cook gently, stirring frequently, for about 5 minutes or until softened.

2 Add the tomato paste and stir for 1–2 minutes, then add the cream and bring to the boil, stirring. Season with salt and pepper to taste and let the sauce bubble until it starts to thicken slightly. Remove from the heat.

3 Cook the pasta according to the instructions on the packet, until *al dente*. When it is almost ready, add the prawns and vodka to the sauce; toss over a medium heat for 2–3 minutes, or until the prawns turn pink.

4 Drain the pasta and turn it into a warmed bowl. Pour the sauce over and toss well. Divide among warmed bowls and serve immediately.

COOK'S TIP

This sauce is best served as soon as it is ready, otherwise the prawns will overcook and become tough. Make sure that the pasta has only a minute or two of cooking time left before adding the prawns to the sauce.

Smoked Salmon and Cream Sauce with Penne

THIS MODERN WAY OF serving pasta is popular all over Italy. The three essential ingredients combine beautifully, and the dish is very quick and easy to make.

Serves 4

INGREDIENTS

350g/12oz penne

For the smoked salmon and cream sauce

115g/4oz thinly sliced smoked salmon
2–3 fresh thyme sprigs
30ml/2 tbsp butter
150ml/¼ pint/⅔ cup double cream
salt and ground black pepper

1 Cook the pasta in boiling salted water until it is *al dente*.

2 Meanwhile, using kitchen scissors, cut the smoked salmon into thin strips, about 5mm/¼in wide. Strip the leaves from the thyme sprigs.

3 Melt the butter in a large saucepan. Stir in the cream with a quarter of the salmon and thyme leaves, then season with pepper. Heat gently for 3–4 minutes, stirring constantly. Do not allow to boil. Taste for seasoning.

4 Drain the pasta and toss it in the cream and salmon sauce. Divide among four warmed bowls and top with the remaining salmon and thyme leaves. Serve immediately.

VARIATION

Although penne is traditional with this sauce, it also goes very well with fresh ravioli stuffed with spinach and ricotta.

Spicy Sausage Sauce with Tortiglioni

SERVE THIS HEADY PASTA DISH with a robust Sicilian red wine.

Serves 4

INGREDIENTS

300g/11oz dried tortiglioni
salt and ground black pepper

For the spicy sausage sauce

30ml/2 tbsp olive oil
1 onion, finely chopped
1 celery stick, finely chopped
2 large garlic cloves, crushed
1 fresh red chilli, deseeded and chopped
450g/1lb ripe plum tomatoes, peeled and finely chopped
30ml/2 tbsp tomato purée
150ml/¼ pint/⅔ cup red wine
5ml/1 tsp sugar
175g/6oz spicy salami, rind removed
30ml/2 tbsp chopped parsley, to garnish
freshly grated Parmesan cheese, to serve

1 Heat the oil in a flameproof casserole or large saucepan, then add the onion, celery, garlic and chilli. Cook gently, stirring frequently, for about 10 minutes, until softened.

2 Add the tomatoes, tomato purée, wine, sugar and salt and pepper to taste and bring to the boil, stirring. Lower the heat, cover and simmer gently, stirring occasionally, for about 20 minutes. Add a few spoonfuls of water if the sauce becomes too thick.

3 Meanwhile, cook the pasta in a large saucepan of rapidly boiling, salted water according to the instructions on the packet, until *al dente*.

4 Chop the salami into bite-size chunks and add to the sauce. Heat through, then taste for seasoning.

5 Drain the pasta, tip it into a large bowl, then pour the sauce over and toss to mix. Scatter over the parsley and serve with grated Parmesan.

COOK'S TIP

Buy the salami for this dish in one piece so that you can chop it into large chunks.

Wild Mushroom Sauce with Fusilli

A VERY RICH DISH with an earthy flavour and lots of garlic, this makes an ideal main course for vegetarians, especially if it is followed by a crisp green salad.

Serves 4

INGREDIENTS

150g/5oz wild mushrooms preserved in olive oil
30ml/2 tbsp butter
150g/5oz fresh wild mushrooms, sliced if large
5ml/1 tsp finely chopped fresh thyme
5ml/1 tsp finely chopped fresh marjoram or oregano, plus extra herbs to serve
4 garlic cloves, crushed
350g/12oz fresh or dried fusilli
200ml/7fl oz/scant 1 cup double cream
salt and ground black pepper

1 Drain about 15ml/1 tbsp of the oil from the mushrooms into a medium saucepan. Slice or chop the preserved mushrooms into bite-size pieces, if they are large.

2 Add the butter to the oil in the pan and heat over a low heat until sizzling. Add the preserved and the fresh mushrooms, the chopped herbs and the garlic. Season to taste.

SAFETY TIP

Unless you're an expert, or know of one who will identify them for you, it's safer not to pick mushrooms in the wild, but buy them instead from a reliable source.

3 Simmer over a medium heat, stirring frequently, for about 10 minutes or until the fresh mushrooms are soft and tender.

4 Meanwhile, cook the pasta in boiling salted water according to the packet instructions, until *al dente*.

5 As soon as the mushrooms are cooked, increase the heat to high and toss the mixture with a wooden spoon to boil off any excess liquid. Pour in the cream and bring to the boil. Season if needed.

6 Drain the pasta and turn it into a warmed bowl. Pour the sauce over and toss well. Serve immediately, sprinkled with chopped fresh herbs.

Sauces for Meat Dishes

The simplest, most basic sauce for meat is traditional gravy. Based on the juices from the cooked meat, this is one of the most widely used, everyday sauces. It is on this, together with a basic brown sauce, that many meat sauces are based, from classic French Sauce Espagnole to the rich Cumberland sauce flavoured with port. But not only brown sauces are used with meat – you'll also find white, creamy sauces and a delicate butter in this section.

Many red meat dishes provide the opportunity for quite robust sauces, using warm spices, garlic or pungent herbs, simmered with red wine or tomato mixtures for added richness. The contrasting flavours of tangy fruits or sweet-and-sour mixtures are particularly successful with rich meats such as beef, lamb, pork, venison or duck, notably the popular combination of duck with orange or venison with cranberries.

Although usually classed as a white meat, pork is also a natural partner for the tangy sweetness of apples or oranges, and pairs well with sweet-and-sour type sauces. More delicately flavoured white meats or poultry, such as veal, chicken and turkey, go well with cream sauces or sauces based on white wine.

Avocado Sauce with Lemon Chicken

THIS GREAT SAUCE IS based on the classic Mexican dip, guacamole. Made without the addition of water, it could be used as a dip with raw vegetables, or even as a sandwich filling. Here it teams perfectly with chicken.

Serves 4

INGREDIENTS

juice of 2 lemons
45ml/3 tbsp olive oil
2 garlic cloves, crushed
5 chicken breasts, about 200g/7oz each
2 beefsteak tomatoes, cored and cut in half
salt and ground black pepper

For the avocado sauce

1 ripe avocado
50ml/2fl oz/¼ cup soured cream
45ml/3 tbsp fresh lemon juice
2.5ml/½ tsp salt
50ml/2fl oz/¼ cup water

To serve

chopped fresh coriander, to garnish

1 Combine the lemon juice, oil, garlic, 2.5ml/½ tsp salt, and a little pepper in a bowl. Stir to mix.

2 Arrange the chicken breasts in one layer in a shallow glass or ceramic dish. Pour over the lemon mixture and turn to coat evenly. Cover and allow to stand for at least 1 hour at room temperature, or chill overnight.

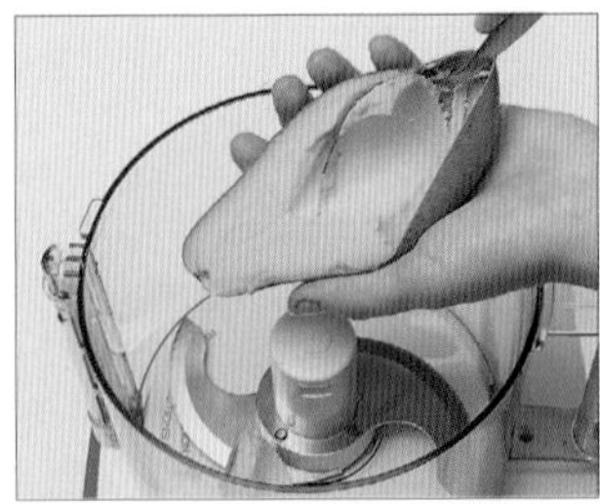

3 For the avocado sauce, cut the avocado in half, remove the stone and scrape the flesh into a food processor or blender.

4 Add the soured cream, lemon juice and salt, and process until smooth. Add the water and process just to blend. If necessary, add more water to thin the sauce. Transfer to a bowl, taste and adjust the seasoning, if necessary. Set aside.

5 Preheat the grill to hot. Heat a ridged griddle or heavy-based frying pan. Remove the chicken from the marinade and pat dry.

6 When the griddle or frying pan is hot, add the chicken breasts and cook, turning often, for about 10 minutes, until they are cooked through.

7 Meanwhile, arrange the tomato halves, cut-sides up, on a baking sheet and season lightly with salt and pepper. Grill for about 5 minutes, until hot and bubbling.

8 To serve, place a chicken breast, tomato half, and a spoonful of avocado sauce on each plate. Sprinkle with coriander and serve.

VARIATION

To barbecue the chicken, prepare the fire, and, when the coals are glowing red and covered with grey ash, spread them in a single layer. Set an oiled grill rack about 13cm/5in above the coals and cook the chicken breasts for 15–20 minutes, until lightly charred and cooked through. Allow extra olive oil for basting.

Salsa Picante with Chicken Enchilladas

THIS "HOT" SALSA IS actually a low-heat version using seeded green chillies, and is also cooled down by the soured cream. As well as accompanying enchilladas it would make a good side dish with kebabs of chicken or pork.

Serves 4

INGREDIENTS

8 wheat tortillas
175g/6oz/1½ cups grated Cheddar cheese
1 onion, finely chopped
350g/12oz cooked chicken, cut into small chunks
300ml/½ pint/1¼ cups soured cream
1 avocado, sliced and tossed in lemon juice, to garnish

For the salsa picante

1–2 green chillies
15ml/1 tbsp vegetable oil
1 onion, chopped
1 garlic clove, crushed
400g/14oz can chopped tomatoes
30ml/2 tbsp tomato purée
salt and ground black pepper

1 To make the salsa picante, cut the chillies in half lengthways and carefully remove the cores and seeds. Slice the chillies very finely. Heat the oil in a frying pan and fry the onion and garlic for about 3–4 minutes until softened. Add the tomatoes, tomato purée and chillies. Simmer gently, uncovered, for 12–15 minutes, stirring the mixture frequently.

2 Pour the sauce into a food processor or blender, and process until smooth. Return to the heat and cook very gently, uncovered, for a further 15 minutes. Season to taste then set aside.

3 Preheat the oven to 180°C/350°F/Gas 4 and butter a shallow ovenproof dish. Take one tortilla and sprinkle with a good pinch of cheese and chopped onion, about 40g/1½oz of the chicken and 15ml/1 tbsp of salsa picante.

4 Pour over 15ml/1 tbsp of soured cream, roll up and place, seam-side down, in the dish. Make seven more enchilladas.

5 Pour the remaining salsa over the top and sprinkle with cheese and onion. Bake for 25–30 minutes until golden. Serve with the remaining cream. Garnish with the sliced avocado.

Marsala Cream Sauce with Turkey

MARSALA MAKES A VERY rich and tasty sauce. The addition of lemon juice gives it a refreshing tang, which helps to offset the richness.

Serves 6

INGREDIENTS

6 turkey breast steaks
45ml/3 tbsp plain flour
30ml/2 tbsp olive oil
25g/1oz/2 tbsp butter
salt and ground black pepper

For the Marsala cream sauce

175ml/6fl oz/¾ cup dry Marsala
60ml/4 tbsp lemon juice
175ml/6fl oz/¾ cup double cream

To serve

lemon wedges and chopped fresh parsley, to garnish
mangetouts and French beans

1 Put each turkey steak between two sheets of clear film and pound with a rolling pin to flatten out evenly. Cut each steak in half or into quarters, cutting away and discarding any sinew.

2 Spread out the flour in a shallow bowl. Season well with salt and pepper and coat the meat.

3 Heat the oil and butter in a wide, heavy-based saucepan or frying pan until sizzling. Add as many pieces of turkey as you can, and sauté over a medium heat for about 3 minutes on each side until crispy and tender.

4 Transfer to a warmed serving dish with tongs and keep hot. Repeat with the remaining turkey. Lower the heat.

5 To make the sauce, mix the Marsala and lemon juice in a jug, add to the oil and butter in the pan and raise the heat. Bring to the boil, stirring in the sediment, then add the cream.

6 Simmer, stirring constantly, until the sauce is reduced and glossy. Taste for seasoning.

7 Spoon the sauce over the turkey, garnish with the lemon wedges and parsley and serve at once.

COOK'S TIP

To make this sauce without using the pan drippings, omit the oil and heat the butter in a pan before adding the other ingredients.

Walnut and Pomegranate Sauce with Duck Breasts

This is an extremely exotic sweet-and-sour sauce which originally comes from Iran.

Serves 4

INGREDIENTS

4 duck breasts, about 225g/8oz each

For the walnut and pomegranate sauce

30ml/2 tbsp olive oil
2 onions, very thinly sliced
2.5ml/½ tsp ground turmeric
400g/14oz/2⅓ cups walnuts, roughly chopped
1 litre/1¾ pints/4 cups duck or chicken stock
6 pomegranates
30ml/2 tbsp caster sugar
60ml/4 tbsp lemon juice
salt and ground black pepper

1 To make the sauce, heat half the oil in a frying pan. Add the onions and turmeric, and cook gently until soft.

2 Transfer to a saucepan, add the walnuts and stock, then season with salt and pepper. Stir, then bring to the boil and simmer the mixture, uncovered, for 20 minutes.

3 Cut the pomegranates in half and scoop out the seeds. Reserve the seeds of one pomegranate. Transfer the remaining seeds to a blender and process to break them up. Strain through a sieve, to extract the juice, and stir in the sugar and lemon juice.

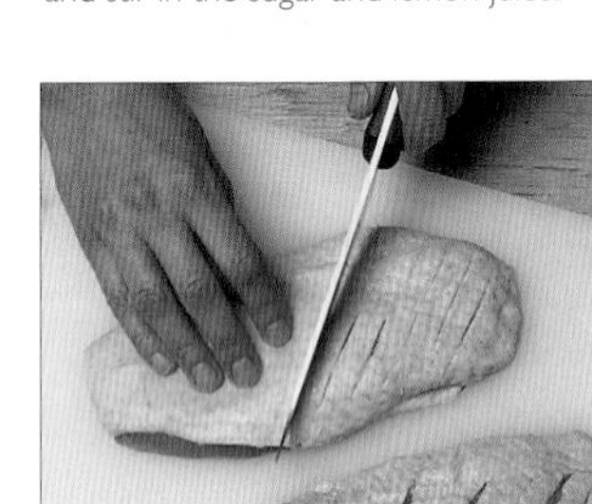

4 Score the skin of the duck breasts in a diamond pattern with a sharp knife. Heat the remaining oil in a frying pan or griddle and place the duck breasts in it, skin-side down.

5 Cook gently for 10 minutes, pouring off the fat, until the skin is dark golden and crisp. Turn the duck breasts over and cook for a further 3–4 minutes. Transfer to a plate and leave to rest. Deglaze the frying pan with the pomegranate juice, then add the walnut and stock mixture and simmer for 15 minutes until thickened.

6 Slice the duck and serve drizzled with a little sauce, and garnished with the reserved pomegranate seeds. Serve the remaining sauce separately.

Redcurrant Sauce with Lamb Burgers

THE SWEET-SOUR redcurrant sauce is the perfect complement to the taste of lamb and would go equally well with grilled or roast lamb steaks.

Serves 4

INGREDIENTS

500g/1¼lb minced lean lamb
1 small onion, finely chopped
30ml/2 tbsp finely chopped fresh mint
30ml/2 tbsp finely chopped fresh parsley
115g/4oz mozzarella cheese
30ml/2 tbsp oil, for basting
salt and ground black pepper

For the redcurrant sauce

115g/4oz/1 cup fresh or frozen redcurrants
10ml/2 tsp clear honey
5ml/1 tsp balsamic vinegar
30ml/2 tbsp finely chopped mint

1 In a large bowl, mix together the minced lamb, chopped onion, mint and parsley until evenly combined. Season well with plenty of salt and ground black pepper.

2 Roughly divide the meat mixture into eight equal pieces and use your hands to press each of the pieces into flat rounds.

3 Cut the mozzarella into four chunks. Place a chunk of cheese on half the lamb rounds. Top each with another round of meat mixture.

4 Press each of the two rounds of meat together firmly, making four flattish burger shapes. Use your fingers to blend the edges and seal in the cheese completely.

5 To make the sauce, place all the ingredients in a bowl and mash them together with a fork. Season well with salt and ground black pepper.

6 Brush the lamb burgers with olive oil and cook over a moderately hot barbecue for about 15 minutes, or grill for 10 minutes turning once, until golden brown. Serve with the sauce.

VARIATION

To make a quick version of the sauce, melt a jar of ready-made redcurrant sauce with balsamic vinegar and mint.

Tomato Sauce with Greek Lamb Sausages

FOR A QUICK AND EASY tomato sauce, passata can be enlivened with the addition of sugar, bay leaves and onions. The sausages will add more flavour as they simmer in the smooth sauce. As an alternative you could try using fresh turkey mince instead of lamb.

Serves 4

INGREDIENTS

50g/2oz/1 cup fresh breadcrumbs
150ml/¼ pint/⅔ cup milk
675g/1½lb minced lamb or minced turkey
30ml/2 tbsp grated onion
3 garlic cloves, crushed
10ml/2 tsp ground cumin
30ml/2 tbsp chopped fresh parsley
flour, for dusting
olive oil, for frying
salt and ground black pepper
fresh flat leaf parsley, to garnish

For the tomato sauce
600ml/1 pint/2½ cups passata
5ml/1 tsp sugar
2 bay leaves
1 small onion, peeled

1 Mix together the breadcrumbs and milk. Add the lamb or turkey, onion, garlic, cumin and parsley and season with salt and pepper.

2 Shape the mixture into little fat sausages, about 5cm/2in long and roll them in flour.

3 Heat about 60ml/4 tbsp olive oil in a pan. Fry the sausages in the oil for about 8 minutes, turning them until evenly browned. Remove and place on kitchen paper to drain.

4 Put the passata, sugar, bay leaves and whole onion in a pan and simmer for 20 minutes.

5 Add the sausages and cook for 10 minutes more. Serve garnished with parsley.

Pesto with Roast Leg of Lamb

THE INTENSE AROMAS OF fresh basil and garlic combine irresistibly with lamb, and the pine nuts and Parmesan make a delectable crunchy crust during roasting.

Serves 6

INGREDIENTS

2.25–2.75kg/5–6lb leg of lamb

For the pesto

90g/3½oz/1¾ cups fresh basil leaves
4 garlic cloves, coarsely chopped
45ml/3 tbsp pine nuts
150ml/¼ pint/⅔ cup olive oil
50g/2oz/⅔ cup freshly grated Parmesan cheese
5ml/1 tsp salt, or to taste

1 To make the pesto, combine the basil, garlic and pine nuts in a food processor, and process until finely chopped. With the motor running, slowly add the oil in a steady stream. Scrape the mixture into a bowl. Stir in the Parmesan and salt.

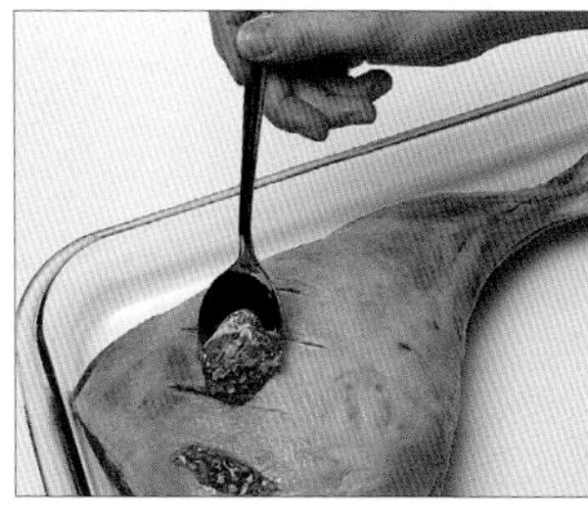

2 Set the lamb in a roasting dish. Make several slits in the meat with a knife, and spoon pesto into each slit.

3 Coat the surface of the lamb in a thick, even layer of the remaining pesto. Cover the meat and leave to stand for 2 hours at room temperature, or chill overnight. Preheat the oven to 180°C/350°F/Gas 4.

4 Place the lamb in the oven and roast, allowing about 20 minutes per 450g/1lb if you like rare meat, or 25 minutes per 450g/1lb if you prefer it medium-rare. Turn the lamb occasionally during roasting.

5 Remove the leg of lamb from the oven, cover it loosely with foil, and let it rest for about 15 minutes before carving and serving.

VARIATION

Lamb steaks or lamb chops could also be coated with this delicious pesto.

Noisettes of Pork with Creamy Calvados and Apple Sauce

This dish is ideal as part of a formal menu to impress guests. Buttered gnocchi or griddled polenta and red cabbage are suitable accompaniments.

Serves 4

INGREDIENTS

30ml/2 tbsp plain flour
4 noisettes of pork, about 175g/6oz each, firmly tied
25g/1oz/2 tbsp butter
4 baby leeks, finely sliced
5ml/1 tsp mustard seeds, coarsely crushed
30ml/2 tbsp Calvados
150ml/¼ pint/⅔ cup dry white wine
2 Golden Delicious apples, peeled, cored and sliced
150ml/¼ pint/⅔ cup double cream
30ml/2 tbsp chopped fresh parsley
salt and ground black pepper

1 Place the flour in a bowl and add plenty of seasoning. Turn the noisettes in the flour mixture to coat them lightly.

2 Melt the butter in a heavy-based frying pan and cook the noisettes until golden on both sides. Remove from the pan and set aside.

3 Add the leeks to the fat remaining in the pan and cook for 5 minutes. Stir in the mustard seeds and pour in the Calvados, then carefully ignite it to burn off the alcohol.

4 When the flames have died down pour in the wine and replace the pork. Cook gently for 10 minutes, turning the pork frequently.

5 Add the apples and cream and simmer for 5 minutes, or until the apples are tender. Taste for seasoning, then stir in the chopped parsley and serve at once.

Chilli-nectarine Relish with Pork Chops

PORK AND FRUIT ARE a classic combination, and this spicy nectarine relish is the perfect partner for griddled pork chops.

Serves 4

INGREDIENTS

250ml/8fl oz/1 cup fresh orange juice
45ml/3 tbsp olive oil
2 garlic cloves, minced
5ml/1 tsp ground cumin
15ml/1 tbsp coarsely ground black pepper
8 pork loin chops, about 2cm/¾in thick, well trimmed
salt

For the chilli-nectarine relish
1 small fresh green chilli pepper
30ml/2 tbsp honey
juice of ½ lemon
250ml/8fl oz/1 cup chicken stock
2 nectarines, pitted and chopped
1 garlic clove, crushed
½ onion, finely chopped
5ml/1 tsp grated fresh ginger root
1.5ml/¼ tsp salt
15ml/1 tbsp chopped fresh coriander

1 Roast the chilli over a gas flame, holding it with tongs, until charred on all sides. (Alternatively, char the skin under the grill.) Cool for 5 minutes.

2 Wearing rubber gloves, remove the charred skin of the chilli. Discard seeds if a less hot flavour is desired. Finely chop the chilli and place in a pan.

3 Add the honey, lemon juice, chicken stock, nectarines, garlic, onion, ginger and salt. Bring to the boil, then simmer, stirring occasionally, for about 30 minutes. Stir in the coriander and set aside.

4 In a small bowl, combine the orange juice, oil, garlic, cumin and pepper. Stir to mix.

5 Arrange the pork chops, in one layer, in a shallow dish. Pour over the orange juice mixture and turn to coat. Cover and leave to stand for at least 1 hour, or chill overnight.

6 Remove the pork from the marinade and pat dry with kitchen paper. Season lightly with salt.

7 Heat a frying pan or ridged griddle. Add the meat and cook for about 5 minutes, or until browned. Turn and cook on the other side for about 10 minutes more. (Work in batches if necessary.) Serve immediately, with the relish.

COOK'S TIP

The relish can be made in advance, then covered and stored in the fridge overnight for the flavours to mature.

Sage and Orange Sauce with Pork Fillet

SAGE IS OFTEN PARTNERED with pork – there seems to be a natural affinity – and the addition of orange to the sauce balances the flavour.

Serves 4

INGREDIENTS

2 pork fillets, about 350g/12oz each
10ml/2 tsp unsalted butter
salt and ground black pepper
orange wedges and sage leaves, to garnish

For the sage and orange sauce
120ml/4fl oz/½ cup dry sherry
175ml/6fl oz/¾ cup chicken stock
2 garlic cloves, very finely chopped
grated rind and juice of 1 unwaxed orange
3 or 4 sage leaves, finely chopped
10ml/2 tsp cornflour

1 Season the pork fillets lightly with salt and pepper.

2 Melt the butter in a heavy, flameproof casserole over a medium-high heat, then add the meat and cook for 5–6 minutes, turning to brown all sides evenly.

3 Add the sherry, boil for about 1 minute, then add the stock, garlic, orange rind and chopped sage. Bring to the boil and reduce the heat to low, then cover and simmer for 20 minutes, turning once.

4 Transfer the pork to a warmed platter and cover to keep warm.

5 Bring the sauce to the boil. Blend the cornflour and orange juice and stir into the sauce, then boil gently over a medium heat for a few minutes, stirring frequently, until the sauce is slightly thickened.

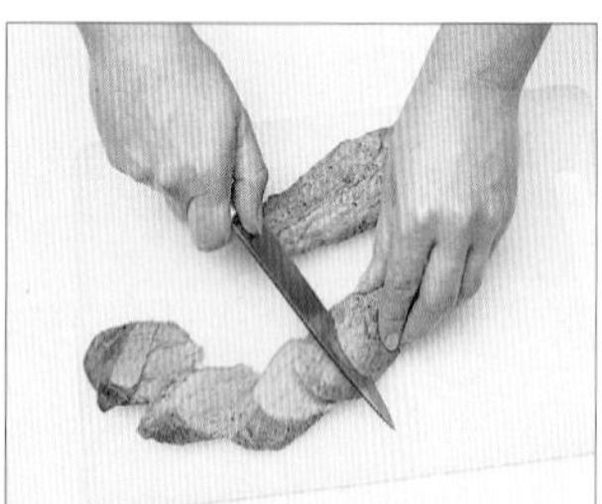

6 Slice the pork diagonally and pour the meat juices into the sauce.

7 Spoon a little sauce over the pork and garnish with orange wedges and sage leaves. Serve the remaining sauce separately.

COOK'S TIP

- *The meat is cooked if the juices run clear when the meat is pierced, or when a meat thermometer inserted into the thickest part of the meat registers 66°C/150°F.*
- *If fresh sage is not available, try using rosemary as a substitute, as this also goes very well with pork.*

Smoked Cheese Sauce with Veal Escalopes

SHEEP'S MILK CHEESE melted with cream makes a simple sauce for serving with pan-fried veal escalopes. The escalopes are used as purchased, not beaten thin.

Serves 4

INGREDIENTS

25g/1oz/2 tbsp butter
15ml/1 tbsp extra virgin olive oil
8 small veal escalopes
2 garlic cloves, crushed
250g/9oz/3½ cups button mushrooms or closed cup mushrooms, sliced
150g/5oz/1¼ cups frozen peas, thawed
60ml/4 tbsp brandy
250ml/8fl oz/1 cup whipping cream
150g/5oz smoked sheep's milk cheese, diced
ground black pepper
sprigs of flat leaf parsley, to garnish

1 Melt half the butter with the oil in a large, heavy-based frying pan. Season the escalopes with plenty of pepper and brown them in batches on each side over a high heat. Reduce the heat and cook for about 5 minutes on each side until just done. The escalopes should feel firm to the touch, with a very light springiness.

2 Lift the escalopes on to a serving dish and keep hot.

3 Add the remaining butter to the pan. When it melts, stir-fry the garlic and mushrooms for about 3 minutes.

4 Add the peas, pour in the brandy and cook until all the pan juices have been absorbed. Season lightly. Using a slotted spoon, remove the mushrooms and peas and place on top of the escalopes. Pour the cream into the pan.

5 Stir in the diced cheese. Heat gently until the cheese has melted. Season with pepper only and pour over the escalopes and vegetables. Serve immediately, garnished with sprigs of flat leaf parsley.

VARIATION

This dish works well with lean pork steaks. Ensure that pork is well cooked, with a slightly longer frying time.

Sweet-and-sour Sauce with Pork

The combination of sweet-and-sour flavours is popular in Venetian cooking, especially with meat and liver. This recipe is given extra bite with the addition of crushed mixed peppercorns. Served with shelled broad beans tossed with grilled bacon, it is delectable.

Serves 2

INGREDIENTS

1 whole pork fillet, about 350g/12oz
25ml/1½ tbsp plain flour
30–45ml/2–3 tbsp olive oil
salt and ground black pepper
broad beans tossed with grilled bacon, to serve

For the sweet-and-sour sauce
250ml/8fl oz/1 cup dry white wine
30ml/2 tbsp white wine vinegar
10ml/2 tsp sugar
15ml/1 tbsp mixed peppercorns, coarsely ground

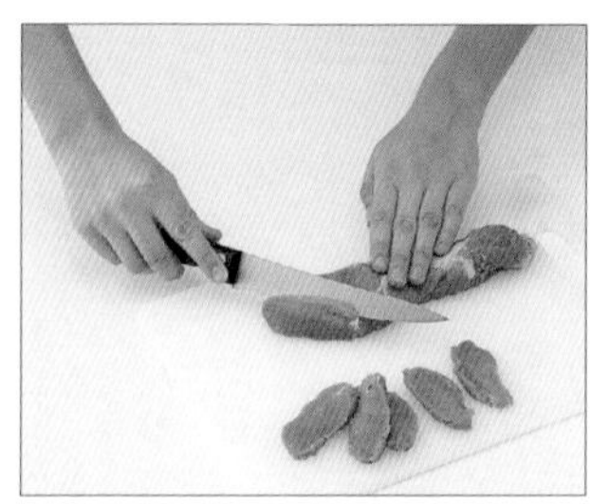

1 Cut the pork diagonally into thin slices. Place between two sheets of clear film and pound lightly with a rolling pin to flatten them evenly.

2 Spread out the flour in a shallow bowl. Season well with salt and pepper and coat the meat.

3 Heat 15ml/1 tbsp of the oil in a wide, heavy-based saucepan or frying pan and add as many slices of pork as the pan will hold. Fry over a medium to high heat for 2–3 minutes on each side, or until crispy and tender. Remove with a fish slice and set aside. Repeat with the remaining pork, adding more oil as necessary.

4 Mix the wine, wine vinegar and sugar in a jug. Pour into the pan and stir vigorously over a high heat until reduced, scraping the pan to incorporate the sediment. Stir in the peppercorns and return the pork to the pan. Spoon the sauce over the pork until it is evenly coated and heated through. Serve with the broad beans tossed with grilled bacon.

Cook's Tip

Grind the peppercorns in a pepper grinder, or crush them with a mortar and pestle.

Gammon with Cumberland Sauce

CUMBERLAND SAUCE WAS INVENTED to honour the Duke of Cumberland, who commanded the troops at the last battle on English soil, against the Scots. It can be served hot or cold, with gammon or venison.

Serves 8–10

INGREDIENTS

2.25kg/5lb smoked or unsmoked gammon joint
1 onion
1 carrot
1 celery stick
bouquet garni sachet
6 peppercorns

For the glaze

whole cloves
50g/2oz/¼ cup soft light brown or demerara sugar
30ml/2 tbsp golden syrup
5ml/1 tsp English mustard powder

For the Cumberland sauce

juice and shredded rind of 1 orange
30ml/2 tbsp lemon juice
120ml/4fl oz/½ cup port or red wine
60ml/4 tbsp redcurrant jelly

1 Soak the gammon overnight in a cool place in plenty of cold water to cover. Discard this water. Put the joint into a large pan and cover it again with more cold water. Bring the water to the boil slowly and skim any scum from the surface with a slotted spoon.

2 Add the vegetables and seasonings, cover and simmer very gently for 2 hours. (The meat can also be cooked in the oven at 180°C/350°F/Gas 4. Allow 30 minutes per 450g/1lb.)

3 Leave the meat to cool in the liquid for 30 minutes. Then remove it from the liquid and strip off the skin neatly with the help of a knife (use rubber gloves if the gammon is too hot to handle).

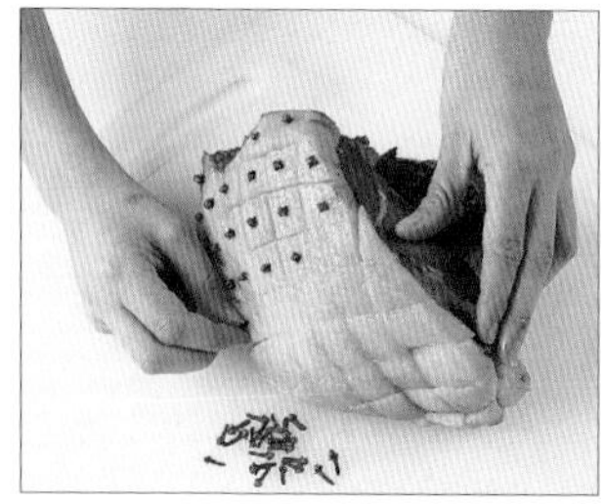

4 Score the fat in diamonds with a sharp knife and stick a clove in the centre of each diamond. Preheat the oven to 180°C/350°F/Gas 4.

5 Put the sugar, golden syrup and mustard powder in a small pan and heat gently to melt them. Place the gammon in a roasting tin and spoon over the hot glaze. Bake it for about 20 minutes, or until golden brown, then put it under a hot grill to colour.

6 Allow the meat to stand in a warm place for 15 minutes before carving (this makes carving much easier and tenderizes the meat).

7 For the Cumberland sauce, put the orange and lemon juice into a pan with the port or wine and redcurrant jelly, and heat gently to melt the jelly. Pour boiling water on to the orange rind, strain, and add the rind to the sauce. Cook gently for 2 minutes. Serve the sauce hot.

COOK'S TIP

Gammon is often not as strongly salted as it once was, so it may not be necessary to soak overnight before cooking to remove the salty flavour.

Cranberry Sauce with Venison

VENISON STEAKS ARE NOW readily available. Lean and low in fat, they make a healthy choice for a special occasion. Served with a sauce of fresh seasonal cranberries, port and ginger, they make a dish with a wonderful combination of flavours.

Serves 4

INGREDIENTS

30ml/2 tbsp sunflower oil
4 venison steaks
2 shallots, finely chopped
salt and ground black pepper
fresh thyme sprigs, to garnish
creamy mashed potatoes and broccoli, to serve

For the cranberry sauce

1 orange
1 lemon
75g/3oz/¾ cup fresh or frozen cranberries
5ml/1 tsp grated fresh root ginger
1 fresh thyme sprig
5ml/1 tsp Dijon mustard
60ml/4 tbsp redcurrant jelly
150ml/¼ pint/⅔ cup ruby port

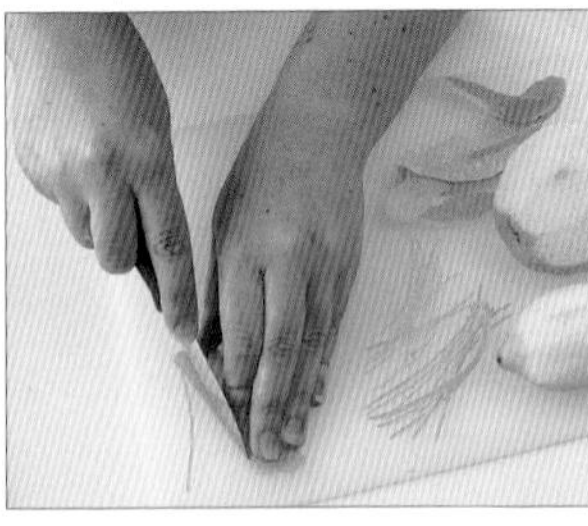

1 For the sauce, pare the rind thinly from half the orange and half the lemon using a vegetable peeler, then cut into very fine strips.

2 Blanch the strips in a small pan of boiling water for about 5 minutes until tender. Strain the strips and refresh under cold water.

3 Squeeze the juice from the orange and lemon and then pour into a small pan. Add the fresh or frozen cranberries, ginger, thyme sprig, mustard, redcurrant jelly and port. Cook the sauce mixture over a low heat until the jelly melts.

4 Bring the sauce to the boil, stirring occasionally, then cover the pan and reduce the heat. Cook gently, for about 15 minutes, or until the cranberries are just tender.

5 Heat the oil in a heavy-based frying pan, add the venison steaks and cook over a high heat for 2–3 minutes.

6 Turn over the steaks and add the shallots to the pan. Cook the steaks on the other side for 2–3 minutes, depending on whether you like rare or medium cooked meat.

7 Just before the end of cooking, pour in the sauce and add the strips of orange and lemon rind. Leave the sauce to bubble for a few seconds to thicken slightly, then remove the thyme sprig and adjust the seasoning to taste.

8 Transfer the venison steaks to warmed plates and spoon over the sauce. Garnish with thyme sprigs and serve accompanied by creamy mashed potatoes and broccoli.

COOK'S TIP

When frying venison, always remember the briefer the better; venison will turn to leather if subjected to fierce heat after it has reached the medium-rare stage. If you dislike any hint of pink, cook it to this stage then let it rest in a low oven for a few minutes.

VARIATION

When fresh cranberries are unavailable, use redcurrants instead. Stir them into the sauce towards the end of cooking with the orange and lemon rinds.

Gravy with Beef Pot Roast

A TRADITIONAL BRITISH DISH which will feed a crowd at low cost. The rich gravy gathers all the flavour from the meat and vegetables, so nothing is wasted.

Serves 8

INGREDIENTS

1.8kg/4lb joint beef suitable for pot roasting, such as brisket
3 garlic cloves, cut in half or in thirds
225g/8oz piece salt pork or bacon
275g/10oz onions, chopped
3 celery sticks, chopped
2 carrots, chopped
115g/4oz turnip, diced
450ml/¾ pint/scant 2 cups beef or chicken stock
450ml/¾ pint/scant 2 cups dry red or white wine
1 bay leaf
5ml/1 tsp fresh thyme, or 2.5ml/½ tsp dried
4–6 small whole potatoes, or 3 large potatoes, quartered
75g/3oz beurre manié
salt and ground black pepper
watercress, to garnish

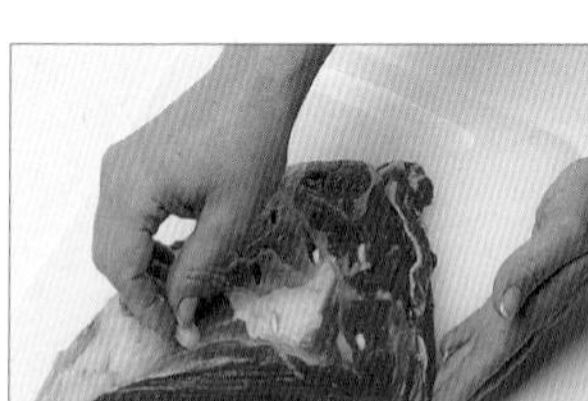

1 Preheat the oven to 160°C/325°F/Gas 3. Make deep incisions in the beef joint on all sides with the tip of a sharp knife and insert the garlic pieces.

2 In a large, flameproof casserole, cook the salt pork or bacon over a low heat until the fat runs and the pork or bacon begins to brown.

3 Remove the meat with a slotted spoon and discard. Increase the heat to medium-high and add the beef joint to the casserole. Brown it evenly on all sides. Remove and set aside on a plate or dish while you prepare the remaining vegetables.

4 Add the chopped onions, celery and carrots to the casserole and cook them for 8–10 minutes, stirring occasionally to avoid sticking, until all the vegetables are softened.

5 Stir in the diced turnips, add the beef or chicken stock, red or white wine, bay leaf and thyme, and mix well. Return the beef joint and any juices to the casserole, cover and cook in the preheated oven for 2 hours.

6 Add the whole or quartered potatoes to the casserole, pushing them down under the other vegetables. Season with salt and ground black pepper to taste. Cover the casserole once more and cook for a further 45 minutes, or until the potatoes are tender.

7 Transfer the meat to a warmed serving dish. Remove the potatoes and other vegetables from the casserole with a slotted spoon and arrange around the joint.

8 Discard the bay leaf and skim off excess fat from the cooking liquid.

9 Bring to the boil on the hob, then stir teaspoonfuls of the beurre manié into the liquid, whisking thoroughly to blend and adding just enough to thicken to taste. Strain into a gravy boat.

10 Serve the meat with some of the gravy poured over and the vegetables alongside. Garnish as desired with watercress. Offer the remaining gravy for pouring.

COOK'S TIP

Suitable cuts of beef for pot roasting include brisket, thin and thick rump, thick flank (top rump) and topside. Your butcher should be able to advise you.

VARIATION

For extra colour, stir 175g/6oz frozen peas into the casserole about 5 minutes before the potatoes are cooked.

Black Bean Sauce with Beef and Broccoli Stir-fry

THIS CHINESE BEEF DISH is a quick stir-fry with a richly flavoured marinade that bubbles down into a luscious, dark sauce.

Serves 4

INGREDIENTS

225g/8oz lean fillet or rump steak
15ml/1 tbsp sunflower oil
225g/8oz broccoli
115g/4oz baby corn, diagonally halved
45–60ml/3–4 tbsp water
2 leeks, diagonally sliced
225g/8oz can water chestnuts, sliced

For the marinade

15ml/1 tbsp fermented black beans
30ml/2 tbsp dark soy sauce
30ml/2 tbsp Chinese rice vinegar or cider vinegar
15ml/1 tbsp sunflower oil
5ml/1 tsp sugar
2 garlic cloves, crushed
2.5cm/1in piece of fresh root ginger, peeled and finely chopped

1 To make the marinade, mash the fermented black beans in a non-metallic bowl. Add the remaining ingredients and stir well.

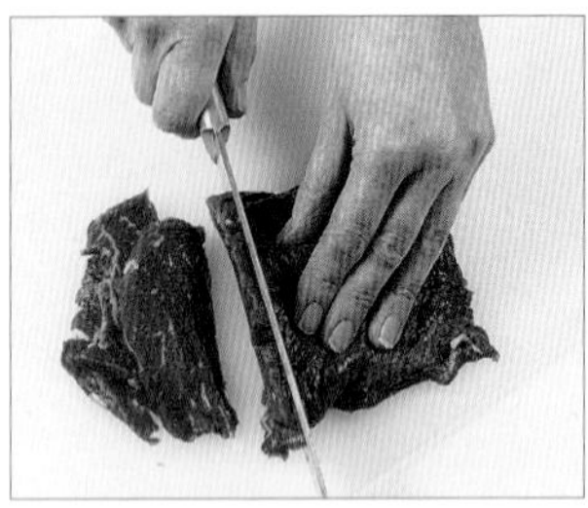

2 Cut the steak into thin slices across the grain, then add them to the marinade. Stir the steak well to coat it in the marinade. Cover the bowl and leave for several hours.

3 Heat the oil in a large frying pan. Drain the steak (reserving the marinade). When the oil is hot, add the meat and stir-fry for 3–4 minutes. Transfer it to a plate and set aside.

4 Cut the broccoli into small florets. Reheat the oil in the pan, add the broccoli, corn and water. Cover and steam gently for 5 minutes.

5 Add the leeks and water chestnuts to the broccoli mixture and toss over the heat for 1–2 minutes. Return the meat to the pan, pour over the reserved marinade and toss briefly over a high heat before serving.

COOK'S TIP

Fermented black beans are cooked, salted and fermented whole soya beans; they are available from Oriental stores.

Roquefort and Walnut Butter with Rump Steak

MAKE A ROLL OF this savoury cheese butter to keep in the fridge, ready to top plain steaks or pork chops.

Serves 4

INGREDIENTS

15ml/1 tbsp finely snipped fresh chives
15ml/1 tbsp olive oil or sunflower oil
4 lean rump steaks, about 130g/4½oz each
120ml/4fl oz/½ cup dry white wine
30ml/2 tbsp crème fraîche or double cream
salt and ground black pepper
fresh chives, to garnish

For the Roquefort and walnut butter
2 shallots, chopped
75g/3oz/6 tbsp butter, slightly softened
150g/5oz Roquefort cheese
30ml/2 tbsp finely chopped walnuts

1 Sauté the shallots in a third of the butter. Tip into a bowl and add half the remaining butter, the cheese, walnuts, snipped chives and pepper to taste. Chill lightly, roll in foil to a sausage shape and chill again until firm.

2 Heat the remaining butter with the oil and cook the steaks to your liking. Season and remove from the pan.

3 Pour the wine into the pan and stir to incorporate any sediment. Bubble up the liquid for a minute or two, then stir in the crème fraîche or cream. Season with salt and pepper and pour over the steaks.

4 Cut pats of the Roquefort butter from the roll and put one on top of each steak. Garnish with chives and serve. Green beans make an ideal accompaniment to this dish.

COOK'S TIP

The butter can also be stored in the freezer, but it is easier to cut it into rounds before freezing, so you can remove just as many as you need, without thawing the rest.

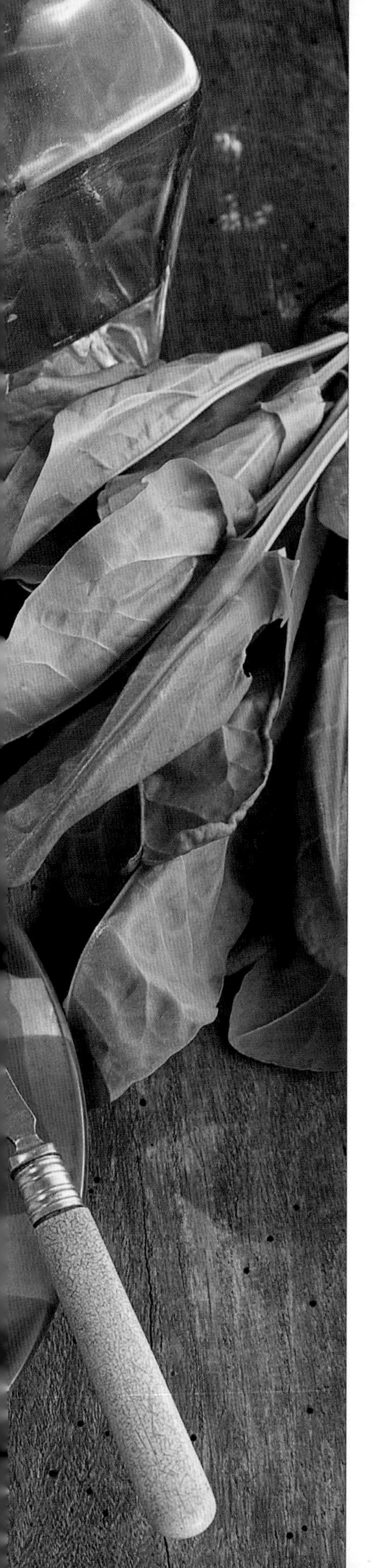

Sauces for Fish Dishes

You might expect all sauces for fish to be very delicate and light in flavour, but that's not always the case. Certainly in this chapter you'll find a classic white Parsley Sauce and a deliciously subtle Lemon and Chive Sauce: the perfect partners for white fish or fishcakes. But you'll also discover some more surprising combinations – a tangy Orange and Caper Sauce to pep up plain white fish, and a Chilli Barbecue Sauce to serve with salmon steaks.

There are some flavours that are natural partners for fish, such as lemon or dill, which can be used in classic white or white wine sauces, or in butters to serve with whole fish, fillets or steaks. Some of the classic pairings which have become enduring favourites cannot be ignored. The rich, oily flesh of mackerel balances perfectly with the tangy acidity of a Gooseberry Sauce, and the slightly sharp flavour of sorrel offsets the richness of salmon and transforms it into a sophisticated dinner-party dish.

As with any sauce, there are no hard-and-fast rules, but the general guideline is that white fish pairs best with subtle cream sauces and herb butters, whereas oily fish can take more robust flavours such as spices or tangy fruits.

Orange and Caper Sauce with Skate

A WONDERFULLY SWEET-SOUR, creamy sauce to add zest to otherwise plain white fish.

Serves 4

INGREDIENTS

4 skate wings, about 200g/7oz each
25g/1oz/2 tbsp butter
350ml/12fl oz/1½ cups fish stock

For the orange and caper sauce

25g/1oz/2 tbsp butter
1 onion, chopped
fish bones and trimmings
5ml/1 tsp black peppercorns
300ml/½ pint/1¼ cups dry white wine
2 small oranges
15ml/1 tbsp capers, drained
60ml/4 tbsp crème fraîche
salt and ground white pepper

1 To make the sauce, melt the butter and add the onion. Sauté over a moderate heat until the onion is lightly browned.

2 To the sauce, add the fish bones and trimmings and peppercorns, then pour in the wine. Cover and simmer gently for 30 minutes.

3 Using a serrated knife, peel the oranges, ensuring all the white pith is removed. Ease the segments away from the membrane.

4 Place the skate in a frying pan, add the butter and the fish stock and poach for 10–15 minutes, depending on thickness.

5 Strain the wine mixture into a clean saucepan. Add the capers and orange segments together with any juice, and heat through. Lower the heat and gently stir in the crème fraîche and seasoning. Serve the skate wings and the sauce, garnished with parsley.

VARIATION

For an unusual change, try using ruby grapefruit instead of the orange – this goes particularly well with oily fish such as trout or tuna.

Parsley Sauce with Haddock

ONE OF THE MOST classic sauces for fish is parsley sauce – a perfect partner for any white fish.

Serves 4

INGREDIENTS

4 haddock fillets, about 175g/6oz each
25g/1oz/2 tbsp butter
150ml/¼ pint/⅔ cup milk
150ml/¼ pint/⅔ cup fish stock
1 bay leaf
salt and ground black pepper

For the parsley sauce
25g/1oz/2 tbsp butter
20ml/4 tsp plain flour
60ml/4 tbsp single cream
1 egg yolk
45ml/3 tbsp chopped fresh parsley
grated rind and juice of ½ lemon

1 Place the fish in a frying pan, add the butter, milk, fish stock, bay leaf and seasoning, and heat to simmering point.

2 Lower the heat, cover the pan and poach the fish for 10–15 minutes, depending on the thickness of the fillets, until the fish is tender and the flesh begins to flake. Transfer to a warm serving plate, cover and keep warm.

3 Make the sauce. Return the cooking liquid to the heat and bring to the boil, stirring. Simmer for about 4 minutes, then remove and discard the bay leaf.

4 Melt the butter in a saucepan, stir in the flour and cook, stirring continuously, for 1 minute.

5 Remove the pan from the heat and gradually stir in the fish cooking liquid.

6 Return to the heat and bring to the boil, stirring. Simmer for about 4 minutes, stirring frequently.

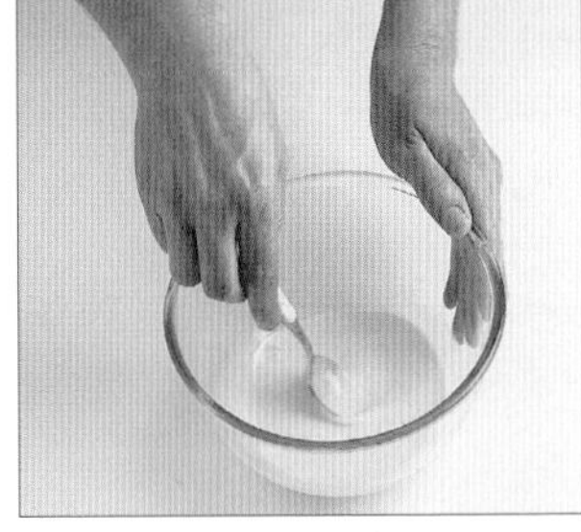

7 Remove the pan from the heat. In a bowl, blend the cream into the egg yolk, then stir this into the sauce with the parsley.

8 Reheat gently, stirring, for a few minutes; do not allow to boil.

9 Remove from the heat and add the lemon juice and rind, and season to taste. Pour into a warmed sauceboat and serve with the fish.

Vermouth and Chèvre Sauce with Pan-fried Cod

A SMOOTH SAUCE OF vermouth and light, creamy chèvre teams deliciously with chunky, white cod.

Serves 4

INGREDIENTS

4 cod fillets, about 150g/5oz each, skinned
15ml/1 tbsp olive oil
salt and ground black pepper
fresh flat leaf parsley, to garnish

For the vermouth and chèvre sauce

15ml/1 tbsp olive oil
4 spring onions, chopped
150ml/¼ pint/⅔ cup dry vermouth, preferably Noilly Prat
300ml/½ pint/1¼ cups fish stock
45ml/3 tbsp crème fraîche or double cream
65g/2½oz chèvre (goat's milk cheese), rind removed, and chopped
30ml/2 tbsp chopped fresh parsley
15ml/1 tbsp chopped fresh chervil

1 Remove any stray bones from the cod fillets. Rinse the fish under cold running water and pat dry with kitchen paper. Place the pieces on a plate and season generously.

VARIATION

Instead of cod you could use salmon, haddock or plaice. The cooking time may change according to the thickness of the fish fillets.

2 Heat a non-stick frying pan, then add the oil, swirling it around to coat the bottom. Add the pieces of cod and cook, without turning or moving them, for 4 minutes, or until nicely caramelized.

3 Turn each piece over and cook the other side for a further 3 minutes, or until just firm. Remove them to a serving plate and keep hot.

4 To make the sauce, heat the oil and stir-fry the spring onions for 1 minute. Add the vermouth and cook until reduced by half. Add the stock and cook again until reduced by half. Stir in the crème fraîche or cream and chèvre (goat's milk cheese) and simmer for 3 minutes.

5 Add salt and pepper to taste, stir in the herbs and spoon over the fish. Garnish with parsley.

Dill and Mustard Sauce with Sole

THIS SAUCE WILL GIVE A TANGY, Scandinavian flavour that is perfect with grilled fish. Sole is used here but the dill and mustard would combine with virtually any fish.

Serves 3–4

INGREDIENTS

3–4 lemon sole fillets
melted butter, for brushing
salt and ground black pepper
lemon slices and dill sprigs, to garnish

For the dill and mustard sauce

25g/1oz/2 tbsp butter
20g/¾oz/3 tbsp plain flour
300ml/½ pint/1¼ cups hot fish stock
15ml/1 tbsp white wine vinegar
45ml/3 tbsp chopped fresh dill
15ml/1 tbsp wholegrain mustard
10ml/2 tsp sugar
2 egg yolks

1 Preheat the grill to medium-high. Brush the fish with melted butter, season on both sides and cut two or three slashes in the flesh. Grill for 4 minutes, then transfer to a warmed place and keep warm while you make the sauce.

2 Melt the butter over a medium heat and stir in the flour. Cook for 1–2 minutes over a low heat, stirring continuously to remove any lumps.

3 Remove from the heat and gradually blend in the hot stock. Return to the heat, bring to the boil, stirring continuously, then simmer for 2–3 minutes.

VARIATION

A fennel and mustard sauce could also be made using chopped fennel leaves instead of the dill. Replace the wholegrain mustard with Dijon.

4 Remove the saucepan from the heat and beat in the vinegar, dill, mustard and sugar.

5 Using a fork, beat the yolks in a small bowl and gradually add a small quantity of hot sauce. Return to the pan, whisking vigorously. Continue whisking over a very low heat for a further minute. Serve immediately with the grilled sole, garnished with lemon slices and dill sprigs.

Gooseberry Sauce with Mackerel

GOOSEBERRIES AND MACKEREL ARE a classic combination; the tart sauce offsets the rich, oily fish.

Serves 4

INGREDIENTS

4 fresh mackerel, about 350g/12oz each, cleaned
salt and ground black pepper

For the gooseberry sauce

15g/½ oz/1 tbsp butter
225g/8oz gooseberries, topped and tailed
1 egg, beaten
pinch of ground mace or ginger, or a few drops of orange flower water (optional)
fresh flat leaf parsley, to garnish

1 Melt the butter in a saucepan, add the gooseberries, then cover and cook over a low heat, shaking the pan until the gooseberries are just tender.

2 Meanwhile, preheat the grill. Season the fish inside and out with salt and black pepper.

3 Cut two or three slashes in the skin on both sides of each mackerel, then grill for 15–20 minutes, or until cooked, turning once.

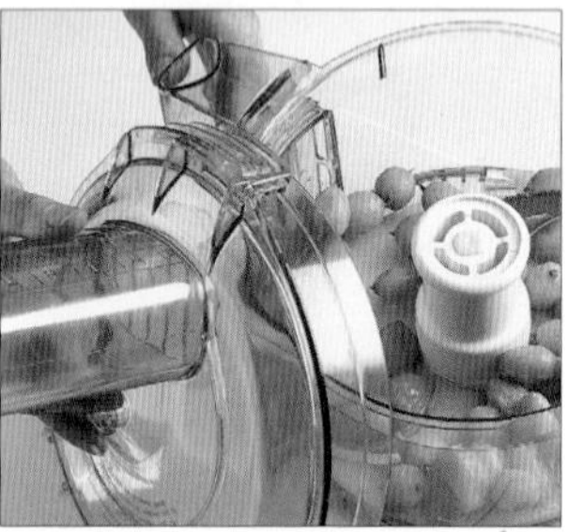

4 Purée the gooseberries with the egg in a food processor or blender, or mash the gooseberries thoroughly in a bowl with the egg. Press the gooseberry mixture through a sieve.

5 Return the gooseberry mixture to the pan and reheat gently, stirring, but do not allow to boil. Add the mace, ginger or orange flower water, if using, and season to taste. Serve the sauce hot with the mackerel, garnished with fresh parsley.

COOK'S TIPS

- *For the best flavour, look for triple strength orange flower water, which can be obtained from chemists and good food shops.*
- *If fresh gooseberries are not in season, canned ones make an alternative. Make sure they do not contain added sugar or the tart flavour will not be achieved.*

Herb Sauce with Sardines

THE ONLY ESSENTIAL ACCOMPANIMENT to this luscious herb sauce is fresh, crusty bread to mop up the tasty juices. The sauce is also quite delicious served with plain, grilled chicken breasts. For the best flavour, barbecue the sardines.

Serves 4

INGREDIENTS

12–16 fresh sardines
oil, for brushing
juice of 1 lemon
crusty bread, to serve

For the herb sauce

15ml/1 tbsp butter
4 spring onions, chopped
1 garlic clove, finely chopped
grated rind of 1 lemon
30ml/2 tbsp finely chopped fresh parsley
30ml/2 tbsp finely snipped fresh chives
30ml/2 tbsp finely chopped fresh basil
30ml/2 tbsp green olive paste
10ml/2 tsp balsamic vinegar
salt and ground black pepper

1 To clean the sardines, use a pair of small kitchen scissors to slit the fish along the belly and pull out the innards. Wipe the fish with kitchen paper and then arrange on a wire rack.

2 To make the sauce, melt the butter in a small pan and gently sauté the spring onions and garlic for about 2 minutes, shaking the pan occasionally, until softened but not browned.

3 Add the lemon rind and remaining sauce ingredients to the onions and garlic in the pan and keep warm on the edge of the hob or barbecue, stirring occasionally. Do not allow the mixture to boil.

4 Brush the sardines lightly with oil and sprinkle with lemon juice, salt and pepper. Barbecue for about 2 minutes on each side, over a medium heat. Serve with the warm sauce and fresh crusty bread.

Orange Butter Sauce with Sea Bream

THIS RICH BUTTER SAUCE, sharpened with tangy orange juice, goes well with the firm white flesh of sea bream.

Serves 2

INGREDIENTS

2 sea bream, about 350g/12oz each, scaled and gutted
10ml/2 tsp Dijon mustard
5ml/1 tsp fennel seeds
30ml/2 tbsp olive oil
50g/2oz watercress
175g/6oz mixed lettuce leaves, such as curly endive or frisée

For the orange butter sauce
30ml/2 tbsp frozen orange juice concentrate
175g/6oz/¾ cup unsalted butter, diced
salt and cayenne pepper

1 Slash the sea bream four times on each side. Combine the mustard and fennel seeds, then spread over both sides of the fish.

2 Brush each side of the fish with olive oil and grill under a preheated grill for 10–12 minutes without burning, turning the fish once midway through the cooking time.

3 Place the orange juice concentrate in a bowl and heat over a saucepan of simmering water. Remove the pan from the heat and gradually whisk in the butter until creamy. Season well.

4 Dress the watercress and lettuce leaves with the remaining olive oil, and arrange with the fish on two plates. Spoon the sauce over the fish and serve.

COOK'S TIP

Alternatively, barbecue the bream on a medium-hot barbecue. This is much easier if you use a hinged wire rack that holds the fish firmly and enables you to turn the fish without it breaking up.

Tahini Sauce with Baked Fish

THIS NORTH AFRICAN RECIPE evokes all the colour and rich flavours of Mediterranean cuisine, and the tahini sauce makes an unusual combination of tastes.

Serves 4

INGREDIENTS

1 whole fish, about 1.2kg/2½lb, scaled and cleaned
10ml/2 tsp coriander seeds
4 garlic cloves, sliced
10ml/2 tsp harissa sauce
90ml/6 tbsp olive oil
6 plum tomatoes, sliced
1 mild onion, sliced
3 preserved lemons or 1 fresh lemon
plenty of fresh herbs, such as bay leaves, thyme and rosemary
salt and ground black pepper
extra herbs, to garnish

For the tahini sauce
75ml/2½fl oz/⅓ cup light tahini
juice of 1 lemon
1 garlic clove, crushed
45ml/3 tbsp finely chopped fresh parsley or coriander

1 Preheat the oven to 200°C/400°F/Gas 6. Grease the base and sides of a large, shallow ovenproof dish.

2 Slash the fish diagonally on both sides with a sharp knife. Finely crush the coriander seeds and garlic with a mortar and pestle. Mix with the harissa sauce and about 60ml/4 tbsp of the olive oil.

3 Spread a little of the harissa, coriander and garlic paste inside the cavity of the fish. Spread the remainder over each side of the fish and set aside.

4 Scatter the tomatoes, onion and preserved or quartered fresh lemon into the dish. Sprinkle with the remaining oil, and season. Put the fish on top. Tuck plenty of herbs around it.

5 Bake the fish, uncovered, for about 25 minutes, or until it has turned opaque – test by piercing the thickest part with a knife.

6 Meanwhile, to make the sauce, put the tahini, lemon juice, garlic and parsley or coriander in a small saucepan with 120ml/4fl oz/½ cup cold water, and add a little salt and ground black pepper to season. Cook gently until smooth and heated through. Garnish the fish with the herbs, and serve the sauce separately.

COOK'S TIP

If you can't get a suitable large fish, use small whole fish such as red mullet or even cod or haddock steaks. Remember to reduce the cooking time slightly.

Tomato Coulis with Marinated Monkfish

A LIGHT BUT WELL-FLAVOURED sauce, this should be made when Italian plum tomatoes are at their ripest. The lime and herb marinade is offset by the sweet tomatoes in the coulis. Serve this delicious dish with a glass of chilled white wine.

Serves 4

INGREDIENTS

30ml/2 tbsp olive oil
finely grated rind and juice of 1 lime
30ml/2 tbsp chopped fresh mixed herbs
5ml/1 tsp Dijon mustard
4 skinless, boneless monkfish fillets
salt and ground black pepper
fresh herb sprigs, to garnish

For the tomato coulis

4 plum tomatoes, peeled and chopped
1 garlic clove, chopped
15ml/1 tbsp olive oil
15ml/1 tbsp tomato purée
30ml/2 tbsp chopped fresh oregano
5ml/1 tsp light soft brown sugar

1 Place the oil, lime rind and juice, herbs, mustard, and salt and pepper in a small bowl or jug and whisk together until thoroughly mixed.

2 Place the monkfish fillets in a shallow, non-metallic container and pour the lime mixture over. Turn the fish several times in the marinade to coat it. Cover and chill in the fridge for 1–2 hours.

3 Meanwhile, make the tomato coulis. Place all the coulis ingredients in a food processor or blender and process until smooth. Season to taste, then cover and chill until required.

4 Preheat the oven to 180°C/350°F/Gas 4. Using a fish slice, place each fish fillet on a sheet of greaseproof paper big enough to hold it in a parcel.

5 Spoon a little marinade over each piece of fish. Gather the paper loosely over the fish and fold over the edges to secure the parcel tightly. Place on a baking sheet.

6 Bake for 20–30 minutes, or until the fish fillets are cooked, tender and just beginning to flake.

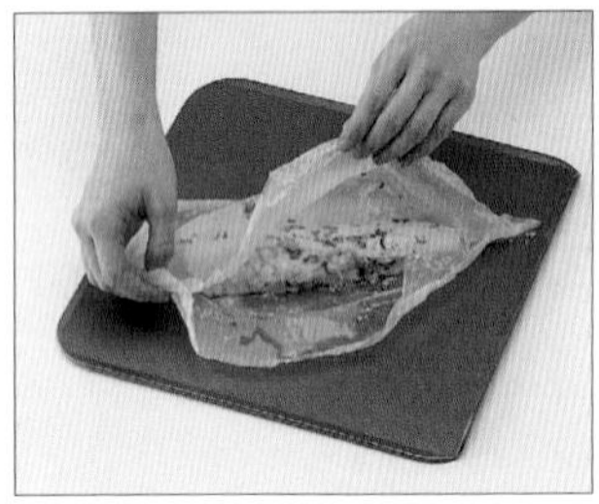

7 Carefully unwrap the parcels and serve the fish fillets immediately with a little of the chilled coulis served alongside, and garnished with a few fresh herb sprigs.

COOK'S TIP

The coulis can be served hot, if you prefer. Simply make as directed in the recipe and heat gently in a saucepan until almost boiling, just before serving.

Watercress Cream with Poached Salmon

THE DELICATE GREEN COLOUR of this cream sauce looks wonderful against pink-fleshed fish such as salmon or salmon trout.

Serves 4

INGREDIENTS

4 salmon fillets, about 175g/6oz each
25g/1oz/2 tbsp butter
150ml/¼ pint/⅔ cup hot fish stock
150ml/¼ pint/⅔ cup dry white wine
1 bay leaf
salt
pinch cayenne pepper

For the watercress cream

2 bunches watercress
25g/1oz/2 tbsp butter
2 shallots, chopped
25g/1oz/¼ cup plain flour
5ml/1 tsp anchovy essence
150ml/¼ pint/⅔ cup single cream
lemon juice

VARIATION

To make rocket cream, replace the watercress with 25g/1oz rocket leaves.

1 Trim the watercress of any bruised leaves and coarse stalks. Blanch in boiling water for 5 minutes. Drain and refresh under cold running water. In a sieve, press with a spoon to remove excess moisture. Chop finely.

2 Place the fish in a saucepan, add the butter, the fish stock, wine, bay leaf and seasoning, and heat over a low-medium heat to simmering point.

3 Lower the heat, cover the pan and poach the fish for 10–15 minutes, depending on thickness, until tender.

4 Transfer the fish to a warmed plate, cover and keep warm. Discard the bay leaf and reserve the cooking liquid for the sauce.

5 To make the sauce, melt the butter and fry the shallots until soft. Stir in the flour and cook for 1–2 minutes.

6 Remove from the heat and gradually blend in the reserved fish cooking liquid. Return to the heat, bring to the boil, stirring continuously, and simmer gently for 2–3 minutes.

7 Strain the sauce into a clean saucepan, then add the watercress, anchovy essence and cream. Warm over a low heat. Season with salt and cayenne pepper and sharpen with lemon juice to taste. Serve immediately with the poached salmon.

Lemon and Chive Sauce with Herby Fishcakes

THIS PIQUANT SAUCE MAKES a delicious accompaniment to fishcakes but would also team with most grilled or baked fish dishes.

Serves 4

INGREDIENTS

350g/12oz potatoes, peeled
75ml/5 tbsp skimmed milk
350g/12oz haddock or hoki fillets, skinned
15ml/1 tbsp lemon juice
15ml/1 tbsp creamed horseradish sauce
30ml/2 tbsp chopped fresh parsley
flour, for dusting
115g/4oz/2 cups fresh wholemeal breadcrumbs
salt and ground black pepper
sprigs of fresh flat leaf parsley, to garnish
vegetables in season, to serve

For the lemon and chive sauce
thinly pared rind and juice of ½ small lemon
120ml/4fl oz/½ cup dry white wine
2 thin slices fresh root ginger
10ml/2 tsp cornflour
30ml/2 tbsp snipped fresh chives

1 Place the potatoes in a large saucepan of boiling water and cook for 15–20 minutes. Drain and mash with the milk, and season to taste.

2 Purée the fish together with the lemon juice and horseradish sauce in a food processor or blender. Mix together with the potatoes and parsley.

3 With floured hands, shape the mixture into eight fishcakes and coat with the breadcrumbs. Chill in the fridge for 30 minutes.

4 Cook the fishcakes under a preheated medium-hot grill for about 5 minutes on each side, until browned.

5 To make the sauce, cut the lemon rind into julienne strips and put into a large saucepan together with the lemon juice, wine and ginger, and season to taste.

6 Simmer the sauce uncovered for 6 minutes.

7 Blend the cornflour with 15ml/1 tbsp of cold water. Add to the ingredients in the saucepan and simmer, stirring, until the sauce has thickened and is clear.

8 Stir in the chives immediately before serving. Serve the sauce hot with the fishcakes. Garnish the dish with sprigs of flat leaf parsley and serve with a selection of vegetables.

Sorrel Sauce with Salmon Steaks

THE SHARP FLAVOUR OF the sorrel sauce balances the richness of the fish. The young plant has the mildest flavour, so try to buy the herb in its spring season when it is at its best.

Serves 2

INGREDIENTS

2 salmon steaks, about 250g/9oz each
5ml/1 tsp olive oil
salt and ground black pepper
fresh sage, to garnish

For the sorrel sauce

15g/½oz/1 tbsp butter
2 shallots, finely chopped
45ml/3 tbsp crème fraîche
90g/3½oz fresh sorrel leaves, washed and patted dry

1 Season the salmon steaks with salt and pepper. Brush a non-stick frying pan with the oil.

2 Make the sauce. In a small saucepan, melt the butter over a medium heat. Add the shallots and fry for 2–3 minutes, stirring frequently, until just softened.

3 Add the crème fraîche and the sorrel leaves to the shallots and cook until the sorrel is completely wilted, stirring constantly.

4 Meanwhile, place the frying pan over a medium heat until hot. Add the salmon steaks and cook for about 5 minutes, turning once, until the flesh is opaque next to the bone. If you're not sure, pierce the flesh with the tip of a sharp knife; the fish should flake easily.

5 Arrange the salmon steaks on two warmed plates, garnish with sage and serve with the sorrel sauce.

COOK'S TIP

If preferred, cook the salmon steaks in the microwave for 4–5 minutes, in a tightly covered dish, or according to the manufacturer's guidelines.

VARIATION

If sorrel is not available, use finely chopped watercress instead.

Chilli Barbecue Sauce with Salmon

THIS SPICY TOMATO AND mustard sauce is delicious served with chargrilled salmon fillets – cook them either on a barbecue or under a hot grill.

Serves 4

INGREDIENTS

4 salmon fillets, about 175g/6oz

For the chilli barbecue sauce

10ml/2 tsp butter
1 small red onion, finely chopped
1 garlic clove, finely chopped
6 plum tomatoes, diced
45ml/3 tbsp tomato ketchup
30ml/2 tbsp Dijon mustard
30ml/2 tbsp dark brown sugar
15ml/1 tbsp runny honey
5ml/1 tsp ground cayenne pepper
15ml/1 tbsp ancho chilli powder
15ml/1 tbsp ground paprika
15ml/1 tbsp Worcestershire sauce

1 To make the barbecue sauce, melt the butter in a large, heavy-based saucepan and gently cook the chopped onion and garlic until they are tender and translucent.

2 Stir in the tomatoes and simmer for 15 minutes, stirring occasionally (to break up the tomato pieces).

3 Add the remaining sauce ingredients and simmer for a further 20 minutes.

4 Process the mixture until smooth, in a food processor fitted with a metal blade. Leave to cool.

5 Brush the salmon with the sauce and chill for at least 2 hours. Barbecue or grill for about 2–3 minutes either side, brushing on the sauce when necessary. Serve drizzled with the remaining sauce.

Butter Sauce with Salmon Cakes

THE LEMONY BUTTER SAUCE keeps the salmon fishcakes deliciously moist; they make a real treat for supper or a leisurely breakfast at the weekend.

Makes 6

INGREDIENTS

225g/8oz tail piece of salmon, cooked
30ml/2 tbsp chopped fresh parsley
2 spring onions, trimmed and chopped
225g/8oz/2⅔ cups firm mashed potato
1 egg, beaten
50g/2oz/1 cup fresh white breadcrumbs
butter and oil, for frying (optional)
salt and ground black pepper

For the butter sauce
75g/3oz/6 tbsp butter
grated rind and juice of ½ lemon

1 Remove all the skin and bones from the fish and mash or flake it well. Add the chopped parsley, onions and 5ml/1 tsp of the lemon rind (from the same ingredients) and season with salt and black pepper.

2 Gently work in the potato and then shape into six rounds.

3 Chill the fishcakes for 20 minutes to allow them to firm up. Coat each fishcake well in egg and then the breadcrumbs. Grill gently for 5 minutes each side, or until golden, or fry in butter and oil over a medium-hot heat.

4 To make the butter sauce, in a saucepan, melt the butter over a gentle heat, then whisk in the remaining lemon rind and the lemon juice, together with 15–30ml/1–2 tbsp cold water. Season with salt and ground black pepper to taste. Simmer the sauce for a few minutes and then serve immediately with the fish cakes.

VARIATION

If you like, use a lime instead of the half lemon for a change of flavour. This butter sauce is a quick and easy accompaniment to virtually any fish.

COOK'S TIP

Tail pieces of salmon fillet are usually a good buy and do not contain bones, but any cut of salmon can be used for this dish, so look out for any which are on special offer.

Seafood with Warm Green Tartare Sauce

A colourful sauce that's good with all kinds of seafood, particularly fresh scallops, and it looks stunning over black pasta.

Serves 4

INGREDIENTS

350g/12oz black tagliatelle
12 large scallops
60ml/4 tbsp white wine
150ml/¼ pint/⅔ cup fish stock
lime wedges and parsley sprigs, to garnish

For the warm green tartare sauce
120ml/4fl oz/½ cup crème fraîche
10ml/2 tsp wholegrain mustard
2 garlic cloves, crushed
30–45ml/2–3 tbsp fresh lime juice
60ml/4 tbsp chopped fresh parsley
30ml/2 tbsp snipped chives
salt and ground black pepper

1 To make the tartare sauce, blend the crème fraîche, mustard, garlic, lime juice, parsley, chives and seasoning together in a food processor or blender.

2 Cook the pasta in a large pan of boiling, salted water according to the instructions on the packet until *al dente*. Drain thoroughly.

3 Meanwhile, slice the scallops in half, horizontally. Keep any corals whole.

4 Put the white wine and fish stock into a saucepan. Heat to simmering point. Add the scallops and cook very gently for 3–4 minutes (no longer or they will become tough).

5 Remove the scallops from the saucepan. Boil the wine and stock to reduce by half and add the tartare sauce to the pan. Heat gently to warm the sauce.

6 Replace the scallops and cook for 1 minute. Spoon over the pasta and garnish with lime wedges and parsley.

COOK'S TIPS

- *If you are removing the scallops from the shells yourself, remember to wash them first in plenty of cold water.*
- *If the scallops are frozen, defrost them before cooking, as they will probably have been glazed with water and will need to be drained well.*

VARIATIONS

- *This sauce could be made equally well with fresh mussels.*
- *Instead of serving over pasta, this sauce would go particularly well with fish dishes, such as monkfish which has a flavour reminiscent of lobster.*

Romesco Sauce with Grilled King Prawns

THIS SAUCE, FROM THE Catalan region of Spain, is served with fish and seafood. Its main ingredients are sweet pepper, tomatoes, garlic and toasted almonds.

Serves 4

INGREDIENTS

24 raw king prawns
30–45ml/2–3 tbsp olive oil
fresh flat leaf parsley, to garnish
lemon wedges, to serve

For the romesco sauce

2 well-flavoured tomatoes
60ml/4 tbsp olive oil
1 onion, chopped
4 garlic cloves, chopped
1 canned pimiento, chopped
2.5ml/½ tsp dried chilli flakes or powder
75ml/5 tbsp fish stock
30ml/2 tbsp sherry or white wine
10 blanched almonds
15ml/1 tbsp red wine vinegar
salt

1 To make the sauce, immerse the tomatoes in boiling water for about 30 seconds, remove from the pan with a slotted spoon, then refresh them under cold water. Peel away the skins and roughly chop the flesh.

2 Heat 30ml/2 tbsp of the oil in a pan, add the onion and 3 of the garlic cloves, and cook until soft.

3 Add the pimiento, tomatoes, chilli, fish stock and sherry or wine, then cover and simmer for 30 minutes. Allow to cool slightly.

4 Meanwhile, toast the almonds under the grill until golden.

5 Transfer the almonds to a blender or food processor and grind coarsely.

6 Add the remaining 30ml/2 tbsp of oil, the vinegar and the last garlic clove and process the mixture until it is evenly combined.

7 Carefully add the tomato and pimiento sauce (in batches if necessary) and process until smooth. Season with salt to taste and return to the rinsed pan to keep warm.

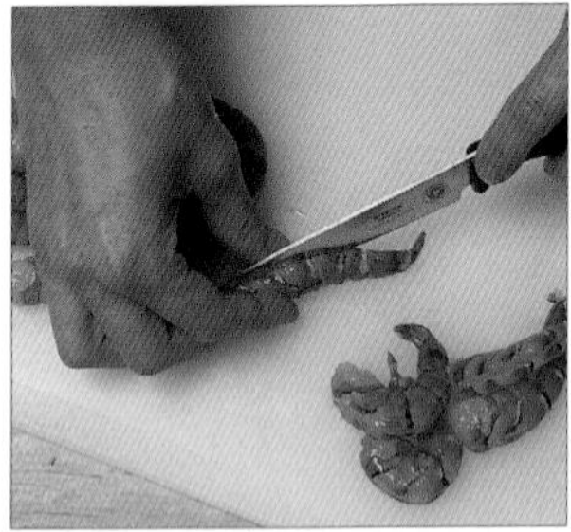

8 Remove the heads from the prawns, leaving them otherwise unshelled. With a sharp knife, slit each one down the back and remove the dark vein. Rinse and pat dry on kitchen paper. Preheat the grill.

9 Toss the prawns in olive oil, then spread out in the grill pan. Grill for about 2–3 minutes on each side, until pink. Arrange the prawns on a serving platter and garnish with parsley. Serve at once with the lemon wedges, and the sauce in a small bowl.

VARIATION

In Catalonia, romesco sauce is also served with local spicy sausages, grilled fish and poultry dishes. Spoonfuls can also be added to enrich a fish or chicken stew, rather like a rouille is used in French cooking.

Five-spice and Black Bean Sauce with Stir-fried Squid

THE SPICY ASIAN SAUCE is the ideal accompaniment for stir-fried squid and is very easy to make. It is important to have all the ingredients ready before you start to cook. The squid must be cooked very quickly or it will toughen.

Serves 6

INGREDIENTS

450g/1lb small squid cleaned
45ml/3 tbsp oil

For the five-spice and black bean sauce

2.5cm/1in piece fresh root ginger, grated
1 garlic clove, crushed
8 spring onions, cut diagonally into 2.5cm/1in lengths
1 red pepper, seeded and cut into strips
1 fresh green chilli, seeded and thinly sliced
6 chestnut mushrooms, sliced
5ml/1 tsp five-spice powder
30ml/2 tbsp black bean sauce
30ml/2 tbsp soy sauce
5ml/1 tsp sugar
15ml/1 tbsp rice wine or dry sherry

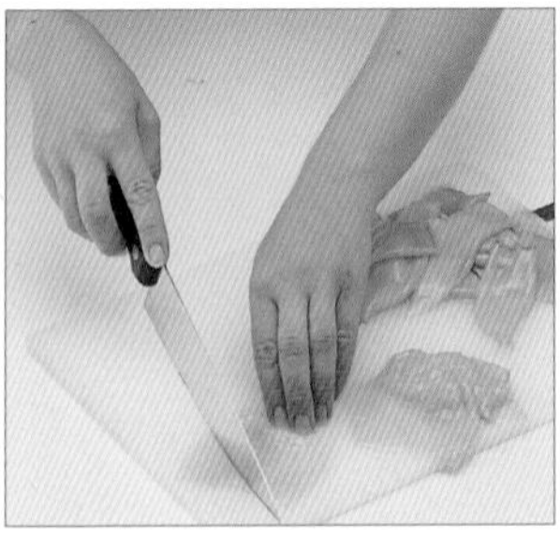

1 Rinse the squid and pull away the outer skin. Dry on kitchen paper. Slit the squid open and score the outside into diamonds with a sharp knife. Cut the squid into strips.

2 Heat a wok and add the oil. When it is hot, stir-fry the squid quickly. Remove the squid strips from the wok with a slotted spoon and set aside.

3 For the sauce, add the ginger, garlic, spring onions, red pepper, chilli and mushrooms to the oil remaining in the wok and stir-fry for 2 minutes.

4 Return the squid to the wok and stir in the five-spice powder. Stir in the black bean sauce, soy sauce, sugar and rice wine or sherry. Bring to the boil and cook, stirring, for 1 minute. Serve immediately.

Tartare Sauce with Crab Cakes

When serving any fried fish, tartare sauce is the traditional accompaniment, but it is also delicious with vegetables. Maryland is renowned for its seafood, and these little crab cakes hail from there.

Serves 4

INGREDIENTS

675g/1½lb fresh white crab meat
1 egg, beaten
30ml/2 tbsp mayonnaise
15ml/1 tbsp Worcestershire sauce
15ml/1 tbsp sherry
30ml/2 tbsp finely chopped fresh parsley
15ml/1 tbsp finely chopped fresh chives
45ml/3 tbsp olive oil
salt and ground black pepper

For the tartare sauce
1 egg yolk
15ml/1 tbsp white wine vinegar
30ml/2 tbsp Dijon-style mustard
250ml/8fl oz/1 cup vegetable or groundnut oil
30ml/2 tbsp fresh lemon juice
45ml/3 tbsp finely chopped spring onions
30ml/2 tbsp chopped drained capers
45ml/3 tbsp finely chopped sour dill pickles
45ml/3 tbsp finely chopped fresh parsley

1 Pick over the crab meat, removing any shell or cartilage. Keep the pieces of crab as large as possible.

2 In a bowl, combine the beaten egg with the mayonnaise, Worcestershire sauce, sherry and herbs. Season to taste. Gently fold in the crab meat.

3 Divide the mixture into eight portions and gently form each into an oval cake.

4 Place on a baking sheet between layers of waxed paper and chill for at least 1 hour.

5 To make the sauce, in a bowl, beat the egg yolk with a wire whisk. Add the vinegar, mustard, and seasoning, and whisk for about 10 seconds. Whisk in the oil in a slow, steady stream.

6 Add the lemon juice, spring onions, capers, sour dill pickles and parsley and mix well. Check the seasoning. Cover and chill.

7 Preheat the grill. Brush the crab cakes with the olive oil. Place on an oiled baking sheet, in one layer. Grill 15cm/6in from the heat until golden brown, about 5 minutes on each side. Alternatively, fry the crab cakes over a medium heat for a few minutes on each side. Serve the crab cakes hot with the tartare sauce.

Cook's Tips

For easier handling and to make the crab meat go further, add 50g/2oz/1 cup fresh breadcrumbs and 1 more egg to the crab mixture. Divide the mixture into 12 cakes to serve 6. Use dill instead of chives if you prefer.

Sauces for Vegetarian Dishes

Vegetable dishes have until recently been considered the poor-relation among other areas of cookery, but it is not only vegetarians that are becoming more interested in making vegetable dishes more appetizing and interesting. Everyone who is interested in healthy eating is including more vegetable-based meals in their diet.

Vegetables are one of the most versatile of all ingredients – they can provide hearty, cold-weather meals, such as Baked Marrow and Parsley Sauce and the family favourite, Cheddar Cheese Sauce with Cauliflower, or light summer dishes consisting of steamed and fresh vegetables, such as the Warm Vegetable Salad served with Peanut Sauce.

The sauces in this chapter, however, are not intended to be served exclusively with vegetable meals. They provide flavour and texture that can be teamed with freshly cooked pasta, such as the Green Vegetable Sauce, or polenta, as in the Wild Mushroom Sauce. Others provide a piquant taste to add flavour to a plainer dish, like the Citrus Sauce or Mustard Sauce, which add spice to liven up courgettes or potatoes but would be equally at home with fish or meat dishes. Any of these sauces will enhance and complement a variety of dishes – whether the flavours are similar or contrasting – if you choose carefully.

Green Vegetable Sauce

THIS SAUCE IS A medley of cooked fresh vegetables. Tossed with pasta, it's ideal for a fresh, light lunch or supper dish.

Serves 4

INGREDIENTS

450g/1lb dried pasta shapes

For the green vegetable sauce

30ml/2 tbsp butter
45ml/3 tbsp extra virgin olive oil
1 small leek, thinly sliced
2 carrots, diced
2.5ml/½ tsp sugar
1 courgette, diced
75g/3oz/generous ½ cup green beans
115g/4oz/1 cup frozen peas
1 handful fresh flat leaf parsley, chopped
2 ripe plum tomatoes, peeled and diced
salt and ground black pepper
fried parsley sprigs, to garnish

1 Melt the butter and oil in a medium frying pan or saucepan. When the mixture sizzles, add the prepared leek and carrots. Sprinkle the sugar over the vegetables and fry over a medium heat, stirring the mixture frequently, for about 5 minutes.

2 Stir the courgette, beans and peas into the sauce, and season with plenty of salt and pepper. Cover and cook over a low to medium heat for 5–8 minutes, or until the vegetables are tender, stirring occasionally.

3 Meanwhile, cook the pasta according to the instructions on the packet.

4 Stir the parsley and chopped tomatoes into the sauce.

5 Serve the sauce immediately, tossed with freshly cooked pasta and garnished with parsley sprigs.

Citrus Sauce with Baby Courgettes

THIS PIQUANT SAUCE IS a refreshing change served with steamed green vegetables, or it would make a tasty dip with roast potato wedges.

Serves 4

INGREDIENTS

350g/12oz baby courgettes

For the citrus sauce

4 spring onions, finely sliced
2.5cm/1in piece fresh root ginger, grated
30ml/2 tbsp cider vinegar
15ml/1 tbsp light soy sauce
5ml/1 tsp soft light brown sugar
45ml/3 tbsp vegetable stock
finely grated rind and juice of ½ lemon and ½ orange
5ml/1 tsp cornflour

1 Cook the courgettes in lightly salted, boiling water for 3–4 minutes, or until just tender. Drain well.

2 Meanwhile, make the sauce. Put all the sauce ingredients, except the cornflour, into a small saucepan and bring to the boil. Simmer for 3 minutes.

3 Blend the cornflour with 10ml/2 tsp cold water and add to the sauce. Bring the sauce to the boil, stirring continuously, until thickened.

4 Pour the sauce over the courgettes and gently heat, shaking the pan to coat evenly. Transfer to a warmed serving dish and serve.

VARIATION

Try this sauce with a mixture of baby vegetables, such as courgettes, carrots, turnips, baby corn, patty pans etc.

Mustard Sauce with Potato Skewers

THIS THICK, GARLIC-RICH dipping sauce is versatile enough to serve with any vegetable kebab or even with crudités.

Serves 4

INGREDIENTS

1kg/2¼lb small new potatoes
200g/7oz shallots, halved
30ml/2 tbsp olive oil
15ml/1 tbsp sea salt

For the mustard sauce
4 garlic cloves, crushed
2 egg yolks
30ml/2 tbsp lemon juice
300ml/½ pint/1¼ cups extra virgin olive oil
10ml/2 tsp wholegrain mustard
salt and ground black pepper

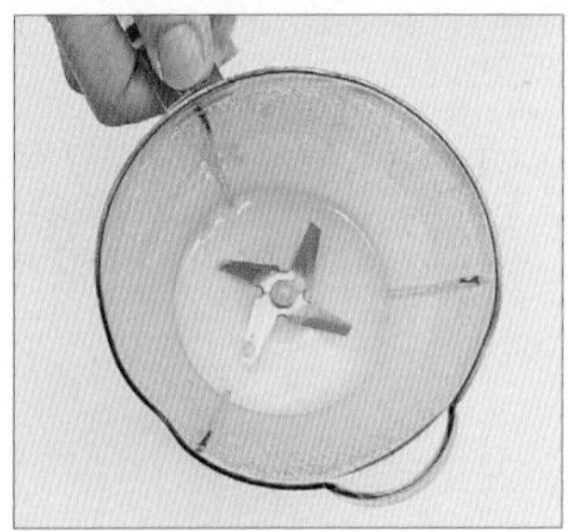

1 To make the mustard sauce, place the garlic, egg yolks and lemon juice in a food processor or blender and process briefly until smooth.

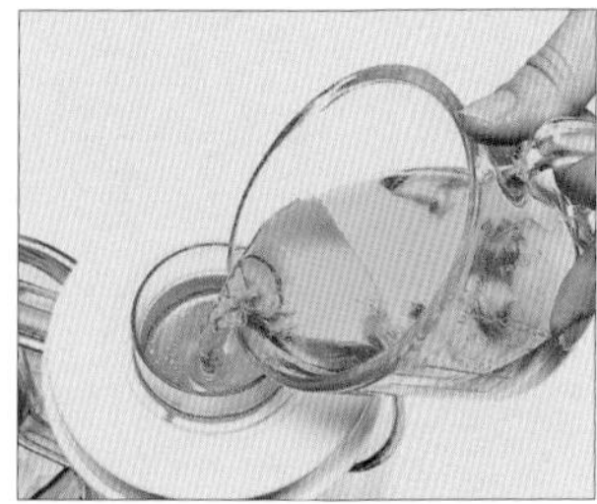

2 With the motor running, add the oil until the mixture forms a thick cream. Add the mustard, and season.

3 Par-boil the potatoes in salted boiling water for about 5 minutes. Drain well and then thread them on to metal skewers with the shallots.

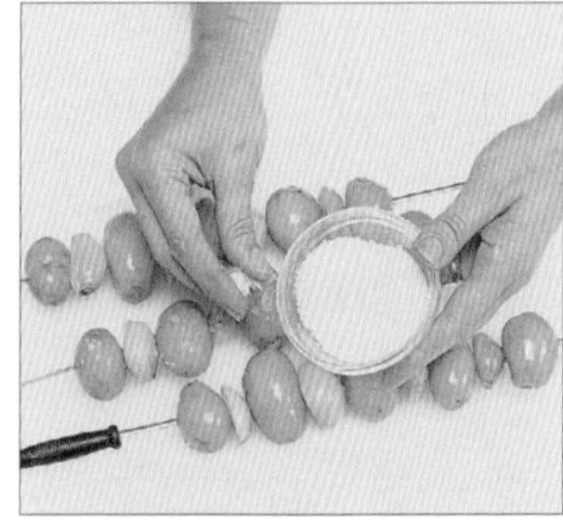

4 Brush the vegetable skewers lightly with olive oil and sprinkle with sea salt.

5 Cook the vegetables for 10–12 minutes over a hot barbecue or under a preheated grill, turning often, until tender. Serve immediately with the mustard dipping sauce.

Chilli Sauce with Spicy Potato Wedges

FOR A HEALTHY SNACK with superb flavour, try these dry-roasted potato wedges. The crisp spice crust makes them irresistible, especially when served with this chilli sauce.

Serves 2

INGREDIENTS

2 baking potatoes, about 225g/8oz each, unpeeled
30ml/2 tbsp olive oil
2 garlic cloves, crushed
5ml/1 tsp ground allspice
5ml/1 tsp ground coriander
15ml/1 tbsp paprika
sea salt and ground black pepper

For the chilli sauce
15ml/1 tbsp olive oil
1 small onion, finely chopped
1 garlic clove, crushed
200g/7oz can chopped tomatoes
1 fresh red chilli, seeded and finely chopped
15ml/1 tbsp balsamic vinegar
15ml/1 tbsp chopped fresh coriander, plus extra to garnish

1 Preheat the oven to 200°C/400°F/Gas 6. Cut the potatoes in half, then into eight wedges.

2 Place the wedges in a saucepan of cold water. Bring to the boil, then lower the heat and simmer gently for 10 minutes or until the potatoes have softened slightly. Drain well and pat dry on kitchen paper.

3 Mix the oil, garlic, allspice, coriander and paprika in a roasting tin. Add salt and pepper to taste. Add the potatoes to the pans and shake to coat them thoroughly. Roast for 20 minutes, turning the potato wedges occasionally, or until they are browned, crisp and fully cooked.

4 Meanwhile, make the chilli sauce. Heat the oil in a saucepan, add the onion and garlic and cook for 5–10 minutes, or until soft. Add the chopped tomatoes, with their juice. Stir in the chilli and vinegar.

5 Cook gently for 10 minutes, or until the mixture has reduced and thickened, then check the seasoning. Stir in the fresh coriander and serve hot, with the potato wedges. Garnish with salt and fresh coriander.

COOK'S TIPS

- *To save time, the potatoes can be par-boiled and tossed with the spices in advance.*
- *Make sure that the potato wedges are perfectly dry and completely covered in the mixture before roasting.*

Peanut Sauce with Warm Vegetable Salad

THIS SPICY SAUCE IS based on the classic Indonesian sauce served with satay, but is equally delicious served with this main-course salad which mixes steamed and raw vegetables. It would also partner barbecued vegetable kebabs.

Serves 2–4

INGREDIENTS

8 new potatoes
225g/8oz broccoli, cut into small florets
200g/7oz/1⅓ cups fine green beans
2 carrots, cut into thin ribbons with a vegetable peeler
1 red pepper, seeded and cut into strips
50g/2oz sprouted beans
sprigs of watercress, to garnish

For the peanut sauce
15ml/1 tbsp sunflower oil
1 birdseye chilli, seeded and sliced
1 garlic clove, crushed
5ml/1 tsp ground coriander
5ml/1 tsp ground cumin
60ml/4 tbsp crunchy peanut butter
75ml/5 tbsp water
15ml/1 tbsp dark soy sauce
1cm/½in piece fresh root ginger, finely grated
5ml/1 tsp soft dark brown sugar
15ml/1 tbsp lime juice
60ml/4 tbsp coconut milk

1 First make the peanut sauce. Heat the oil in a saucepan, add the chilli and garlic, and cook for 1 minute, or until softened. Add the spices and cook for 1 minute.

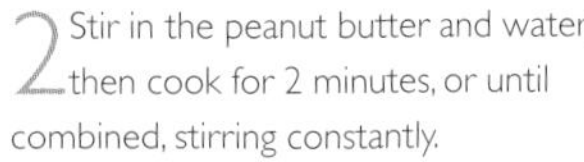

2 Stir in the peanut butter and water, then cook for 2 minutes, or until combined, stirring constantly.

3 Add the soy sauce, ginger, sugar, lime juice and coconut milk, then cook over a low heat until smooth and heated through, stirring frequently. Transfer to a bowl.

4 Bring a saucepan of lightly salted water to the boil, add the potatoes and cook for 10–15 minutes, or until tender. Drain, then halve or thickly slice the potatoes, depending on their size.

5 Meanwhile, steam the broccoli and green beans for 4–5 minutes, or until tender but still crisp. Add the carrots 2 minutes before the end of the cooking time.

6 Arrange the cooked vegetables on a serving platter with the red pepper and sprouted beans. Garnish with watercress and serve with the peanut sauce.

COOK'S TIP

Adjust the dipping consistency by adding slightly less water than recommended; you can always stir in a little more at the last minute. Serve the sauce either warm or cold.

Baked Marrow and Parsley Sauce

THIS IS A REALLY glorious way with a simple and modest vegetable. Try to find a small, firm and unblemished marrow for this recipe, as the flavour will be sweet, fresh and delicate. Young marrows do not need peeling; more mature ones do.

Serves 4

INGREDIENTS

1 small young marrow, about 900g/2lb
30ml/2 tbsp olive oil
15g/½oz/1 tbsp butter
1 onion, chopped
15ml/1 tbsp plain flour
300ml/½ pint/1¼ cups milk and single cream, mixed
30ml/2 tbsp chopped fresh parsley
salt and ground black pepper

1 Preheat the oven to 180°C/350°F/Gas 4 and cut the marrow into pieces measuring about 5 x 2.5cm/2 x 1in.

2 Heat the oil and butter in a flameproof casserole and fry the onion over a gentle heat until very soft.

3 Add the marrow and sauté for 1–2 minutes and then stir in the flour. Cook for a few minutes.

4 Stir the milk and cream into the vegetable mixture.

5 Add the parsley and seasoning, and stir well.

6 Cover and cook in the oven for 30–35 minutes. If liked, uncover for the final 5 minutes of cooking to brown the top. Alternatively, serve the marrow in its rich, pale sauce.

VARIATION

Chopped fresh basil or a mixture of basil and chervil also tastes good in this dish.

Roasted Pepper Sauce with Malfatti

A SMOKY PEPPER AND tomato sauce adds the finishing touch to spinach and ricotta dumplings. The Italians call these malfatti (badly made) because of their uneven shape.

Serves 4

INGREDIENTS

500g/1¼lb young leaf spinach
1 onion, finely chopped
1 garlic clove, crushed
15ml/1 tbsp extra virgin olive oil
350g/12oz/1½ cups ricotta cheese
3 eggs, beaten
50g/2oz/scant 1 cup undyed dried breadcrumbs
50g/2oz/½ cup plain flour
50g/2oz/⅔ cup freshly grated Parmesan cheese
freshly grated nutmeg
25g/1oz/2 tbsp butter, melted

For the roasted pepper sauce
2 red peppers, seeded and quartered
30ml/2 tbsp extra virgin olive oil
1 onion, chopped
400g/14oz can chopped tomatoes
150ml/¼ pint/⅔ cup water
salt and ground black pepper

1 Make the sauce. Preheat the grill and grill the pepper quarters skin-side up until they blister and blacken. Cool slightly, then peel off the skins and chop the flesh.

2 Heat the oil in a saucepan and lightly sauté the onion and peppers for 5 minutes.

3 Add the tomatoes and water, with salt and pepper to taste. Bring to the boil, lower the heat and simmer gently for 15 minutes.

4 Purée the mixture in a food processor or blender, in batches if necessary, then return to the clean pan and set aside.

5 Trim any thick stalks from the spinach, wash it well if necessary, then blanch in a pan of boiling water for about 1 minute. Drain, refresh under cold water and drain again. Squeeze dry, then chop finely.

6 Put the finely chopped onion, garlic, olive oil, ricotta, eggs and breadcrumbs in a bowl. Add the spinach and mix well. Stir in the flour and 5ml/1 tsp salt with half the Parmesan, then season to taste with pepper and nutmeg.

7 Roll the mixture into 16 small logs and chill lightly.

8 Bring a large saucepan of water to the boil. Carefully drop in the malfatti in batches and cook them for 5 minutes. Remove with a fish slice and toss with the melted butter.

9 To serve, reheat the sauce and divide it among four plates. Arrange four malfatti on each and sprinkle the remaining Parmesan over. Serve at once.

Quick Tomato Sauce with Baked Cheese Polenta

THIS QUICK TOMATO SAUCE can be prepared from store-cupboard ingredients. The rich flavour of the sauce enhances baked polenta.

Serves 4

INGREDIENTS

5ml/1 tsp salt
250g/9oz/2¼ cups quick-cook polenta
5ml/1 tsp paprika
2.5ml/½ tsp ground nutmeg
75g/3oz/¾ cup grated Gruyère cheese

For the quick tomato sauce

30ml/2 tbsp olive oil
1 large onion, finely chopped
2 garlic cloves, crushed
2 x 400g/14oz cans chopped tomatoes
15ml/1 tbsp tomato purée
5ml/1 tsp sugar
salt and ground black pepper

1 Preheat the oven to 200°C/400°F/Gas 6. Line a 28 x 18cm/11 x 7in baking tin with clear film. Bring 1 litre/1¾ pints/4 cups water to the boil with the measured salt.

2 Pour in the quick-cook polenta in a steady stream and cook, stirring continuously, for 5 minutes. Beat in the paprika and nutmeg, then pour into the prepared tin and smooth the surface. Leave to cool.

3 To make the quick tomato sauce, heat the oil in a pan and cook the onion and garlic until soft. Add the chopped tomatoes, tomato purée and sugar. Season, and simmer for 20 minutes.

4 Turn out the polenta on to a board, and cut into 5cm/2in squares. Place half the squares in a greased ovenproof dish. Spoon over half the tomato sauce, and sprinkle with half the cheese. Repeat the layers. Bake for 25 minutes.

Fresh Tomato and Ginger Sauce with Tofu and Potato Rösti

IN THIS RECIPE, the tofu is marinated in a mixture of tamari, honey and oil, flavoured with garlic and ginger. This marinade is then added to the fresh tomatoes to make a thick, creamy tomato sauce with a delicious tang, and the method ensures that the tofu is infused with the same flavours.

Serves 4

INGREDIENTS

425g/15oz tofu, cut into 1cm/½in cubes
4 large potatoes, about 900g/2lb total weight, peeled
sunflower oil, for frying
salt and ground black pepper
30ml/2 tsp sesame seeds, toasted

For the fresh tomato and ginger sauce
30ml/2 tbsp tamari or dark soy sauce
15ml/1 tbsp clear honey
2 garlic cloves, crushed
4cm/1½in piece fresh root ginger, grated
5ml/1 tsp toasted sesame oil
15ml/1 tbsp olive oil
8 tomatoes, halved, seeded and chopped

1 For the sauce, mix together the tamari or dark soy sauce, clear honey, garlic, root ginger and toasted sesame oil in a shallow dish.

2 Add the tofu, then spoon the liquid over the tofu and leave to marinate in the fridge for at least 1 hour. Turn the tofu occasionally in the marinade to allow the flavours to infuse.

3 To make the rösti, par-boil the potatoes for 10–15 minutes until almost tender. Leave to cool, then grate coarsely. Season well with salt and fresly ground black pepper. Preheat the oven to 200°C/400°F/Gas 6.

4 Using a slotted spoon, remove the tofu from the marinade and reserve the marinade on one side. Spread out the tofu on a baking tray and bake for 20 minutes, turning occasionally, until golden and crisp on all sides.

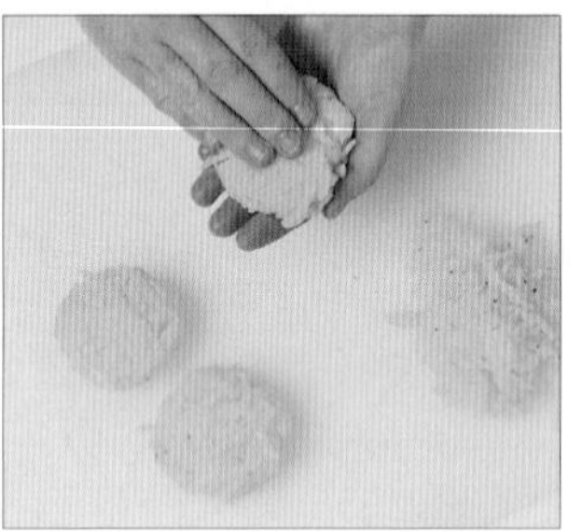

5 Take a quarter of the potato mixture in your hands at a time and form into rough cakes.

6 Heat a frying pan with just enough oil to cover the base. Place the cakes in the frying pan and flatten the mixture, using your hands or a spatula to form rounds about 1cm/½in thick.

7 Cook for about 6 minutes, or until golden and crisp underneath. Carefully turn the rösti over and cook for a further 6 minutes, or until golden brown in colour.

8 Meanwhile, complete the sauce. Heat the oil in a saucepan, add the reserved marinade and then the tomatoes and cook for 2 minutes, stirring continuously.

9 Reduce the heat and simmer, covered, for 10 minutes, stirring occasionally, until the tomatoes break down. Press the mixture through a sieve to make a thick, smooth sauce.

10 To serve, place a rösti on each of four warm serving plates. Scatter the tofu on top, spoon over the tomato sauce and sprinkle with sesame seeds.

COOK'S TIPS

- *Tamari is a thick, mellow-flavoured Japanese soy sauce, which is sold in Japanese food shops and some larger health-food stores.*
- *Tofu can be rather bland so allow it to marinate for 2–3 hours if possible, to ensure that it is full of flavour.*

Cheddar Cheese Sauce with Cauliflower

SELECT A MATURE FARMHOUSE Cheddar to give this popular dish a full flavour, and season with plenty of ground black pepper.

Serves 4

INGREDIENTS

1.2kg/2½lb cauliflower florets (about 1 large head)
3 bay leaves

For the Cheddar cheese sauce
45ml/3 tbsp butter
45ml/3 tbsp flour
450ml/¾ pint/scant 2 cups milk
50g/2oz/3 cups grated mature Cheddar cheese
salt and ground black pepper

1 Preheat the oven to 180°C/350°F/Gas 4. Grease a 30cm/12in round ovenproof dish.

2 Bring a large pan of lightly salted water to a boil. Add the cauliflower florets and cook for 7–8 minutes, or until just tender but still firm. Drain well.

3 To make the sauce, melt the butter in a heavy saucepan. Whisk in the flour until blended with the butter. Cook until smooth and bubbling, stirring continuously.

4 Gradually add the milk. Bring to a boil and continue cooking, stirring constantly, until the sauce is thickened and smooth.

5 Remove from the heat and stir in the cheese. Season the sauce to taste with salt and pepper.

6 Place the bay leaves on the bottom of the prepared dish. Arrange the cauliflower florets on top in an even layer. Pour the cheese sauce evenly over the cauliflower.

7 Bake for 20–25 minutes, or until golden brown and bubbling. Serve immediately.

VARIATION

You might like to try this with broccoli in place of cauliflower, or with a mixture of the two for a colourful change.

Wild Mushroom Sauce with Polenta and Gorgonzola

THE FLAVOUR OF WILD mushrooms combines well with mascarpone in this sauce to heighten the taste of the polenta. It also makes a delicious topping for baked potatoes.

Serves 4–6

INGREDIENTS

900ml/1½ pints/3¾ cups milk
900ml/1½ pints/3¾ cups water
5ml/1 tsp salt
300g/11oz/2¾ cups polenta
50g/2oz/¼ cup butter
115g/4oz Gorgonzola cheese
fresh thyme sprigs, to garnish

For the wild mushroom sauce
40g/1½oz/scant 1 cup dried porcini mushrooms
150ml/¼ pint/⅔ cup hot water
25g/1oz/2 tbsp butter
115g/4oz/1½ cups button mushrooms, chopped
60ml/4 tbsp dry white wine
generous pinch of dried thyme
60ml/4 tbsp mascarpone cheese
salt and ground black pepper

1 Pour the milk and water into a large, heavy-based saucepan. Add the salt and bring to the boil. Using a long-handled spoon, stir the liquid briskly with one hand while drizzling in the polenta with the other. When the mixture is thick and smooth, lower the heat to a gentle simmer and cook for about 20 minutes, stirring occasionally.

2 Remove from the heat and stir in the butter and Gorgonzola. Spoon the polenta mixture into a shallow dish and level the surface.

3 Let the polenta set until solid, then cut into wedges.

4 Meanwhile, make the sauce. Soak the porcini in the hot water for 15 minutes. Drain, reserving the liquid. Finely chop the porcini and strain the soaking liquid through a sieve lined with kitchen paper. Discard the kitchen paper.

5 Melt half the butter in a small saucepan. Sauté the chopped fresh mushrooms for about 5 minutes.

6 Add the wine, porcini and strained soaking liquid, with the dried thyme. Season to taste. Cook for 2 minutes more. Stir in the mascarpone and simmer for a few minutes, until reduced by a third. Set aside to cool.

7 Heat a ridged grill pan or grill, and grill the polenta until crisp. Brush with melted butter and serve hot with the sauce. Garnish with thyme.

COOK'S TIP

If fresh porcini mushrooms are available, use instead of dried and do not soak. You would need about 175g/6oz fresh porcini for this recipe. They are also sold under the name cèpes.

Salsas

"Salsa" is simply translated as "sauce", but since the sauces we refer to as salsas originated in the rich, colourful tradition of Mexican cooking, they have a very different style to the familiar types of classic sauces we've covered in other chapters. They're perfect for summer eating, and an ideal choice to accompany barbecued or grilled foods.

Fresh, colourful chillies are finely chopped and tossed imaginatively with fruits, vegetables or herbs to create highly individual combinations which enliven any dish or simple meal, from fish to meat, and from vegetables to eggs. Salsas may be fiery-hot, or delicately spiced hot, sweet and sour, or just hot and sweet – depending on your taste and the food it will accompany.

The most basic salsas are "crudo" which simply means raw, so the ingredients take no more preparation than fine chopping or whizzing in a blender to combine. The most typical Mexican salsa crudo would have chillies, onions, tomatoes or peppers with fresh coriander, for a simple, vibrant, zesty mix. Others can be more elaborate, sometimes simmered to soften ingredients and mingle flavours, or with the addition of exotic fruits or spices. Above all, salsas are an opportunity to show your creative flair – try some of our varied recipes, then start experimenting with your own.

Salsa Verde

THERE ARE MANY VERSIONS of this classic green salsa. Try this one drizzled over chargrilled squid, or with jacket potatoes served with a green salad.

Serves 4

INGREDIENTS

2–4 green chillies, halved
8 spring onions
2 garlic cloves
50g/2oz salted capers
sprig of fresh tarragon
bunch of fresh parsley
grated rind and juice of 1 lime
juice of 1 lemon
90ml/6 tbsp olive oil
about 15ml/1 tbsp green Tabasco sauce
ground black pepper

1 Halve and seed the chillies and trim the spring onions. Halve the garlic cloves. Place in a food processor and pulse briefly.

COOK'S TIP

Some salted capers are quite strong and may need rinsing before use. If you prefer, you may use pickled capers instead.

2 Use your fingers to rub the excess salt off the capers. Add them, with the tarragon and parsley, to the food processor and pulse again until the ingredients are quite finely chopped.

3 Transfer the mixture to a bowl. Mix in the lime rind and juice, lemon juice and olive oil, stirring lightly so the citrus juice and oil do not emulsify.

4 Add green Tabasco sauce, a little at a time, and black pepper to taste.

5 Chill the salsa in the fridge until ready to serve, but do not prepare it more than 8 hours in advance.

Coriander Pesto Salsa

THIS AROMATIC SALSA IS delicious drizzled over fish and chicken, tossed with pasta ribbons or used to dress a fresh avocado and tomato salad. To transform it into a dip, simply mix with a little mayonnaise or soured cream.

Serves 4

INGREDIENTS

50g/2oz fresh coriander leaves
15g/½ oz fresh parsley
2 red chillies
1 garlic clove
50g/2oz/⅓ cup shelled pistachio nuts
25g/1oz/⅓ cup finely grated Parmesan cheese, plus extra to garnish
90ml/6 tbsp olive oil
juice of 2 limes
salt and ground black pepper

1 Process the fresh coriander and parsley in a food processor or blender until finely chopped.

2 Halve the chillies lengthways and remove their seeds. Add to the herbs together with the garlic, and process until finely chopped.

3 Add the pistachio nuts to the herb mixture and pulse the power until they are roughly chopped. Stir in the Parmesan cheese, olive oil and lime juice.

4 Add salt and pepper to taste. Spoon the mixture into a serving bowl and cover and chill until ready to serve, garnished with Parmesan.

VARIATION

Any number of different herbs or nuts may be used to make a similar salsa to this one – try a mixture of rosemary and parsley, or add a handful of black olives.

Double Chilli Salsa

THIS IS A SCORCHINGLY hot salsa for only the very brave! Spread it sparingly on to cooked meats and burgers for a real kick.

Serves 4–6

INGREDIENTS

6 habanero chillies or Scotch bonnets
2 ripe tomatoes
4 standard green jalapeño chillies
30ml/2 tbsp chopped fresh parsley
30ml/2 tbsp olive oil
15ml/1 tbsp balsamic or sherry vinegar
salt

1 Skewer a habanero or Scotch bonnet chilli on to a metal fork and hold it in a gas flame for 2–3 minutes, turning the chilli until the skin blackens and blisters. Repeat with all the habaneros or Scotch bonnets, then set aside until cool.

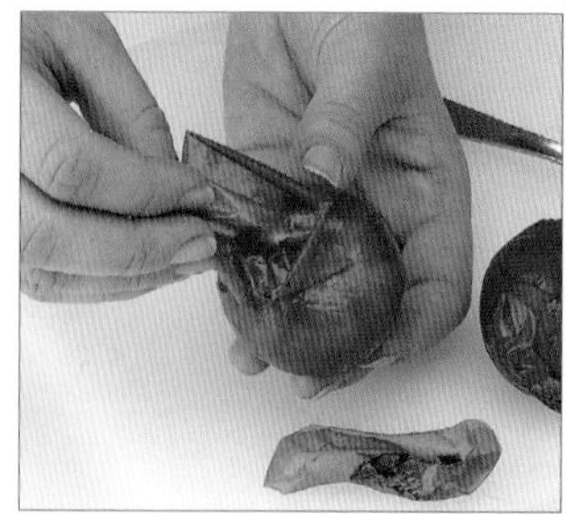

2 Skewer the tomatoes, one at a time, and hold them in the gas flame for 1–2 minutes, or until the skin wrinkles. Slip off the skins and halve. Use a teaspoon to scoop out and discard the seeds. Finely chop the flesh.

3 Rub the skins off the cooled chillies with a clean dish towel. Do not touch the chillies with your hands: use a fork to hold them and slice them open with a sharp knife. Scrape out and discard the seeds, then finely chop the flesh.

4 Halve the jalapeño chillies, remove their seeds and finely slice them widthways into tiny strips.

5 Mix together both types of chilli, the tomatoes and chopped parsley.

6 Mix the olive oil, vinegar and a little salt, pour this over the salsa and cover the dish. Chill for up to 3 days.

VARIATION

Habanero chillies and Scotch bonnets are among the hottest fresh chillies available. You may prefer to tone down the heat of this salsa by using a milder variety.

Tomato Salsa

THIS SIMPLE SIDE DISH is very versatile and really enhances a wide range of hot and cold dishes.

Serves 6

INGREDIENTS

6 medium tomatoes
1 green Kenyan chilli
2 spring onions, chopped
10cm/4in length cucumber, diced
30ml/2 tbsp lemon juice
30ml/2 tbsp fresh coriander, chopped
15ml/1 tbsp fresh parsley, chopped
salt and ground black pepper

1 Cut a small cross in the stalk end of each tomato. Place in a bowl and cover with boiling water.

2 After 30 seconds or as soon as the skins split, drain and plunge into cold water. Gently slide off the skins. Quarter the tomatoes, remove the seeds and dice the flesh.

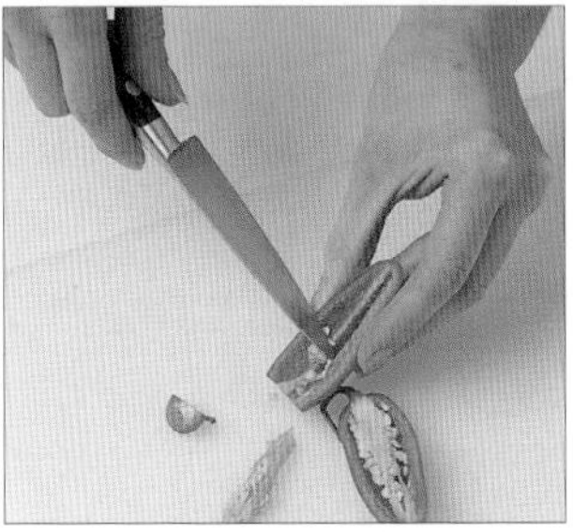

3 Halve the chilli, remove the stalk, seeds and the membrane, and chop finely.

4 Mix together all the ingredients and transfer to a serving bowl. Chill for 1–2 hours before serving.

VARIATIONS

To make Tomato and Caper Salsa

Prepare the tomatoes and stir in the onion and lemon juice. Add six torn sprigs of basil and 15ml/1 tbsp roughly chopped capers. Season to taste.

To make Tomato and Pepper Salsa

Prepare 4 tomatoes and stir in the chilli, onion and herbs. Add a roasted, peeled and diced orange pepper and a crushed garlic clove. Season to taste.

Chilli and Coconut Salsa

A SWEET-AND-SOUR SALSA, spiked with chillies, that goes well with grilled or barbecued fish.

Serves 6–8

INGREDIENTS

1 small coconut
1 small pineapple
2 green Kenyan chillies
5cm/2in piece lemon grass
60ml/4 tbsp natural yogurt
2.5ml/½ tsp salt
30ml/2 tbsp chopped fresh coriander
fresh coriander sprigs, to garnish

1 Puncture two of the coconut eyes with a screwdriver and drain the milk out from the shell.

2 Crack the coconut shell, prise away the flesh, and then coarsely grate the coconut into a medium-size bowl.

COOK'S TIP

When buying a fresh coconut, check its freshness by shaking gently – you should hear the liquid swishing about inside. If not, it's dried out and stale.

3 Cut the rind from the pineapple with a sharp knife and remove the eyes with a potato peeler. Finely chop the flesh and add to the coconut together with any juice.

4 Halve the chillies lengthways and remove the stalks, seeds and membrane. Chop very finely and stir into the coconut mixture.

5 Finely chop the lemon grass with a very sharp knife. Add to the coconut mixture and stir in.

6 Add the remaining ingredients and stir well. Spoon into a serving dish and garnish with coriander sprigs.

Fiery Citrus Salsa

THIS VERY UNUSUAL SALSA makes a fantastic marinade for shellfish, and it is also delicious drizzled over barbecued meat.

Serves 4

INGREDIENTS

1 orange
1 green apple
2 fresh red chillies, halved and seeded
1 garlic clove
8 fresh mint leaves
juice of 1 lemon
salt and ground black pepper

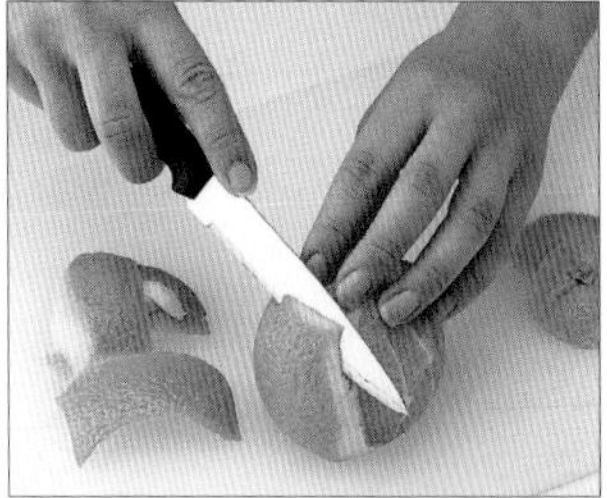

1 Slice the bottom off the orange so that it will stand firmly on a chopping board. Using a sharp knife, remove the peel by slicing from the top to the bottom of the orange.

2 Hold the orange in one hand over a bowl. Slice towards the middle of the fruit, to one side of a segment, and then gently twist the knife to ease the segment away from the membrane and out of the orange. Remove all the segments. Squeeze any juice from the remaining membrane into the bowl.

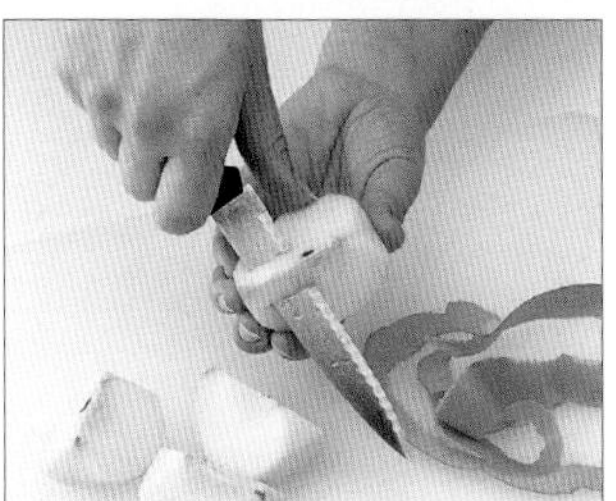

3 Peel the apple, slice it into wedges and remove the core.

4 Place the chillies in a blender or food processor with the orange segments and juice, apple wedges, garlic and fresh mint. Process for a few seconds until smooth. Then, with the motor running, slowly pour the lemon juice into the mixture.

5 Season to taste with a little salt and ground black pepper. Pour the salsa mixture into a bowl or small jug and serve immediately.

VARIATION

If you're feeling really fiery, don't seed the chillies! The seeds will make the salsa particularly hot and fierce.

Sweet Pepper Salsa

ROASTING PEPPERS ENHANCES THEIR sweet flavour, making them perfect for salsas. This is delicious served with poached salmon.

Serves 4

INGREDIENTS

1 red pepper
1 yellow pepper
5ml/1 tsp cumin seeds
1 red chilli, seeded
30ml/2 tbsp chopped fresh coriander leaves, plus extra to garnish
30ml/2 tbsp olive oil
15ml/1 tbsp red wine vinegar
salt and ground black pepper

1 Preheat the grill to medium. Place the peppers on a baking sheet and grill them for 8–10 minutes, turning regularly, until their skins have blackened and are blistered.

2 Place the peppers in a bowl and cover with a clean dish towel. Leave for 5 minutes so the steam helps to lift the skin away from the flesh. Remove the dish towel.

3 Meanwhile, place the cumin seeds in a small frying pan. Heat gently, stirring, until the seeds start to splutter and release their aroma. Remove the pan from the heat, then tip out the seeds into a mortar and crush them lightly with a pestle.

4 When the peppers are cool enough to handle, pierce a hole in the bottom of each and squeeze out all of the juices into a bowl. Peel, core and seed the peppers, then process the flesh and juices in a blender or food processor with the chilli and coriander until finely chopped.

5 Stir in the oil, vinegar and cumin with salt and pepper to taste. Serve the salsa at room temperature, garnished with coriander.

COOK'S TIP

Choose red, yellow or orange peppers for this salsa as the green variety is less ripe and therefore not so sweet.

Pineapple and Passion Fruit Salsa

PILE THIS SWEET, FRUITY salsa into brandy snap baskets or meringue nests for a luxurious dessert.

Serves 6

INGREDIENTS

1 small fresh pineapple
2 passion fruit
150ml/¼ pint/⅔ cup Greek-style yogurt
30ml/2 tbsp light muscovado sugar

1 Cut off the top and bottom of the pineapple so that it will stand firmly on a chopping board. Using a large, sharp knife, slice off the peel.

2 Use a small, sharp knife to carefully cut out the eyes. Slice the peeled pineapple and use a small pastry cutter to cut out the tough core. Finely chop the flesh.

3 Halve the passion fruit and use a spoon to scoop out the seeds and pulp into a bowl.

4 Stir in the chopped pineapple and the Greek-style yogurt. Cover and chill until required.

5 Stir in the muscovado sugar just before serving the salsa.

VARIATION

Lightly whipped double cream can be used instead of Greek-style yogurt.

Plantain Salsa

HERE IS A SUMMERY SALSA which is perfect for lazy outdoor eating. Serve with barbecued meat or fish or with potato or vegetable crisps or taco chips for dipping.

Serves 4

INGREDIENTS

knob of butter
4 ripe plantains
handful of fresh coriander, plus extra to garnish
30ml/2 tbsp olive oil
5ml/1 tsp cayenne pepper
salt and ground black pepper

COOK'S TIP

Be sure to choose ripe plantains with blackened skins for this recipe as they will be at their sweetest and most tender.

1 Preheat the oven to 200°C/400°F/ Gas 6.

2 Grease four pieces of foil, each measuring roughly 15 x 20cm/ 6 x 8in, with a knob of butter.

3 Peel the plantains and place one on each piece of buttered foil. Carefully fold the pieces of foil over the plantain sealing them tightly to form four parcels.

4 Bake the plantain for 25 minutes, or until tender. Alternatively, the plantain may be cooked in the embers of a charcoal barbecue.

5 Allow the parcels to cool slightly, then remove the plantains, discarding any liquid, and place in a food processor or blender.

6 Process the plantains with the coriander until fairly smooth. Stir in the olive oil, cayenne pepper, and salt and pepper to taste.

7 Serve immediately as the salsa will discolour and over-thicken if left to cool for too long. Garnish with torn coriander leaves.

Barbecued Sweetcorn Salsa

SERVE THIS SUCCULENT SALSA with smoked meats or a juicy grilled gammon steak.

Serves 4

INGREDIENTS

2 corn cobs
30ml/2 tbsp melted butter
4 tomatoes
6 spring onions, finely chopped
1 garlic clove, finely chopped
30ml/2 tbsp fresh lemon juice
30ml/2 tbsp olive oil
red Tabasco sauce, to taste
salt and ground black pepper
spring onion slices, to garnish

1 Remove the husks and silky threads covering the corn cobs. Brush the cobs with the melted butter and gently barbecue or grill for 20–30 minutes, turning occasionally, until tender and tinged brown.

2 To remove the kernels, stand the cob upright on a chopping board and use a large, heavy knife to slice down the length of the cob.

3 Skewer the tomatoes in turn on a metal fork and hold in a gas flame for 1–2 minutes, turning, until the skin splits and wrinkles. Slip off the skin and dice the tomato flesh.

4 Mix the spring onions and garlic with the corn and tomato in a small bowl.

5 Mix the lemon juice, olive oil and Tabasco together. Season to taste.

6 Pour this over the salsa and stir well. Cover the salsa and leave to infuse at room temperature for 1–2 hours before serving, garnished with slices of spring onion.

COOK'S TIP

Make this salsa in late summer when fresh cobs of corn are readily available and at the peak of their flavour.

Berry Salsa

THIS UNUSUAL, RICHLY COLOURED fruit salsa is the perfect choice for a summer *al fresco* meal, to serve with grilled or barbecued fish or poultry.

Serves 4

INGREDIENTS

1 fresh jalapeño pepper
½ red onion, minced
2 spring onions, chopped
1 tomato, finely diced
1 small yellow pepper, seeded and minced
45ml/3 tbsp chopped fresh coriander
1.5ml/¼ tsp salt
15ml/1 tbsp raspberry vinegar
15ml/1 tbsp fresh orange juice
5ml/1 tsp honey
15ml/1 tbsp olive oil
175g/6oz/1½ cups strawberries, hulled
175g/6oz/1½ cups blueberries or blackberries
200g/7oz/generous 1 cup raspberries

1 Wearing rubber gloves, finely chop the jalapeño pepper (discard the seeds and membrane if a less hot flavour is desired). Place the pepper in a medium-size bowl.

2 Add the red onion, spring onions, tomato, pepper and coriander, and stir to blend.

3 In a small bowl, whisk together the salt, vinegar, orange juice, honey and olive oil. Pour over the jalapeño mixture and stir well.

4 Coarsely chop the strawberries. Add to the jalapeño mixture with the other berries and stir to blend.

5 Allow to stand at room temperature for 3 hours, then serve.

COOK'S TIP

Defrosted frozen berries can be used in the salsa, but the texture will be softer.

Mixed Melon Salsa

A combination of two very different melons gives this salsa an exciting flavour and texture. Try it with thinly sliced Parma ham or smoked salmon.

Serves 10

INGREDIENTS

1 small orange-fleshed melon, such as Charentais
1 large wedge watermelon
2 oranges

Variation

Other melons can be used for this salsa. Try cantaloupe, Galia or Ogen.

1 Quarter the orange-fleshed melon and remove the seeds. Use a large, sharp knife to cut off the skin. Dice the melon flesh.

2 Pick out the seeds from the watermelon, then remove the skin. Dice the flesh into small chunks.

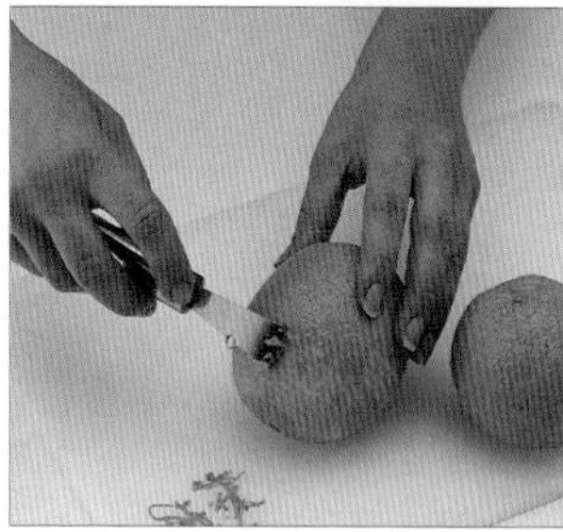

3 Use a zester to pare long strips of rind from both oranges. Halve the oranges and squeeze out all their juice.

4 Mix both types of the melon and the orange rind and juice together in a bowl. Chill for about 30 minutes and serve.

Roasted Pepper and Ginger Salsa

CHARGRILLING TO REMOVE the skins will take away any bitterness from the peppers and soften the flesh. Serve the salsa with grilled vegetable kebabs.

Serves 6

INGREDIENTS

1 large red pepper
1 large yellow pepper
1 large orange pepper
2.5ml/½ tsp coriander seeds
5ml/1 tsp cumin seeds
2.5cm/1in piece root ginger, chopped
1 small garlic clove, chopped
30ml/2 tbsp lime or lemon juice
1 small red onion, finely chopped
30ml/2 tbsp fresh coriander, chopped
5ml/1 tsp fresh thyme, chopped
salt and ground black pepper

1 Preheat the grill to hot. Quarter the peppers and remove the stalk, seeds and membranes. Grill the quarters, skin-side up, until charred and blistered. Rub away the skins and slice very finely.

COOK'S TIP

If you don't have a pestle and mortar, crush the garlic and grate the ginger. The spices can be ground in a pepper mill or crushed with a rolling pin.

2 Over a moderate heat, gently dry-fry the coriander and cumin for 30 seconds to 1 minute, shaking the pan to make sure they don't scorch.

3 Crush the spices in a pestle and mortar. Add the ginger and garlic and continue to work to a pulp. Work in the lime or lemon juice.

4 Mix together the peppers, spice mixture, onion and herbs. Season to taste with salt and ground black pepper and spoon into a serving bowl. Chill for 1–2 hours before serving as an accompaniment to barbecued meats or kebabs.

Orange and Chive Salsa

FRESH CHIVES AND SWEET oranges provide a refreshing combination of flavours. This salsa can be used to cool down spicy barbecued meat or poultry.

Serves 4

INGREDIENTS

2 large oranges
1 beefsteak tomato
bunch of chives
1 garlic clove, thinly sliced
30ml/2 tbsp olive oil
sea salt

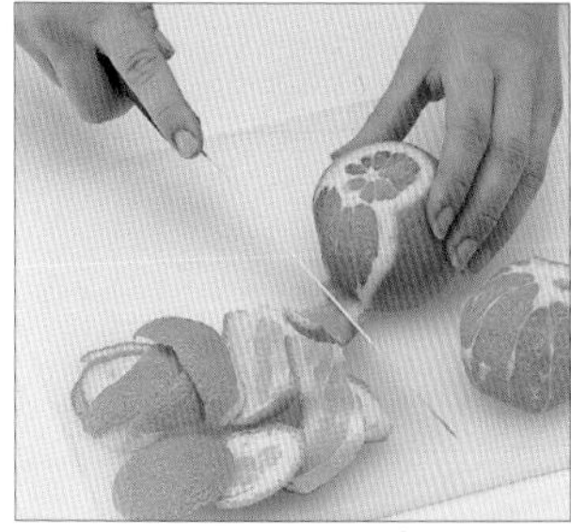

1 Slice the bottom off one orange so that it will stand firmly on a chopping board. Using a large, sharp knife, remove the peel by slicing from the top to the bottom of the orange.

2 Hold the orange over a bowl. Slice towards the middle of the fruit, to one side of a segment, and then twist the knife to ease the segment away from the membrane and out of the orange. Repeat to remove all segments. Squeeze any juice from the membrane.

3 Prepare the second orange in the same way. Roughly chop the orange segments and place them in the bowl with the collected juice.

4 Halve the tomato and use a teaspoon to scoop the seeds into the bowl. Finely dice the flesh and add it to the oranges, juice and seeds in the bowl.

5 Hold the bunch of chives together and use a pair of scissors to snip them into the bowl. Stir in the garlic.

6 Pour the olive oil over, season with sea salt to taste and stir well to mix. Serve within 2 hours.

Mango and Red Onion Salsa

A VERY SIMPLE TROPICAL salsa, which is livened up by the addition of passion fruit pulp. This salsa goes well with salmon and poultry.

Serves 4

INGREDIENTS

1 large ripe mango
1 red onion
2 passion fruit
6 large fresh basil leaves
juice of 1 lime, to taste
sea salt

1 Holding the mango upright on a chopping board, use a large knife to slice the flesh away from each side of the large flat stone in two portions.

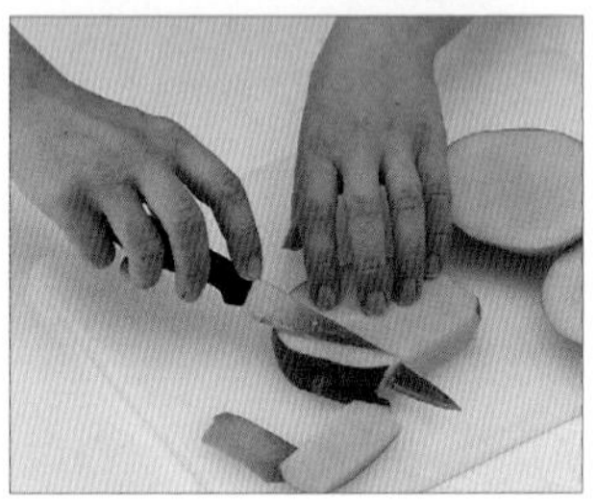

2 Using a smaller knife, trim away any flesh still clinging to the top and bottom of the stone.

3 Score the flesh of the mango halves deeply, taking care to avoid cutting through the skin: make parallel incisions about 1cm/½in apart; turn and cut lines in the opposite direction.

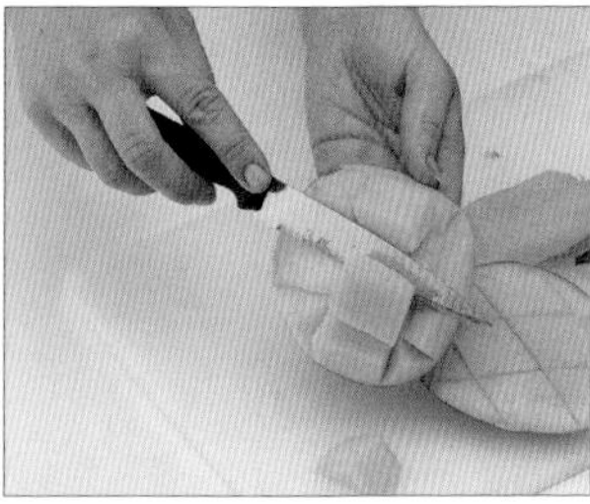

4 Carefully turn the skin inside out so the flesh stands out. Slice the dice away from the skin. Place in a bowl.

5 Finely chop the red onion and place it in the bowl with the mango. Halve the passion fruit, scoop out the seeds and pulp, and add to the mango mixture in the bowl.

6 Tear the basil leaves coarsely and stir them into the mixture with lime juice and a little sea salt to taste. Mix well and serve the salsa immediately.

VARIATION

Freshly cooked sweetcorn kernels are a delicious addition to this salsa.

Aromatic Peach and Cucumber Salsa

ANGOSTURA BITTERS ADD AN unusual and very pleasing flavour to this salsa. The distinctive, sweet taste of the mint complements chicken and other meat dishes.

Serves 4

INGREDIENTS

2 peaches
1 mini cucumber
2.5ml/½ tsp angostura bitters
15ml/1 tbsp olive oil
10ml/2 tsp fresh lemon juice
30ml/2 tbsp chopped fresh mint
salt and ground black pepper

1 Using a small, sharp knife, carefully score a line right around the centre of each peach, taking care to cut just through the skin.

2 Bring a large pan of water to the boil. Add the peaches and blanch them for 1 minute. Drain and briefly refresh in cold water. Peel off and discard the skin. Halve the peaches and remove their stones. Finely dice the flesh and place in a bowl.

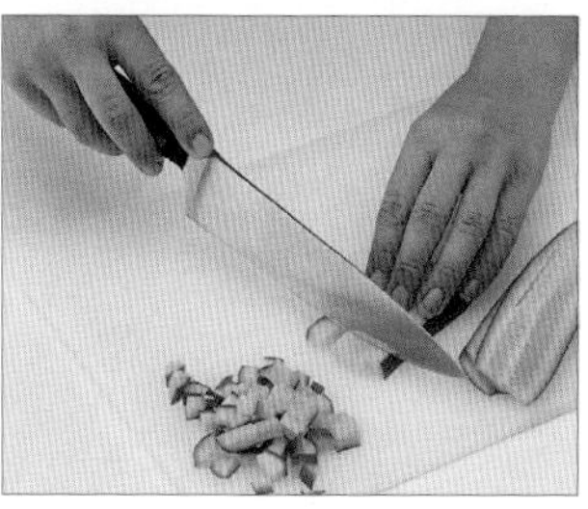

3 Trim the ends off the cucumber, then finely dice the flesh and stir it into the peaches. Stir the angostura bitters, olive oil and lemon juice together and then stir this dressing into the peach mixture.

4 Stir in the mint with salt and pepper to taste. Chill and serve within 1 hour.

VARIATION

Use diced mango in place of the peaches for an alternative.

COOK'S TIP

The texture of the peach and the crispness of the cucumber will fade fairly rapidly, so try to prepare this salsa as close to serving time as possible.

Dips

Far from being just for parties, dips are for any occasion, any time of day, and any season. They are an opportunity for informal eating, an appetite teaser, and a very healthy way to snack. They're also a good choice for packed lunches and picnics, as they travel well and can be served in so many ways.

Hot or cold, dips are a very versatile food; they are invariably quick to make and uncomplicated, so they're easily rustled up at a moment's notice. For a satisfying treat, try a warm, creamy cheese Fonduta with crusty bread for dipping, or Hot Chilli Bean Dip. Or, as a light, refreshing summer snack, Blue Cheese Dip or creamy Guacamole with fresh crudités will fit the bill. For parties, choose a selection of different dips for variety, so there's something for everyone's taste.

Serve your favourite dips with raw vegetable crudités such as carrot, cucumber or celery sticks, raw mushrooms or cauliflower florets. Cooked vegetables such as asparagus or artichokes or deep-fried mushrooms are just incomplete without a creamy or tangy savoury dip. Or, try dipping fingers of pitta breads, breadsticks and taco chips, perfect for easy snacking.

Saffron Dip

SERVE THIS MILD DIP with fresh vegetable crudités – it is particularly good with florets of cauliflower.

Serves 4

INGREDIENTS

15ml/1 tbsp boiling water
small pinch of saffron threads
200g/7oz/scant 1 cup fromage frais
10 fresh chives
10 fresh basil leaves
salt and ground black pepper

VARIATION

Leave out the saffron and add a squeeze of lemon or lime juice instead. A pinch of turmeric gives a good colour.

1 Pour the boiling water into a small container and add the saffron strands. Leave to infuse for 3 minutes.

2 Beat the fromage frais until smooth, then stir in the infused saffron liquid.

3 Use a pair of scissors to snip the chives into the dip. Tear the basil leaves into small pieces and stir them in.

4 Add salt and pepper to taste. Serve the dip immediately.

Basil and Lemon Mayonnaise

THIS FRESH MAYONNAISE is flavoured with lemon and two types of basil. Serve as a dip with potato wedges or crudités, or as an accompaniment to salads and jacket potatoes.

Serves 4

INGREDIENTS

2 large egg yolks
15ml/1 tbsp lemon juice
150ml/¼ pint/⅔ cup olive oil
150ml/¼ pint/⅔ cup sunflower oil
handful of green basil leaves
handful of dark opal (purple) basil leaves
4 garlic cloves, crushed
salt and ground black pepper
green and dark opal basil leaves and sea salt, to garnish

COOK'S TIP

Dark opal basil has crinkled, deep-purple leaves and a richly scented flavour, with a hint of blackcurrants.

1 Place the egg yolks and lemon juice in a food processor or blender and process them briefly together.

2 In a jug, stir the two oils together. With the machine running, pour in the oil very slowly, a drop at a time.

3 Once half the oil has been added, the remainder can be incorporated more quickly. Continue processing the mixture to form a thick and creamy mayonnaise.

4 Tear both types of basil into small pieces and stir into the mayonnaise with the crushed garlic and seasoning. Transfer to a serving dish, cover and chill until ready to serve, garnished with basil leaves and sea salt.

Blue Cheese Dip

2 Add the soft cheese and beat well to blend the two cheeses together.

3 Gradually beat in the Greek-style yogurt, adding enough to give you the consistency you prefer.

4 Season with lots of black pepper and a little salt. Chill the dip until you are ready to serve it.

THIS DIP CAN BE mixed up in next to no time and is delicious served with pears, or with fresh vegetable crudités. Add more yogurt to make a great dressing. This is a very thick dip to which you can add a little more Greek-style yogurt, or stir in a little milk, for a softer consistency.

Serves 4

INGREDIENTS

150g/5oz blue cheese, such as Stilton or Danish blue
150g/5oz/⅔ cup soft cheese
75ml/5 tbsp Greek-style yogurt
salt and ground black pepper

1 Crumble the blue cheese into a bowl. Using a wooden spoon, beat the cheese to soften it.

Mellow Garlic Dip

TWO WHOLE HEADS OF garlic may seem like a lot, but roasting transforms the flesh to a tender, sweet and mellow pulp. Serve with crunchy breadsticks and crisps. For a low-fat version of this dip, use reduced-fat mayonnaise and low-fat natural yogurt.

Serves 4

INGREDIENTS

2 whole garlic heads
15ml/1 tbsp olive oil
60ml/4 tbsp mayonnaise
75ml/5 tbsp Greek-style yogurt
5ml/1 tsp wholegrain mustard
salt and ground black pepper

1 Preheat the oven to 200°C/400°F/Gas 6. Separate the garlic cloves and place them in a small roasting tin.

2 Pour the olive oil over the garlic cloves and turn them with a spoon to coat them evenly. Roast them for 20–30 minutes, or until tender and softened. Leave to cool for 5 minutes.

3 Trim off the root end of each roasted garlic clove. Peel the cloves and discard the skins. Place the roasted garlic on a chopping board and sprinkle with salt. Mash with a fork until puréed.

4 Place the garlic in a small bowl and stir in the mayonnaise, yogurt and wholegrain mustard.

5 Check and adjust the seasoning, then spoon the dip into a bowl. Cover and chill until ready to serve.

COOK'S TIP

If you are cooking on a barbecue, leave the garlic heads whole and cook until tender, turning occasionally. Peel and mash.

Butternut Squash and Parmesan Dip

THE RICH, NUTTY FLAVOUR of butternut squash is enhanced by roasting. Serve this dip with melba toast or cheese straws.

Serves 4

INGREDIENTS

1 butternut squash
15g/½oz/1 tbsp butter
4 garlic cloves, unpeeled
30ml/2 tbsp freshly grated Parmesan cheese
45–75ml/3–5 tbsp double cream
salt and ground black pepper

1 Preheat the oven to 200°C/400°F/Gas 6.

2 Halve the butternut squash, then scoop out and discard the seeds.

3 Use a small, sharp knife to deeply score the flesh in a criss-cross pattern: cut as close to the skin as possible, without cutting through it.

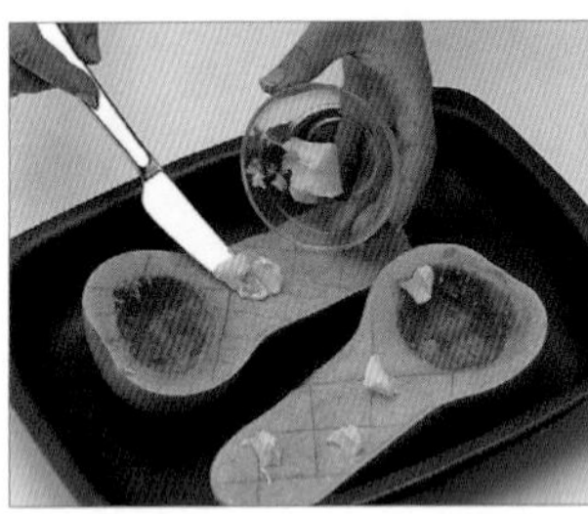

4 Arrange both halves in a small roasting tin and dot them with the butter. Sprinkle the butternut squash with salt and ground black pepper and roast on a high heat near the top of the oven for 20 minutes.

5 Tuck the unpeeled garlic cloves around the squash in the roasting tin and continue baking for 20 minutes, until the butternut squash is tender and softened.

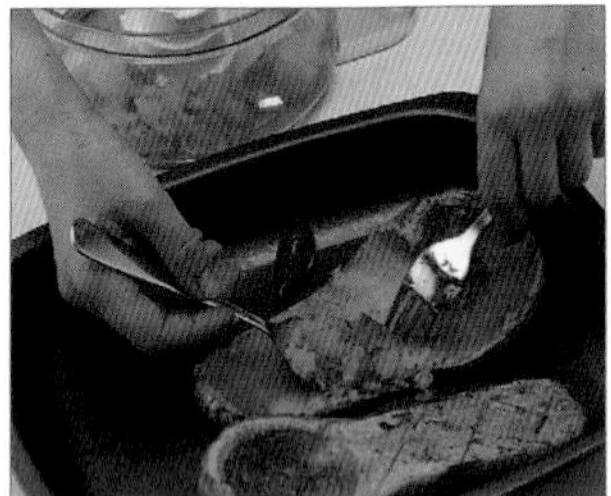

6 Scoop the flesh out of the squash shells and place it in a food processor or blender. Slip the garlic cloves out of their skins and add to the squash. Process until smooth.

7 With the motor running, add all but 15ml/1 tbsp of the Parmesan cheese and then the cream. Check the seasoning and spoon the dip into a serving bowl; it is at its best served warm. Scatter the reserved cheese over the top. If you don't have a food processor or blender, mash the squash in a bowl using a potato masher, then beat in the cheese and cream with a wooden spoon.

VARIATION

Try making this dip with pumpkin or other types of squash, such as acorn squash or New Zealand kabocha. Adjust the cooking time depending on size.

Thousand Island Dip

THIS VARIATION ON THE classic dressing is far removed from the original version, but can be served in the same way – with grilled king prawns laced on to bamboo skewers for dipping or with a simple mixed seafood salad.

Serves 4

INGREDIENTS

4 sun-dried tomatoes in oil
4 tomatoes
150g/5oz/⅔ cup soft cheese
60ml/4 tbsp mayonnaise
30ml/2 tbsp tomato purée
30ml/2 tbsp chopped fresh parsley
grated rind and juice of 1 lemon
red Tabasco sauce, to taste
5ml/1 tsp Worcestershire or soy sauce
salt and ground black pepper

1 Drain the sun-dried tomatoes on kitchen paper to remove excess oil, then finely chop them.

2 Skewer each tomato in turn on a metal fork and hold in a gas flame for 1–2 minutes, or until the skin wrinkles and splits. Allow to cool, then slip off and discard the skins. Halve the tomatoes and scoop out the seeds with a teaspoon. Finely chop the tomato flesh and set aside.

3 In a bowl, beat the soft cheese, then gradually beat in the mayonnaise and tomato purée to a smooth mixture.

4 Stir in the chopped parsley and sun-dried tomatoes, then add the chopped tomatoes and their seeds, and mix well.

5 Add the lemon rind and juice and Tabasco sauce to taste. Stir in the Worcestershire or soy sauce, and salt and pepper to taste.

6 Transfer the dip to a serving bowl, cover and chill until ready to serve.

VARIATION

Stir in cayenne pepper or a chopped fresh chilli for a more fiery dip. Garnish with a small piece of lemon, if liked.

Guacamole

THIS IS QUITE A fiery version of the popular Mexican dish, although probably nowhere near as hot as the dish you would be served in Mexico, where it often seems that heat knows no bounds! Serve it as a snack with tortilla chips or breadsticks.

Serves 4

INGREDIENTS

2 ripe avocados
2 tomatoes, peeled, seeded and finely chopped
6 spring onions, finely chopped
1–2 chillies, seeded and finely chopped
30ml/2 tbsp fresh lime or lemon juice
15ml/1 tbsp chopped fresh coriander
salt and ground black pepper
fresh coriander sprigs, to garnish

1 Cut the avocados in half and remove the stones and discard. Scoop the flesh into a large bowl and mash it roughly with a large fork.

COOK'S TIP

Unless you are going to serve the dip immediately, cover the surface closely with a piece of clear film to prevent browning. If the surface should still start to brown, stir lightly before serving.

2 Add the tomatoes, spring onions, chillies, lime or lemon juice and coriander. Mix well and season with salt and ground black pepper to taste.

3 Serve as soon as possible, garnished with fresh coriander.

VARIATION

For extra flavour, stir in a crushed garlic clove, or season with garlic salt.

Spiced Carrot Dip

THIS IS A DELICIOUS dip with a sweet and spicy flavour. Serve wheat crackers or fiery tortilla chips as accompaniments for dipping.

Serves 4

INGREDIENTS

1 onion
3 carrots, plus extra to garnish
grated rind and juice of 2 oranges
15ml/1 tbsp hot curry paste
150ml/¼ pint/⅔ cup natural yogurt
handful of fresh basil leaves
15–30ml/1–2 tbsp fresh lemon juice, to taste
red Tabasco sauce, to taste
salt and ground black pepper

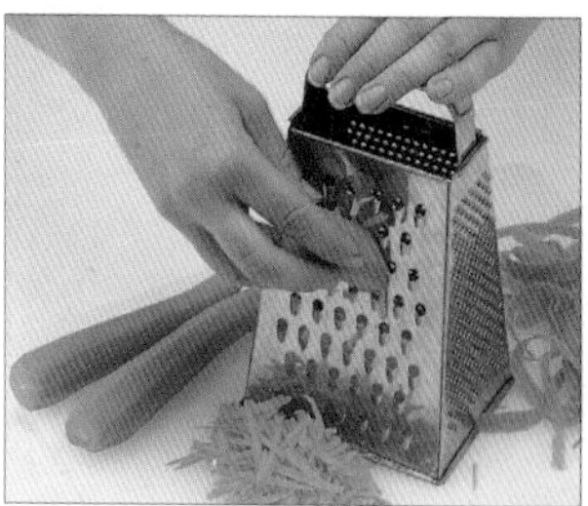

1 Finely chop the onion. Peel and grate the carrots. Place the onion, carrots, orange rind and juice, and curry paste in a small pan. Bring to the boil, cover and simmer for 10 minutes.

2 Process the mixture in a blender until smooth. Leave to cool.

3 Stir in the yogurt. Tear the basil leaves into small pieces and add most of them to the carrot mixture.

4 Add the lemon juice, Tabasco and seasoning. Serve within a few hours at room temperature, garnished with grated carrot and basil.

VARIATION

Greek-style yogurt or soured cream may be used in place of the natural yogurt to make a richer, creamier-textured dip.

Creamy Aubergine Dip

SPREAD THIS VELVET-TEXTURED DIP thickly on to toasted rounds of bread, then top them with slivers of sun-dried tomato to make wonderful, Italian-style crostini.

Serves 4

INGREDIENTS

1 large aubergine
30ml/2 tbsp olive oil
1 small onion, finely chopped
2 garlic cloves, finely chopped
60ml/4 tbsp chopped fresh parsley
75ml/5 tbsp crème fraîche
red Tabasco sauce, to taste
juice of 1 lemon, to taste
salt and ground black pepper

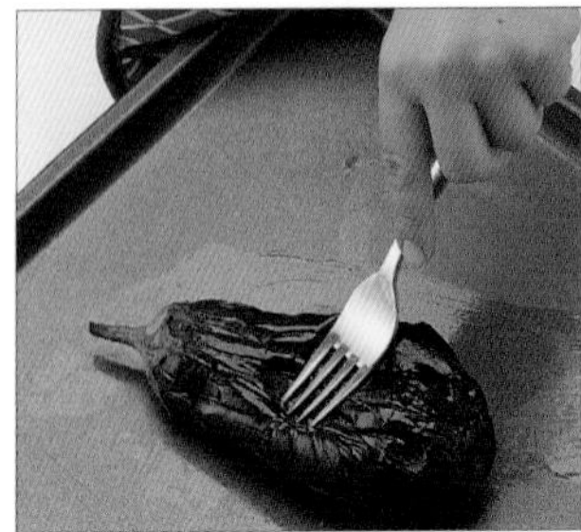

1 Preheat the grill to medium. Place the whole aubergine on a non-stick baking sheet and grill it for 20–30 minutes under a medium-high heat, turning occasionally, until the skin is blackened and wrinkled, and the aubergine feels soft when squeezed.

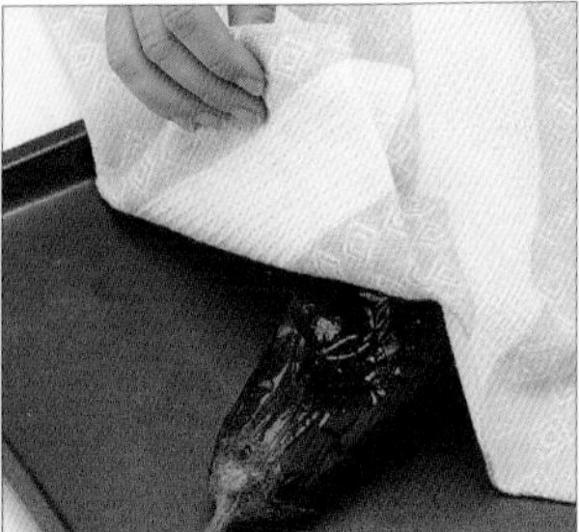

2 Cover the aubergine with a clean dish towel and leave it to cool for about 5 minutes.

3 Heat the oil in a frying pan and cook the onion and garlic for 5 minutes, until they are softened, but not browned.

4 Peel the skin from the aubergine. Mash the flesh with a large fork or potato masher to make a pulpy purée.

5 Stir in the onion and garlic, parsley and crème fraîche. Add Tabasco, lemon juice, and salt and pepper to taste.

6 Transfer the dip to a serving bowl and serve warm or leave to cool and serve at room temperature.

COOK'S TIP

The aubergine can be roasted in the oven at 200°C/400°F/Gas 6 for 20 minutes, or until tender, if preferred.

Hot Chilli Bean Dip

MAKE THIS ONE AS hot as you like – the soured cream helps to balance the heat of the chillies. Serve it with tortilla chips or vegetable crudités.

Serves 4

INGREDIENTS

275g/10oz/1½ cups dried pinto beans, soaked overnight and drained
1 bay leaf
45ml/3 tbsp sea salt
15ml/1 tbsp vegetable oil
1 small onion, sliced
1 garlic clove, minced
2–4 canned hot green chillies (optional)
75ml/5 tbsp soured cream, plus extra to garnish
2.5ml/½ tsp ground cumin
hot pepper sauce, to taste
15ml/1 tbsp chopped fresh coriander

1 Place the beans in a large pan. Add fresh cold water to cover and the bay leaf. Bring to a boil, then cover, and simmer for 30 minutes.

2 Add the sea salt and continue simmering for about 30 minutes, or until the beans are tender.

3 Drain the cooked beans, reserving 120ml/4fl oz/½ cup of the liquid. Let cool slightly. Discard the bay leaf.

4 Heat the oil in a non-stick frying pan. Add the onion and garlic and cook over low heat for 8–10 minutes, or until just softened, stirring occasionally.

5 In a food processor or blender, combine the beans, onion mixture, chillies, if using, and the reserved cooking liquid. Process until the mixture is a coarse purée.

6 Transfer to a bowl and stir in the soured cream, cumin, and hot pepper sauce to taste. Stir in the coriander, garnish with soured cream, and serve warm.

VARIATION

To save time, use 2½ x 400g/14oz cans beans instead of the dried beans.

Hummus

THIS NUTRITIOUS DIP CAN be served with vegetable crudités or packed into salad-filled pitta, but it is best spread thickly on hot buttered toast. Tahini is a thick, smooth and oily paste made from sesame seeds. It is a classic ingredient in hummus, this Middle-Eastern dip.

Serves 4

INGREDIENTS

400g/14oz can chick-peas, drained
2 garlic cloves
30ml/2 tbsp tahini or smooth peanut butter
60ml/4 tbsp olive oil
juice of 1 lemon
2.5ml/½ tsp cayenne pepper
15ml/1 tbsp sesame seeds
sea salt

1 Rinse the chick-peas well and place in a food processor or blender with the garlic and a good pinch of sea salt. Process until very finely chopped.

2 Add the tahini or peanut butter, and process until fairly smooth. With the motor still running, slowly pour in the oil and lemon juice.

3 Stir in the cayenne pepper and add more salt to taste. If the mixture is too thick, stir in a little cold water. Transfer the purée to a serving bowl.

4 Heat a small non-stick pan and add the sesame seeds. Cook them for 2–3 minutes, shaking the pan, until they are golden brown in colour. Allow them to cool, then sprinkle them over the purée.

Cannellini Bean Dip

THIS SOFT BEAN DIP or pâté is good spread on wheaten crackers or toasted muffins. Alternatively, it can be served with wedges of tomato and a crisp green salad.

Serves 4

INGREDIENTS

400g/14oz can cannellini beans
grated rind and juice of 1 lemon
30ml/2 tbsp olive oil
1 garlic clove, finely chopped
30ml/2 tbsp chopped fresh parsley
red Tabasco sauce, to taste
salt and ground black pepper
cayenne pepper, to garnish

1 Drain the beans in a sieve and rinse them well under cold water. Drain well and transfer to a bowl.

2 Use a potato masher to roughly purée the beans, then stir in the lemon rind, juice and olive oil.

3 Stir in the chopped garlic and parsley. Add Tabasco sauce, salt and pepper to taste.

4 Spoon the mixture into a small bowl and dust lightly with cayenne pepper. Chill until ready to serve.

VARIATION

Canned or cooked butter beans or kidney beans can also be used for this dip.

Soured Cream Cooler

THIS COOLING DIP MAKES the perfect accompaniment to hot and spicy Mexican dishes. Alternatively, serve it as a snack with the fieriest tortilla chips you can find.

Serves 2

INGREDIENTS

1 small yellow pepper
2 small tomatoes
30ml/2 tbsp chopped fresh parsley, plus extra to garnish
150ml/¼ pint/⅔ cup soured cream
grated lemon rind, to garnish

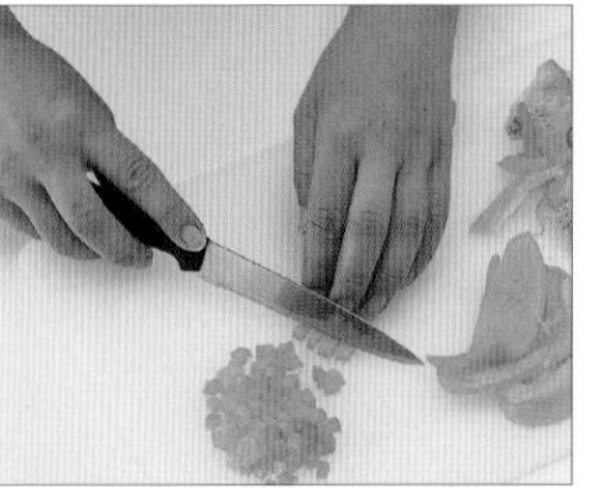

1 Halve the pepper lengthways. With a sharp knife, remove the core and scoop out the seeds, then cut the flesh into tiny dice.

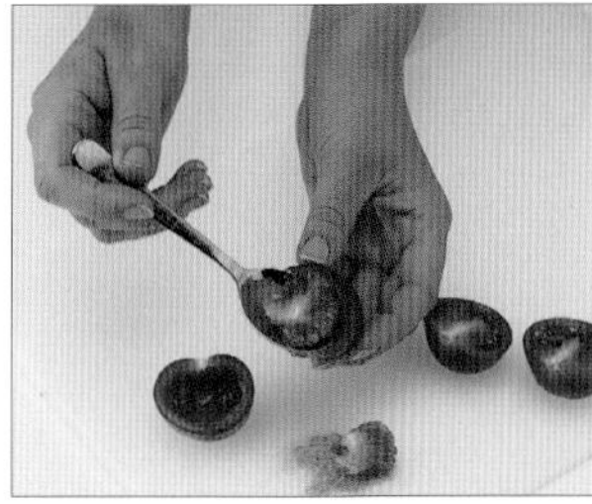

2 Cut the tomatoes in half, then use a teaspoon to scoop out and discard the seeds. Cut the tomato flesh into tiny dice.

3 Stir the pepper and tomato dice and the chopped parsley into the soured cream and mix well.

4 Spoon the dip into a small bowl and chill. Garnish with grated lemon rind and parsley before serving.

VARIATION

Use finely diced avocado or cucumber in place of the pepper or tomato.

Tzatziki

THIS CLASSIC GREEK DIP is a cooling mix of yogurt, cucumber and mint, perfect for a hot summer's day. Serve it with strips of lightly toasted pitta bread.

Serves 4

INGREDIENTS

1 mini cucumber
4 spring onions
1 garlic clove
200ml/7fl oz/scant 1 cup Greek-style yogurt
45ml/3 tbsp chopped fresh mint
salt and ground black pepper
fresh mint sprig, to garnish (optional)

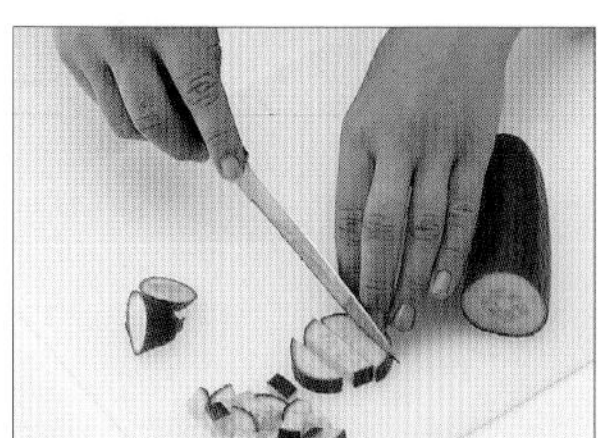

1 Trim the ends from the cucumber, then cut it into 5mm/¼in dice. Set aside.

2 Trim the spring onions and garlic, then chop both very finely.

COOK'S TIP

Choose Greek-style yogurt for this dip – it has a higher fat content than most yogurts, but this gives it a deliciously rich, creamy texture.

3 Beat the yogurt until smooth, if necessary, then gently stir in the cucumber, onions, garlic and mint.

4 Add salt and plenty of ground black pepper to taste, then transfer the mixture to a serving bowl. Chill until ready to serve and then garnish with a small mint sprig, if liked.

Red Onion Raita

RAITA IS A TRADITIONAL Indian side dish served as an accompaniment for hot curries. It is also delicious served with poppadums as a dip.

Serves 4

INGREDIENTS

5ml/1 tsp cumin seeds
1 small garlic clove
1 small green chilli
1 large red onion
150ml/¼ pint/⅔ cup natural yogurt
30ml/2 tbsp chopped fresh coriander, plus extra to garnish
2.5ml/½ tsp sugar
salt

1 Heat a small frying pan and dry-fry the cumin seeds for 1–2 minutes, until they release their aroma and begin to pop.

VARIATION

For an extra tangy raita stir in 15ml/1 tbsp lemon juice.

2 Lightly crush the seeds in a mortar and pestle or flatten them with the heel of a heavy-bladed knife.

3 Finely chop the garlic. Remove the fiery seeds from the chilli and chop the flesh finely, along with the red onion.

4 Place the natural yogurt in a bowl and add the garlic, chilli and red onion, along with the crushed cumin seeds and fresh coriander. Stir to combine.

5 Add sugar and salt to taste. Spoon the raita into a small bowl and chill until ready to serve. Garnish with extra coriander before serving.

Satay Dip

A DELICIOUSLY PUNGENT SAUCE which tastes great served with spicy chicken on skewers but is equally good as a dip for crisp vegetables.

Serves 6

INGREDIENTS

150g/5oz/scant 1 cup roasted, unsalted peanuts
45ml/3 tbsp vegetable oil
1 small onion, roughly chopped
2 garlic cloves, crushed
1 red chilli, seeded and chopped
2.5cm/1in piece root ginger, peeled and chopped
5cm/2in piece lemon grass, roughly chopped
2.5ml/½ tsp ground cumin
45ml/3 tbsp chopped fresh coriander stalks
15ml/1 tbsp sesame oil
175ml/6fl oz/¾ cup coconut milk
30ml/2 tbsp thick soy sauce (kecap manis)
10ml/2 tsp lime juice
salt and ground black pepper
lime wedges and chives, to garnish

1 Rub the husks from the peanuts in a clean dish towel.

2 Place the nuts in a food processor or blender with 30ml/2 tbsp vegetable oil, and process to a smooth paste. Transfer to a bowl.

3 Place the next seven ingredients in the food processor or blender and process to a fairly smooth paste.

4 Heat the remaining vegetable oil with the sesame oil in a frying pan and add the onion paste. Cook over a low heat for about 10–15 minutes, stirring occasionally.

5 Stir in the peanuts, coconut milk, soy sauce and lime juice, and keep stirring while it heats through.

6 Add salt and ground black pepper to taste, then spoon the mixture into small bowls or saucers. Serve warm, garnished with lime wedges and chives.

Spicy Tuna Dip

A PIQUANT DIP, DELICIOUS served with breadsticks – use more oil for a sauce, less for filling hard-boiled eggs, tomatoes or celery sticks.

Serves 6

INGREDIENTS

90g/3¼oz can tuna fish in oil
olive oil
3 hard-boiled eggs
75g/3oz/¾ cup pitted green olives
50g/2oz can anchovy fillets, drained
45ml/3 tbsp capers, drained
10ml/2 tsp Dijon mustard
ground black pepper
fresh parsley sprigs, to garnish

1 Drain the oil from the tuna into a small bowl and make up the quantity to 90ml/6 tbsp with olive oil.

2 Halve the hard-boiled eggs, remove the yolks and then place in a food processor or blender. Discard the whites or use in another dish.

3 Reserve a few olives for garnishing, then add the rest to the processor or blender together with the remaining ingredients. Process together until smooth. Season with pepper to taste.

4 Spoon into a bowl and garnish with the reserved olives and the parsley.

COOK'S TIP

Choose a good quality, light olive oil for this dip – richly flavoured extra virgin oils may dominate the flavour.

Lemon and Coconut Dahl

A WARM, SPICY DISH, this can be served either as a dip with poppadums or to accompany an Indian main dish.

Serves 8

INGREDIENTS

30ml/2 tbsp sunflower oil
5cm/2in piece fresh root ginger, finely chopped
1 onion, finely chopped
2 garlic cloves, finely chopped
2 small red chillies, seeded and finely chopped
5ml/1 tsp cumin seeds
150g/5oz/⅔ cup red lentils
250ml/8fl oz/1 cup water
15ml/1 tbsp hot curry paste
200ml/7fl oz/scant 1 cup coconut cream
juice of 1 lemon
handful of fresh coriander leaves
25g/1oz/¼ cup flaked almonds
salt and ground black pepper

1 Heat the oil in a large, shallow saucepan. Add the chopped ginger, onion, garlic, chillies and the cumin seeds. Cook for 5 minutes, until softened but not coloured.

2 Stir the lentils, water and curry paste into the pan. Bring to the boil, cover and cook gently over a low heat for 15–20 minutes, stirring the mixture occasionally, until the lentils are just tender and not yet broken.

3 Stir in all but 30ml/2 tbsp of the coconut cream. Bring to the boil and cook, uncovered, for a further 15–20 minutes, or until thick and pulpy. Remove from the heat, then stir in the lemon juice and the whole coriander leaves. Add salt and pepper to taste.

VARIATION

Try making this dhal with yellow split peas: they take longer to cook and a little extra water has to be added but the result is equally tasty.

4 Heat a large pan and cook the flaked almonds for one or two minutes on each side until golden brown. Stir about three-quarters of the toasted almonds into the dhal.

5 Transfer the dhal to a serving bowl and swirl in the remaining coconut cream. Scatter the reserved almonds on top and serve warm.

Fonduta

FONTINA IS AN ITALIAN medium-fat cheese with a mild nutty flavour, which melts easily and smoothly. It is a little like Gruyère, which makes a good substitute. This delicious cheese dip needs only some warm ciabatta bread or focaccia, a crisp salad and some robust red wine to complete the meal.

Serves 4

INGREDIENTS

225g/8oz/2 cups diced Fontina cheese
250ml/8fl oz/1 cup milk
15g/½ oz/1 tbsp butter
2 eggs, lightly beaten
ground black pepper

1 Put the cheese in a bowl with the milk and leave to soak for 2–3 hours. Transfer to a double boiler or a heatproof bowl set over a pan of simmering water.

2 Add the butter and eggs and cook gently, stirring until the cheese has melted to a smooth sauce with the consistency of custard.

3 Remove from the heat and season with pepper. Transfer to a serving dish and serve immediately.

COOK'S TIP

Don't overheat the sauce, or the eggs might curdle. A very gentle heat will produce a lovely smooth sauce.

VARIATION

Pour the Fonduta over hot pasta or polenta for a really satisfying main dish.

Tahini Yogurt Dip with Sesame seed-coated Falafel

SESAME SEEDS ARE USED to give a crunchy coating to these spicy bean patties. Serve with the tahini yogurt dip and warm pitta bread as a light lunch or supper dish.

Serves 4

INGREDIENTS

250g/9oz/1⅓ cups dried chick-peas
2 garlic cloves, crushed
1 red chilli, seeded and finely sliced
5ml/1 tsp ground coriander
5ml/1 tsp ground cumin
15ml/1 tbsp chopped fresh mint
15ml/1 tbsp chopped fresh parsley
2 spring onions, finely chopped
1 large egg, beaten
sesame seeds, for coating
sunflower oil, for frying
salt and ground black pepper

For the tahini yogurt dip
30ml/2 tbsp light tahini
200g/7oz/scant 1 cup natural live yogurt
5ml/1 tsp cayenne pepper, plus extra for sprinkling
15ml/1 tbsp chopped fresh mint
1 spring onion, finely sliced

1 Place the chick-peas in a bowl, cover with cold water and leave to soak overnight. Drain and rinse the chick-peas, then place in a saucepan and cover with cold water. Bring to the boil and boil rapidly for 10 minutes, then reduce the heat and simmer for 1½–2 hours, or until tender.

2 Meanwhile, make the tahini yogurt dip. Mix together the tahini, yogurt, cayenne pepper and mint in a small bowl. Sprinkle the spring onion and extra cayenne pepper on top and chill until required.

3 Combine the chick-peas with the garlic, chilli, ground spices, herbs, spring onions and seasoning, then mix in the egg. Place in a food processor and blend until the mixture forms a coarse paste. If the paste seems too soft, chill it for 30 minutes.

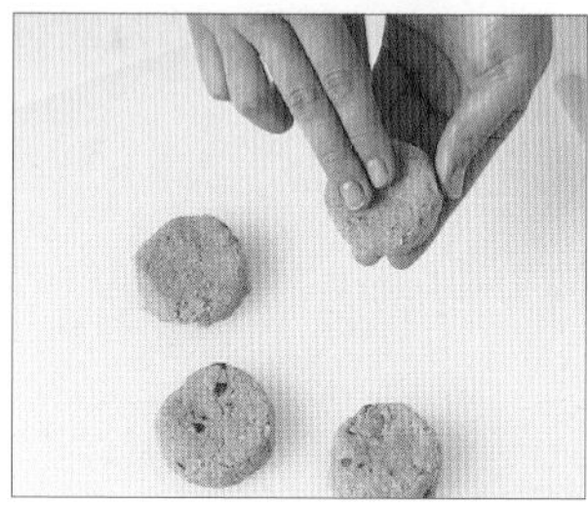

4 Form the chilled chick-pea paste into 12 patties with your hands, then roll each one in the sesame seeds to coat thoroughly.

5 Heat enough oil to cover the base of a large frying pan. Fry the falafel, in batches if necessary, for 6 minutes, turning once.

VARIATION

The dip is also marvellous served with vegetable crisps.

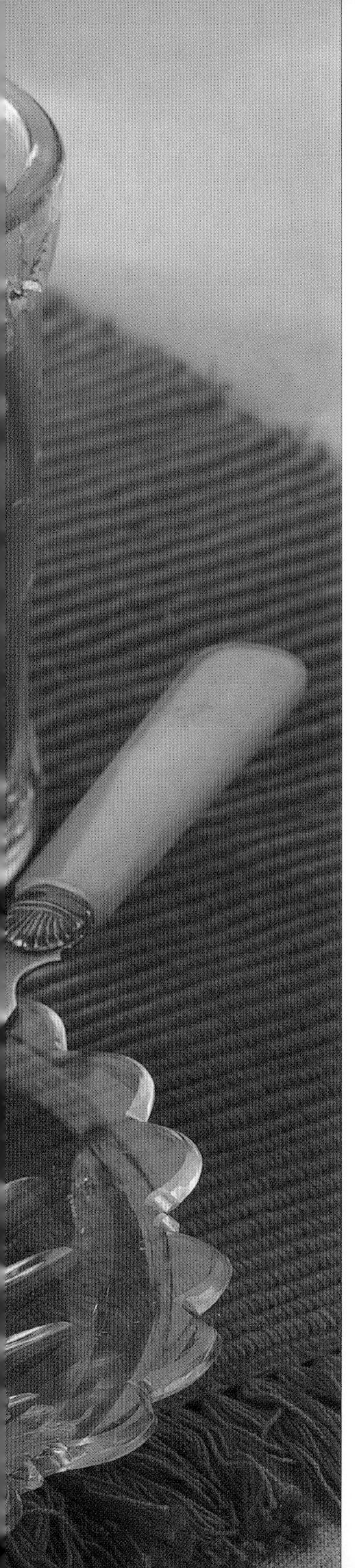

Relishes and Chutneys

It's a myth that preserving is an art – the preparation of a simple chutney or relish is within the reach of any cook, and it's such a worthwhile task. When you line up the jars on your kitchen shelf – and maybe even give a few jars as gifts, you'll feel a real glow of satisfaction.

Once you open the jar, the benefits are even more evident – a spoonful of fruity, spicy chutney or relish can lift the appetite and transform the flavour of the plainest hunk of bread and cheese or meat into a tasty lunch. If your taste is for the exotic, Indian curries are traditionally accompanied by a spoonful of fruity chutney, often made with mangoes, and spiced with chilli or ginger.

Almost any cooked meat will benefit from a spicy spoonful of rich chutney on the side – every burger needs it's relish, and even a plateful of fresh oysters can be lifted to another level by adding a spoonful of Bloody Mary Relish.

The flavour of most chutneys and relishes improves with keeping, so, however tempting it may be, store them carefully for 3–4 weeks before opening the jar to enjoy them at their best.

Classic Quick Recipes

Curried Fruit Chutney

A PIQUANT FRUIT CHUTNEY that is delicious with cold sliced turkey and ham over the Christmas season.

Makes about 1.2kg/2½lb

INGREDIENTS

225g/8oz/1 cup dried apricots
225g/8oz/1⅓ cups dried peaches
225g/8oz/1⅓ cups dates, stoned
225g/8oz/1⅓ cups raisins
1–2 garlic cloves, crushed
225g/8oz/1 cup light muscovado sugar
300ml/½ pint/1¼ cups white malt vinegar
300ml/½ pint/1¼ cups water
5ml/1 tsp salt
10ml/2 tsp mild curry powder

VARIATION

For a different flavour and colour, stoned prunes can be used instead of the raisins.

1 Put all the ingredients in a large pan, cover and simmer very gently for 10–15 minutes, or until tender.

2 Transfer the mixture to a food processor in batches and chop or mince coarsely.

3 Spoon into clean jam jars. Seal the jars and label them. Store in a cool place for 4 weeks before using.

Ginger, Date and Apple Chutney

SERVE THIS RICH, SPICY chutney with cold sliced meats or pies. Make it well ahead to allow time for the warming flavours to mature, and store in airtight jars.

Makes about 1.6kg/3–3½lb

INGREDIENTS

450g/1lb cooking apples
450g/1lb/3¼ cups dates, stoned
225g/8oz/1 cup dried apricots
115g/4oz glacé ginger, chopped
1–2 garlic cloves, crushed
225g/8oz/1⅓ cups sultanas
225g/8oz/1 cup light muscovado sugar
5ml/1 tsp salt
300ml/½ pint/1¼ cups white malt vinegar

VARIATION

If you prefer, drained pieces of preserved stem ginger in syrup can be used instead of the glacé ginger.

1 Peel, core and chop the apples into small chunks. Roughly chop the dates and apricots.

2 Put all the fruit together in a large, saucepan, with all the remaining ingredients. Cover and simmer gently for 10–15 minutes, or until the fruit is tender and the liquid is well reduced.

3 Spoon into clean jam jars. Seal the jars and label them. Store in a cool place for 4 weeks before using.

Anchovy and Parsley Relish

ANCHOVIES AND PARSLEY make a flavourful relish to serve as a topping for fresh vegetables. Serve these fresh-tasting nibbles as a starter to a rich meal, or with drinks.

Makes about 225g/8oz

INGREDIENTS

50g/2oz flat leaf parsley
50g/2oz/½ cup black olives, stoned
25g/1oz/½ cup sun-dried tomatoes
4 canned anchovy fillets, drained
50g/2oz red onion, finely chopped
25g/1oz small pickled capers, rinsed
1 garlic clove, finely chopped
15ml/1 tbsp olive oil
juice of ½ lime
1.5ml/¼ tsp ground black pepper
a selection of cherry tomatoes, radishes, celery and cucumber, to serve

1 Coarsely chop the parsley, black olives, sun-dried tomatoes and anchovy fillets and mix in a bowl with the onion, capers, garlic, olive oil, lime juice and black pepper.

2 Halve the cherry tomatoes and radishes, chop the celery into bite-size chunks and cut the cucumber into 1cm/½ in slices. Top each of the prepared vegetables with a generous amount of relish and serve immediately.

Spiced Cranberry and Orange Relish

THIS COLOURFUL, FESTIVE RELISH is excellent served with roast turkey, goose or duck.

Makes about 450g/1lb

INGREDIENTS

225g/8oz/2 cups fresh cranberries
1 onion, finely chopped
150ml/¼ pint/⅔ cup port
115g/4oz/generous ½ cup caster sugar
finely grated rind and juice of 1 orange
2.5ml/½ tsp English mustard powder
1.5ml/¼ tsp ground ginger
1.5ml/¼ tsp ground cinnamon
5ml/1 tsp cornflour
50g/2oz/scant ½ cup raisins

COOK'S TIP

Frozen cranberries can be used instead of fresh – simply add them straight from the freezer.

1 Put the cranberries, onion, port and sugar in a pan. Cook the mixture gently for 10 minutes, or until tender.

2 Mix the orange juice, mustard powder, ginger, cinnamon and cornflour together. Stir them into the cranberries.

3 Add the raisins and orange rind. Allow to thicken over the heat, stirring, and then simmer for 2 minutes. Cool, cover and chill ready for serving.

Pickled Peach and Chilli Chutney

This is a really spicy, rich chutney that is great served with cold roast meats such as ham, pork or turkey. It is also good with a strong farmhouse Cheddar cheese.

Makes about 450g/1lb

INGREDIENTS

475ml/16fl oz/2 cups cider vinegar
275g/10oz/1¼ cups light muscovado sugar
225g/8oz/1½ cups stoned and finely chopped dried dates
5ml/1 tsp ground allspice
5ml/1 tsp ground mace
450g/1lb ripe peaches, stoned
3 onions, thinly sliced
4 fresh red chillies, seeded and finely chopped
4 garlic cloves, crushed
5cm/2in piece of fresh root ginger, finely grated
5ml/1 tsp salt

1 Place the vinegar, sugar, chopped dates and spices in a large, heavy-based saucepan and bring to the boil, stirring occasionally.

2 Cut the peaches into small chunks. Add to the pan with all the remaining ingredients and return the mixture to the boil. Lower the heat and simmer for 40–50 minutes, or until thick. Stir frequently to prevent the mixture from burning on the base of the saucepan.

3 Spoon the chutney into clean, sterilized jars and seal. When cold, store the jars in the fridge and use within 2 months.

Cook's Tip

To test the consistency of the finished chutney before bottling, spoon a little of the mixture on to a plate: the chutney is ready once it holds its shape.

Nectarine Relish

This sweet and tangy fruit relish goes very well with hot roast meats and game birds, such as guinea fowl, pheasant and pork. Make it while nectarines are plentiful and keep tightly covered in the fridge to serve at a later date.

Makes about 450g/1lb

INGREDIENTS

45ml/3 tbsp olive oil
2 Spanish onions, thinly sliced
1 fresh green chilli, seeded and finely chopped
5ml/1 tsp finely chopped fresh rosemary
2 bay leaves
450g/1lb nectarines, stoned and diced
150g/5oz/1 cup raisins
10ml/2 tsp crushed coriander seeds
350g/12 oz/1½ cups demerara sugar
200ml/7fl oz/scant 1 cup red wine vinegar

1 Heat the oil in a large, heavy-based saucepan. Add the sliced onions, chopped chilli and rosemary, and the bay leaves. Cook, stirring frequently, for 15–20 minutes, or until the onions are soft but not browned.

Cook's Tip

Jars of this relish make a welcome gift. Add a colourful tag reminding the recipient to keep it in the fridge.

2 Add all the remaining ingredients and bring to the boil slowly, stirring often. Lower the heat and simmer for 1 hour, or until the relish is thick and sticky, stirring occasionally.

3 Remove and discard the bay leaves. Spoon into sterilized jars, and seal. Cool, then chill. The relish will keep in the fridge for up to 5 months.

Piquant Pineapple Relish

THIS FRUITY SWEET-AND-SOUR relish is excellent served with grilled chicken, gammon or bacon.

Serves 4

INGREDIENTS

400g/14oz can crushed pineapple in natural juice
30ml/2 tbsp light muscovado sugar
30ml/2 tbsp wine vinegar
1 garlic clove, finely chopped
4 spring onions, finely chopped
2 red chillies, seeded and chopped
10 fresh basil leaves, finely shredded
salt and ground black pepper

1 Drain the pineapple and reserve 60ml/4 tbsp of the juice.

2 Place the juice in a small saucepan with the sugar and vinegar, then heat gently, stirring frequently, until the sugar dissolves. Remove the pan from the heat and season with salt and pepper to taste.

3 Place the pineapple, garlic, spring onions and chillies in a bowl. Mix well and stir in the juice. Allow to cool for 5 minutes, then stir in the basil and serve.

VARIATION

This relish tastes extra special when made with fresh pineapple.

Papaya and Lemon Relish

THIS CHUNKY RELISH IS best made with a firm, unripe papaya.Leave for a week before eating to allow all the flavours to mellow. Store unopened jars in a cool place, away from sunlight. Serve with roast meats or with a robust cheese and crackers.

Makes about 450g/1lb

INGREDIENTS

1 large unripe papaya
1 onion, thinly sliced
40g/1½oz/⅓ cup raisins
250ml/8fl oz/1 cup red wine vinegar
juice of 2 lemons
150ml/¼ pint/⅔ cup elderflower cordial
150g/5oz/¾ cup golden granulated sugar
1 cinnamon stick
1 fresh bay leaf
2.5ml/½ tsp hot paprika
2.5ml/½ tsp salt

1 Peel the papaya and cut lengthways in half. Remove the seeds with a teaspoon. Use a sharp knife to cut the flesh into small chunks and place them in a saucepan. Add the onion slices and raisins, then stir in the red wine vinegar.

2 Bring the liquid to the boil, then immediately lower the heat and allow to simmer for 10 minutes.

COOK'S TIP

The seeds of papaya are often discarded when the ripe fruit is used, but they have a peppery taste and make a delicious addition to a salad dressing.

3 Add all the remaining ingredients to the saucepan and bring to the boil, stirring all the time. Check that all the sugar has dissolved, then lower the heat and simmer for 50–60 minutes, or until the relish is thick and syrupy.

4 Remove and discard the bay leaf. Ladle the relish into hot, sterilized jars. Seal and label, and store in a cool, dark place for 1 week before using. Keep the relish chilled after opening.

Spicy Sweetcorn Relish

SERVE THIS SIMPLE SPICY relish with bowls of Red Onion Raita, Sweet Mango Relish and a plateful of crisp onion bhajis for a fabulous Indian-style starter.

Serves 4

INGREDIENTS

30ml/2 tbsp vegetable oil
1 large onion, chopped
1 red chilli, seeded and chopped
2 garlic cloves, chopped
5ml/1 tsp black mustard seeds
10ml/2 tsp hot curry powder
320g/11¼oz can sweetcorn, drained
grated rind and juice of 1 lime
45ml/3 tbsp chopped fresh coriander
salt and ground black pepper

1 Heat the oil in a large frying pan and cook the onion, chilli and garlic over a high heat for 5 minutes, until the onions are just beginning to brown.

COOK'S TIP

Use frozen rather than canned sweetcorn as the kernels are plump and moist.

2 Stir in the mustard seeds and curry powder, then cook for 2 minutes more, stirring, until the seeds start to splutter and the onions are browned.

3 Remove the fried onion and spice mixture from the heat and allow to cool completely. Transfer the mixture to a glass bowl.

4 Add the drained sweetcorn to the bowl containing the onion mixture and stir to mix.

5 Add the lime rind and juice, coriander and seasoning. Mix well, then cover and serve at room temperature.

Sweet Mango Relish

STIR A SPOONFUL OF this relish into soups and stews for added flavour or serve it with a wedge of Cheddar cheese and chunks of crusty bread.

Makes 750ml/1¼ pints/3 cups

INGREDIENTS

2 large mangoes
1 cooking apple, peeled and chopped
2 shallots, chopped
4cm/1½in piece fresh root ginger, chopped
2 garlic cloves, crushed
115g/4oz/⅔ cup small sultanas
2 star anise
5ml/1 tsp ground cinnamon
2.5ml/½ tsp dried chilli flakes
2.5ml/½ tsp salt
175ml/6fl oz/¾ cup cider vinegar
130g/4½oz/generous ½ cup light muscovado sugar

1 One at a time, hold the mangoes upright on a chopping board and use a large knife to slice the flesh away from each side of the large, flat stone.

2 Using a smaller knife, carefully trim away any flesh still clinging to the top and bottom of the stone.

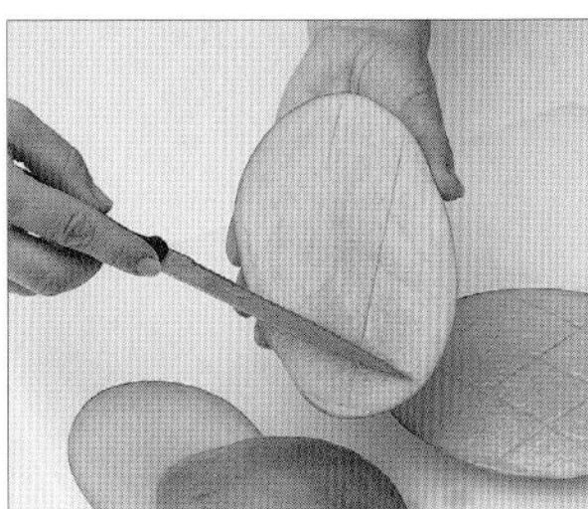

3 Score the flesh of the mango halves deeply, taking care to avoid cutting through the skin: make parallel incisions about 1cm/½in apart, then turn and cut parallel lines in the opposite direction.

4 Carefully turn the skin inside out so that the mango flesh stands out like hedgehog spikes. Slice the dice away from the skin.

5 Place the diced mango, chopped apple, shallots, ginger, garlic and sultanas in a large, heavy-based saucepan. Add the star anise, cinnamon, chilli, salt, vinegar and sugar.

6 Bring to the boil, stirring continuously, until the sugar has dissolved. Reduce the heat and simmer gently for a further 4 minutes, stirring occasionally, until the chutney has reduced and thickened.

7 Allow the relish to cool for about 5 minutes, then ladle it into warm, sterilized jars. Cool completely, cover and label. The relish may be stored in the fridge for up to 2 months. Keep the relish chilled after opening.

VARIATION

Select alternative spices according to your own taste: for example, you can add juniper berries or cumin seeds in place of the star anise.

Chilli Relish

THIS SPICY RELISH will keep for at least a week in the fridge. Serve it with barbecued sausages or with burgers in a sesame bun.

Serves 8

INGREDIENTS

6 tomatoes
30ml/2 tbsp olive oil
1 onion, roughly chopped
1 red pepper, seeded and chopped
2 garlic cloves, chopped
5ml/1 tsp ground cinnamon
5ml/1 tsp chilli flakes
5ml/1 tsp ground ginger
5ml/1 tsp salt
2.5ml/½ tsp ground black pepper
75g/3oz/6 tbsp light muscovado sugar
75ml/5 tbsp cider vinegar
handful of fresh basil leaves, chopped

1 Skewer each of the tomatoes in turn on a metal fork and hold in a gas flame for 1–2 minutes, turning, until the skin splits and wrinkles.

2 Slip off the tomato skins, then roughly chop the flesh.

3 Heat the olive oil in a saucepan. Add the chopped onion, red pepper and garlic to the pan.

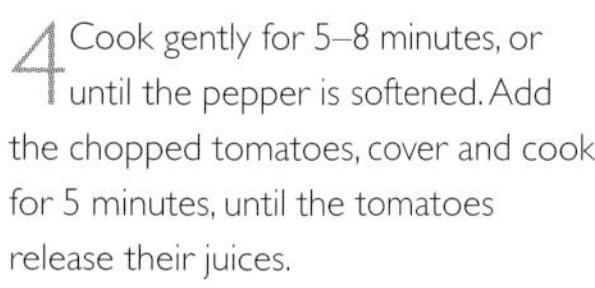

4 Cook gently for 5–8 minutes, or until the pepper is softened. Add the chopped tomatoes, cover and cook for 5 minutes, until the tomatoes release their juices.

5 Stir in the cinnamon, chilli flakes, ginger, salt, pepper, sugar and vinegar. Bring gently to the boil, stirring, until the sugar dissolves.

6 Simmer, uncovered, for 20 minutes, or until the mixture is pulpy. Stir in the basil leaves and check the seasoning.

7 Allow to cool completely, then transfer to a glass jar or a plastic container with a tightly fitting lid. Store, covered, in the fridge.

COOK'S TIP

This relish thickens slightly on cooling so do not worry if the mixture seems a little wet at the end of step 6.

VARIATION

Replace the fresh garlic with smoked garlic for a really smoky, barbecue flavour.

Bloody Mary Relish

SERVE THIS PERFECT PARTY relish with sticks of crunchy cucumber or, on a really special occasion, with freshly shucked oysters.

Serves 2

INGREDIENTS

4 ripe tomatoes
1 celery stalk
1 garlic clove
2 spring onions
45ml/3 tbsp tomato juice
Worcestershire sauce, to taste
red Tabasco sauce, to taste
10ml/2 tsp horseradish sauce
15ml/1 tbsp vodka
juice of 1 lemon
salt and ground black pepper

1 Halve the tomatoes, celery and garlic. Trim the spring onions.

2 Process the vegetables in a food processor or blender until very finely chopped. Transfer to a bowl.

3 Stir in the tomato juice and add a few drops of Worcestershire sauce and Tabasco to taste.

4 Stir in the horseradish sauce, vodka and lemon juice. Season with salt and ground black pepper, to taste.

VARIATION

In the food processor or blender add 1–2 fresh, seeded, red chillies with the tomatoes, celery and garlic instead of adding Tabasco sauce.

Tart Tomato Relish

THE WHOLE LIME used in this recipe adds a pleasantly sour aftertaste. This is delicious served with grilled or roast pork or lamb.

Serves 4

INGREDIENTS

1 lime
450g/1lb cherry tomatoes
115g/4oz/½ cup dark muscovado sugar
105ml/7 tbsp white wine vinegar
5ml/1 tsp salt
2 pieces stem ginger, chopped

1 Slice the whole lime thinly, then chop it into small pieces; do not remove the rind.

VARIATION

If preferred, use ordinary tomatoes, roughly chopped, in place of the cherry tomatoes used here.

2 Place the whole tomatoes, sugar, vinegar, salt, ginger and lime together in a saucepan.

3 Bring to the boil, stirring until the sugar dissolves, then simmer rapidly for 45 minutes. Stir regularly until the liquid has evaporated and the relish is thickened and pulpy.

4 Allow the relish to cool for about 5 minutes, then spoon it into clean jars. Cool completely, cover and store in the fridge for up to 1 month.

Toffee Onion Relish

SLOW, GENTLE COOKING reduces the onions to a soft, caramelized golden brown relish in this recipe. This relish adds a sweet flavour to a mature cheese in a ploughman's lunch or makes an idea accompaniment to flans and quiches.

Serves 4

INGREDIENTS

3 large onions
50g/2oz/¼ cup butter
30ml/2 tbsp olive oil
30ml/2 tbsp light muscovado sugar
30ml/2 tbsp pickled capers
30ml/2 tbsp chopped fresh parsley
salt and ground black pepper

1 Peel the onions and cut them in half vertically through the core, then slice them thinly.

2 Heat the butter and oil together in a large, heavy-based saucepan. Add the sliced onions and sugar and cook very gently for about 30 minutes over a low heat, stirring occasionally, until the onions are reduced to a soft rich-brown, toffee-like mixture.

3 Roughly chop the capers and stir into the browned onion mixture. Allow to cool completely and transfer to a bowl.

4 Stir in the chopped parsley and add salt and freshly ground black pepper to taste. Cover and chill until ready to serve.

COOK'S TIP

Choose a heavy-based pan to cook the relish in, to get an evenly browned toffee mixture without the risk of burning.

VARIATION

Try making this recipe with red onions or shallots for a subtle variation in flavour.

Red Onion Marmalade

THIS IS A RICH and delicious marmalade, and makes a particularly good accompaniment to barbecued or grilled salmon.

Serves 4

INGREDIENTS

5 red onions
50g/2oz/¼ cup butter
175ml/6fl oz/¾ cup red wine vinegar
50ml/2fl oz/¼ cup crème de cassis
50ml/2fl oz/¼ cup grenadine
50ml/2fl oz/¼ cup red wine
salt and ground black pepper

1 Remove the skins from the red onions and slice them finely.

2 Melt the butter in a large, heavy-based saucepan and add the sliced onions. Sauté the onions for 5 minutes, or until golden brown.

3 Stir in the wine vinegar, crème de cassis, grenadine and wine and continue to cook for about 10 minutes, or until the liquid has almost entirely evaporated and the onions are glazed. Season well with salt and freshly ground black pepper.

COOK'S TIP

If serving this marmalade with barbecued salmon, try to find pieces that are at least 2.5cm/1in thick. Brush the fish with olive oil, season with salt and ground black pepper, and cook on a medium barbecue for about 6–8 minutes, turning once during cooking.

Apple and Red Onion Marmalade

THIS MARMALADE CHUTNEY is good enough to eat on its own. Serve it with good quality pork sausages for thoroughly modern hot dogs, or in a ham sandwich instead of mustard.

Makes about 450g/1lb

INGREDIENTS

60ml/4 tbsp extra virgin olive oil
900g/2lb red onions, thinly sliced
75g/3oz/6 tbsp demerara sugar
2 Cox's Orange Pippin apples
90ml/6 tbsp cider vinegar

1 Heat the oil in a large, heavy-based saucepan and add the onions.

2 Stir in the sugar and allow to cook, uncovered, over a medium heat for about 40 minutes, stirring occasionally, or until the onions have softened.

3 Peel, core and grate the apples. Add them to the pan with the vinegar and continue to cook for 20 minutes, or until the chutney is thick and sticky. Spoon into sterilized jars and cover.

4 When cool, label and store in the fridge for up to 1 month.

VARIATION

If you like, add a cinnamon stick to the pan during cooking to impart a mild, sweet spice flavour. Remove the spice before bottling the marmalade chutney in sterilized jars.

Old-fashioned Pickle

THIS SIMPLE, OLD-FASHIONED pickle is quite delicious with cold meats or cheese, with a hunk of fresh crusty bread and butter on the side.

Makes about 1.3–1.6kg/3–3½lb

INGREDIENTS

900g/2lb cucumbers, scrubbed and cut in 5mm/¼in slices
4 onions, very thinly sliced
30ml/2 tbsp salt
350ml/12fl oz/1½ cups cider vinegar
300g/11oz/generous 1½ cups sugar
30ml/2 tbsp mustard seeds
30ml/2 tbsp celery seeds
1.5ml/¼ tsp turmeric
1.5ml/¼ tsp cayenne

COOK'S TIP

Avoid using metal lids or seals, as these may react with the acid in the pickle.

1 Put the sliced cucumbers and onions in a large bowl and sprinkle with the salt. Mix well. Cover loosely and leave to stand for 3 hours.

2 Drain the vegetables. Rinse well under cold running water and then drain again.

3 Prepare some heatproof glass jars (such as preserving jars). Wash them well in warm soapy water and rinse thoroughly in clean warm water.

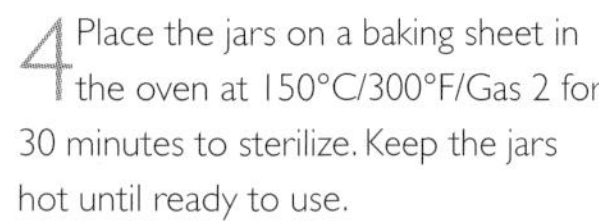

4 Place the jars on a baking sheet in the oven at 150°C/300°F/Gas 2 for 30 minutes to sterilize. Keep the jars hot until ready to use.

5 Combine the remaining ingredients in a large, non-reactive saucepan and bring to the boil. Add the drained cucumbers and onions. Reduce the heat and simmer for 2–3 minutes. Do not boil or the pickles will be limp.

6 Spoon the hot vegetables into the hot jars. Add enough of the liquid to come to 1cm/½in from the top. Carefully wipe the jars with a clean damp cloth.

7 To seal, cover the surface of the pickles with a waxed disc, waxed side down, then put on the jar lids. The pickles should be sealed immediately. If the lid does not have a ring gasket, first cover the top of the jar with a plastic wrap or cellophane cover then screw the plastic top down tightly. Leave in a cool dark place for at least 4 weeks.

Christmas Chutney

THIS SAVOURY MIXTURE OF spices and dried fruit takes its inspiration from mincemeat, and makes a delicious traditional addition to the Boxing Day buffet. Serve with cold meats.

Makes about 1–1.6kg/2¼–3½lb

INGREDIENTS

450g/1lb cooking apples, peeled, cored and chopped
500g/1¼lb/3⅓ cups luxury mixed dried fruit
grated rind of 1 orange
30ml/2 tbsp mixed spice
150ml/¼ pint/⅔ cup cider vinegar
350g/12oz/1½ cups light muscovado sugar

1 Place the chopped apples, dried fruit and grated orange rind in a large, heavy-based saucepan. Stir in the mixed spice, cider vinegar and sugar. Heat the ingredients gently, stirring until all the sugar has dissolved.

2 Bring to the boil, then lower the heat and simmer the mixture for 40–45 minutes, stirring occasionally, until thick.

3 Ladle into warm, sterilized jars, cover and seal. Keep for 1 month before using.

COOK'S TIPS

- *Watch the chutney carefully towards the end of the cooking time, as it has a tendency to catch on the bottom of the pan. Stir frequently at this stage.*
- *Store jars in the fridge after opening.*

Fig and Date Chutney

THIS RECIPE IS USUALLY made with dried figs and dates, but fresh fruit provides a superb flavour and texture.

Makes about 450g/1lb

INGREDIENTS

1 orange
5 large fresh figs, coarsely chopped
350g/12oz/2½ cups fresh dates, peeled, stoned and chopped
2 onions, chopped
5cm/2in piece of fresh root ginger, peeled and finely grated
5ml/1 tsp dried crushed chillies
300g/11oz/generous 1½ cups golden granulated sugar
300ml/½ pint/1¼ cups spiced preserving vinegar
2.5ml/½ tsp salt

COOK'S TIP

Figs are in season for only a short time, so buy when you see them in the shops.

1 Finely grate the rind of the orange, then cut off the remaining pith.

VARIATION

If you would rather use dried figs and dates to make the chutney, you will need to increase the amount of preserving vinegar to 450ml/¾ pint/scant 2 cups. Remove the stones from the dates and then coarsely chop both the figs and the dates.

2 Place the orange segments in a large, heavy-based saucepan with the chopped figs and dates. Add the rind, then stir in the remaining ingredients. Bring to the boil, stirring until the sugar has dissolved, then lower the heat and simmer gently for 1 hour or until thickened and pulpy, stirring frequently.

3 Spoon into hot sterilized jars. Seal while the chutney is still hot and label when cold. Store in a cool dark place for 1 week before using. Keep opened jars in the fridge.

Fresh Pineapple and Mint Chutney

THIS REFRESHING, LIGHT FRUIT chutney has a fresh flavour; it is good with rich meat dishes, particularly lamb or pork.

Makes about 1kg/2¼lb

INGREDIENTS

250ml/8fl oz/1 cup raspberry vinegar
250ml/8fl oz/1 cup dry white wine
1 small pineapple, peeled and chopped
2 medium-size oranges, peeled and chopped
2 dessert apples, peeled and chopped
1 red pepper, seeded and diced
1½ onions, finely chopped
60ml/4 tbsp honey
pinch of salt
1 whole clove
4 black peppercorns
30ml/2 tbsp chopped fresh mint

1 In a large saucepan, combine the raspberry vinegar and white wine, and bring to a boil. Boil for 3 minutes.

2 Add the remaining ingredients, except the mint, and stir to blend. Simmer gently for about 30 minutes, stirring occasionally.

3 Transfer to a strainer set over a bowl and drain, pressing down to extract the liquid. Remove and discard the clove and peppercorns. Set the fruit mixture aside.

4 Return the strained juice to the pan and boil until reduced by two-thirds. Pour over the fruit mixture.

5 Stir in the mint. Allow to stand for 6–8 hours before serving.

COOK'S TIP

The chutney will keep for about 1 week in the fridge. If you can get pineapple mint, this adds a delightful fresh pineapple scent to the finished chutney.

Mango Chutney

THIS CLASSIC CHUTNEY IS frequently served with curries and Indian poppadums, but it is also delicious with baked ham or a traditional cheese ploughman's lunch.

Makes about 450g/1lb

INGREDIENTS

3 firm green mangoes
150ml/¼ pint/⅔ cup cider vinegar
130g/4½oz/generous ½ cup light muscovado sugar
1 small red finger chilli or jalapeño chilli, split
2.5cm/1in piece of fresh root ginger, peeled and finely chopped
1 garlic clove, finely chopped
5 cardamom pods, bruised
2.5ml/½ tsp coriander seeds, crushed
1 bay leaf
2.5ml/½ tsp salt

1 Peel the mangoes and cut the flesh off the stone. Slice them lengthways, then cut into small chunks or wedges.

COOK'S TIP

Green, under-ripe mangoes have quite a sharp, tangy flavour, quite unlike the fragrant sweetness of ripe ones, but ideal for relishes and chutneys to serve with savoury foods.

2 Place these in a large saucepan, add the vinegar and cover. Cook over a low heat for 10 minutes.

3 Stir in the muscovado sugar, chilli, ginger, garlic, bruised cardamom pods and coriander seeds. Add the bay leaf and salt. Bring to the boil slowly, stirring the mixture often.

4 Lower the heat and simmer, uncovered, for 30 minutes, or until the mixture is thick and syrupy. Remove the cardamom pods if you prefer and remove and discard the bay leaf.

5 Ladle into hot, sterilized jars. Leave to cool, then seal and label. Store in a cool, dark place for 1 week before eating. Keep chilled after opening.

Roasted Red Pepper and Chilli Jelly

THE HINT OF CHILLI in this glowing red jelly makes it ideal for spicing up hot or cold roast meat. The jelly is also good stirred into sauces.

Makes about 900g/2lb

INGREDIENTS

8 red peppers, quartered and seeded
4 fresh red chillies, halved and seeded
1 onion, roughly chopped
2 garlic cloves, roughly chopped
250ml/8fl oz/1 cup water
250ml/8fl oz/1 cup white wine vinegar
7.5ml/1½ tsp salt
450g/1lb/2¼ cups preserving sugar
13g/⅓oz sachet powdered pectin (about 25ml/1½ tbsp)

COOK'S TIP

It is not essential to use preserving sugar, but it produces less scum.

1 Place the peppers, skin side up, on a rack in a grill pan. Grill until the skins blister and blacken. Place in a polythene bag until cool enough to handle, then remove the skins.

2 Purée the red peppers with the chillies, onion, garlic and water in a food processor or blender. Press the purée through a nylon sieve set over a bowl, pressing hard with a wooden spoon, to extract as much juice as possible. There should be roughly 750ml/1¼ pints/3 cups.

3 Scrape the purée into a large, stainless steel pan. Add the vinegar and salt. In a bowl, mix the sugar and pectin, then stir into the liquid.

4 Heat gently until both the sugar and pectin have dissolved, then bring to a full rolling boil. Boil, stirring frequently, for exactly 4 minutes.

5 Remove the jelly from the heat and pour into warm, sterilized jars. Leave to cool and set, then cover. Keep opened jars in the fridge.

Dressings and Marinades

The primary function of dressings and marinades is to add or balance flavour, and this can make all the difference to even the simplest foods. Both are usually based on a mix of oil and an acidic ingredient such as vinegar or fruit juice, with aromatic additions such as herbs, garlic or spices for a more individual flavour.

Dressings are used to moisten foods, add variety and lift the flavour of any type of salad, from simple green leaves to substantial main meal salads. They are also of benefit to other foods, such as lightly cooked spears of asparagus, pak choi, or crudités.

Marinades are used not only to add flavour to foods, but can also tenderize meats or add moisture to dry foods, either before cooking or as a baste during cooking. A light summer herb marinade makes the world of difference to the flavour of a simple piece of fish or meat, or try a peppered citrus marinade to add a delicious zip to meaty-textured monkfish. The tenderizing effect, caused by the acid content in marinades, is particularly beneficial for tough meats or poultry. A yogurt marinade has a tenderizing effect, too, with the added benefit of forming a deliciously tangy crust on the outside of grilled food.

Avocado Dressing with Crudités

THIS CREAMY-TEXTURED DRESSING is actually quite light, and also makes a good dressing for tomato salads.

Makes about 450ml/¾ pint/ scant 2 cups

INGREDIENTS

30ml/2 tbsp wine vinegar
2.5ml/½ tsp salt, or to taste
4ml/¾ tsp white pepper
½ red onion, coarsely chopped
45ml/3 tbsp olive oil
1 large ripe avocado, halved and stoned
15ml/1 tbsp fresh lemon juice
45ml/3 tbsp natural yogurt
45ml/3 tbsp water, or as needed
30ml/2 tbsp chopped fresh coriander
raw or briefly cooked cold vegetables, to serve

1 In a bowl, combine the vinegar and salt and stir with a fork to dissolve. Stir in the pepper, chopped red onion, and olive oil.

2 Scoop the avocado flesh into a food processor or blender. Add the lemon juice and onion dressing and process just to blend.

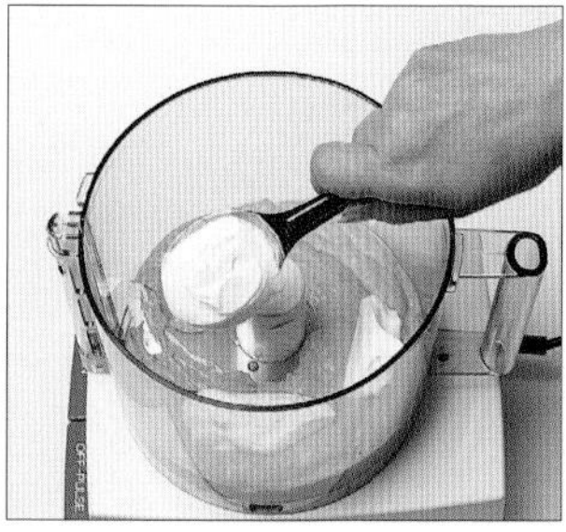

3 Add the yogurt and water and process until the mixture is smooth. If desired, add more water to thin. Taste and adjust the seasoning according to taste.

4 Spoon the mixture into a bowl. Stir in the coriander. Serve immediately with the raw or briefly cooked cold vegetables.

COOK'S TIP

This versatile dressing need not be limited to serving with crudités and salads. Serve it as a sauce with grilled chicken or fish, or use it on sandwiches in place of mayonnaise or mustard, or to provide a cool contrast to any sort of spicy food.

Lime Dressing with Pak Choi

For this Thai recipe, the lime dressing is traditionally made using fish sauce, but vegetarians could use mushroom ketchup instead. Beware, this is a fiery dish!

Serves 4

INGREDIENTS

6 spring onions
2 pak choi
30ml/2 tbsp oil
3 fresh red chillies, cut into thin strips
4 garlic cloves, thinly sliced
15ml/1 tbsp crushed peanuts
salt

For the lime dressing

15–30ml/1–2 tbsp fish sauce
30ml/2 tbsp lime juice
250ml/8fl oz/1 cup coconut milk

Cook's Tip

Coconut milk is available in cans. Alternatively, creamed coconut is available in packets. To use creamed coconut, place about 115g/4 oz in a jug and pour over 250ml/8fl oz/1 cup boiling water. Stir well until dissolved.

1 To make the dressing, blend together the fish sauce and lime juice, and then stir in the coconut milk.

2 Cut the spring onions diagonally into slices, including all but the tips of the green parts. Keep the white parts separate from the green.

3 Using a large, sharp knife, cut the pak choi into very fine shreds.

4 Heat the oil in a wok and stir-fry the chillies for 2–3 minutes, or until crisp. Transfer to a plate using a slotted spoon. Stir-fry the garlic for 30–60 seconds, or until golden brown, and transfer to the plate with the chillies.

5 Stir-fry the white parts of the spring onions for 2–3 minutes and then add the green parts and stir-fry for a further 1 minute. Add to the plate with the chillies and garlic.

6 Bring a large pan of salted water to the boil and add the shredded pak choi. Stir twice and then drain in a sieve or colander immediately.

7 Place the warmed pak choi in a large bowl, add the dressing and stir well.

8 Spoon into a large serving bowl and sprinkle with the crushed peanuts and the stir-fried chilli mixture. Serve either warm or cold, as an accompaniment to rice dishes.

Creamy Raspberry Dressing with Asparagus

RASPBERRY VINEGAR gives this quick dressing a refreshing, tangy fruit flavour – an ideal accompaniment to asparagus.

Serves 4

INGREDIENTS

675g/1½ lb thin asparagus spears
115g/4oz/1½ cups fresh raspberries, to garnish

For the creamy raspberry dressing

30ml/2 tbsp raspberry vinegar
2.5ml/½ tsp salt
5ml/1 tsp Dijon-style mustard
60ml/4 tbsp crème fraîche or natural yogurt
ground white pepper

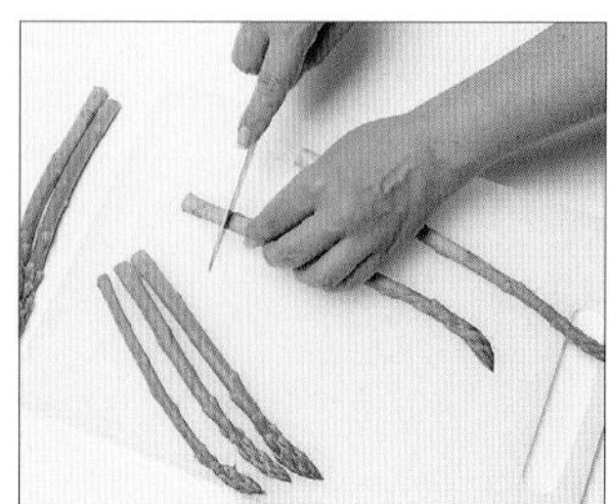

1 Fill a saucepan with water about 10cm/4in deep and bring to the boil. Trim the tough ends of the asparagus spears.

COOK'S TIP

Cook the asparagus and make the sauce in advance, then chill in the fridge until needed. Serve cold.

2 Tie the asparagus spears into two bundles. Lower the bundles into the boiling water and cook for 3–5 minutes, or until just tender.

3 Remove the asparagus and immerse it in cold water to stop the cooking. Drain and untie the bundles. Pat dry. Chill for 1 hour.

4 To make the dressing, mix the vinegar and salt in a bowl and stir with a fork until dissolved. Stir in the mustard, crème fraîche or yogurt. Add pepper to taste. Place the asparagus on individual plates and drizzle the dressing across the middle of the spears. Garnish with fresh raspberries.

Coriander Dressing with Chicken Salad

SERVE THIS SALAD WARM to make the most of the wonderful flavour of barbecued chicken basted with a marinade of coriander, sesame and mustard, and finished with a matching dressing.

Serves 6

INGREDIENTS

4 medium boneless chicken breasts, skinned
225g/8oz mangetouts
2 heads decorative lettuce such as lollo rosso or feuille de chêne
3 carrots, cut into matchsticks
175g/6oz/2¼ cups button mushrooms, sliced
6 bacon rashers, fried and chopped
15ml/1 tbsp chopped fresh coriander, to garnish

For the coriander dressing
120ml/4fl oz/½ cup lemon juice
30ml/2 tbsp wholegrain mustard
250ml/8fl oz/1 cup olive oil
75ml/5 tbsp sesame oil
5ml/1 tsp coriander seeds, crushed

1 Mix all the dressing ingredients in a bowl. Place the chicken breasts in a dish and pour over half the dressing. Marinate overnight in the fridge. Refrigerate the remaining dressing.

2 Cook the mangetouts for about 2 minutes in boiling water, then refresh in cold water.

3 Tear the lettuces into small pieces and mix with all the other salad ingredients and the bacon. Arrange in individual bowls.

4 Cook the chicken breasts on a medium barbecue or grill for 10–15 minutes, basting with the marinade and turning once, until cooked through.

COOK'S TIP

If you have any spare dressing left over, store it in a screw-topped jar in the fridge for up to 4 days. Use the dressing for drizzling over other salads.

5 Slice the chicken on the diagonal into thin pieces. Divide among the bowls of salad and add some of the dressing to each dish. Combine quickly and scatter some fresh coriander over each bowl.

Ginger and Lime Marinade for Prawns

THIS FRAGRANT MARINADE will guarantee a mouth-watering aroma from the barbecue, and is as delicious with chicken or pork as it is with prawns.

Serves 4

INGREDIENTS

225g/8oz peeled raw tiger prawns
1/3 cucumber
15ml/1 tbsp sunflower oil
15ml/1 tbsp sesame seed oil
175g/6oz mangetouts, trimmed
4 spring onons, diagonally sliced
30ml/2 tbsp chopped fresh coriander, to garnish

For the ginger and lime marinade
15ml/1 tbsp clear honey
15ml/1 tbsp light soy sauce
15ml/1 tbsp dry sherry
2 garlic cloves, crushed
small piece of fresh root ginger, peeled and finely chopped
juice of 1 lime

1 Mix together the marinade ingredients, add the prawns and leave to marinate for 1-2 hours.

2 Prepare the cucumber. Slice it in half lengthways, scoop out the seeds, then slice each half neatly into crescents. Set aside.

3 Heat both oils in a large, heavy-based frying pan or wok. Drain the prawns (reserving the marinade) and stir-fry over a high heat for 4 minutes, or until they begin to turn pink. Add the mangetouts and the cucumber and stir-fry for 2 minutes more.

4 Stir in the reserved marinade, heat through, then stir in the spring onions and sprinkle with chopped fresh coriander to garnish.

VARIATION

This marinade is also a good one to use with larger pieces of fish for grilling, such as salmon, trout or tuna.

Peppered Citrus Marinade for Monkfish

MONKFISH IS A FIRM, meaty fish that cooks well on the barbecue. Serve with a green salad.

Serves 4

INGREDIENTS

2 monkfish tails, about 350g/12oz each
1 lime
1 lemon
2 oranges
handful of fresh thyme sprigs
30ml/2 tbsp olive oil
15ml/1 tbsp mixed peppercorns, roughly crushed
salt and ground black pepper

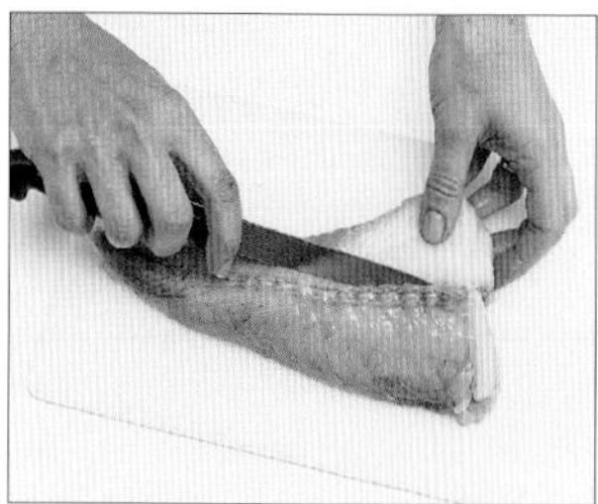

1 Using a sharp kitchen knife, remove any skin from the monkfish tails. Cut the fish carefully down one side of the backbone, sliding the knife between the bone and flesh, to remove the fillet on one side.

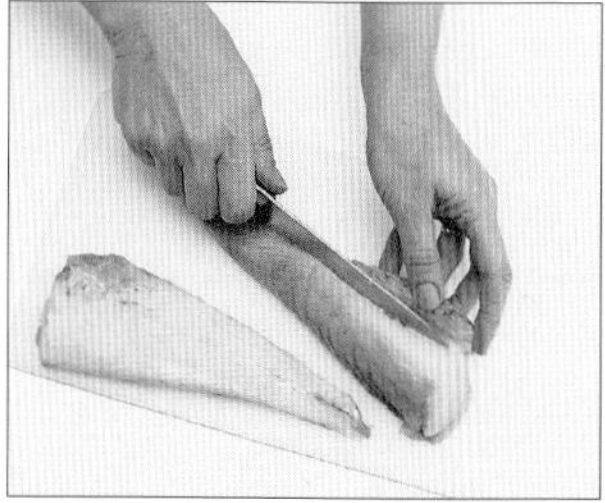

2 Turn the fish and repeat on the other side, to remove the second fillet. Repeat on the second tail. Place the four fillets flat on a chopping board.

3 Cut two slices from each of the citrus fruits and arrange them over two of the fillets.

4 Add a few sprigs of fresh thyme, and sprinkle with plenty of salt and ground black pepper. Finely grate the rind from the remaining fruit and sprinkle it over the fish.

5 Lay the other two fillets on top and tie them firmly at intervals.

6 Squeeze the juice from the citrus fruits and mix it with the olive oil and more salt and pepper. Spoon over the fish. Cover with clear film and leave it to marinate in the fridge for about 1 hour, turning the fish occasionally and spooning the marinade over it.

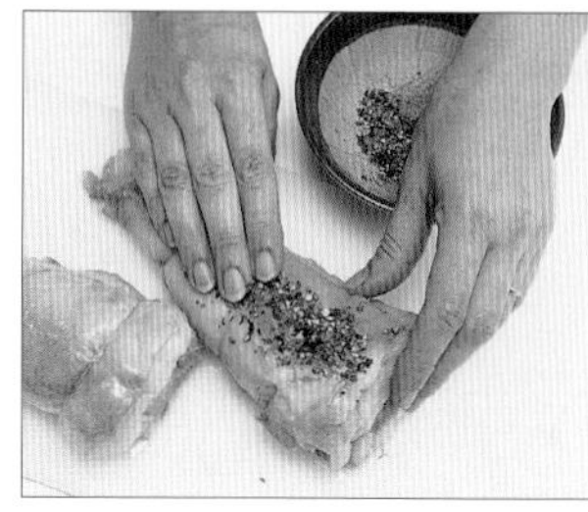

7 Drain the monkfish, reserving the marinade, and sprinkle with the crushed peppercorns. Cook on a medium-hot grill for 15–20 minutes, basting with the marinade.

VARIATION

If you prefer, remove the peel from the fruit before placing between the fillets.

Orange and Green Peppercorn Marinade for Bass

THIS IS AN EXCELLENT light marinade for using with whole fish. The cooked fish, in the lovely soft-coloured marinade, needs only a fresh herb sprig as garnish. Other suitable fish for this recipe are salmon trout or sea bream.

Serves 4

INGREDIENTS

1 medium whole sea bass, cleaned

For the peppercorn marinade

1 red onion
2 small oranges
90ml/6 tbsp light olive oil
30ml/2 tbsp cider vinegar
30ml/2 tbsp green peppercorns in brine, drained
30ml/2 tbsp chopped fresh parsley
salt and sugar, to taste

1 With a sharp knife, slash the sea bass three or four times on both sides.

2 Line an ovenproof dish with foil. Peel and slice the onion and oranges. Place half in the bottom of the dish, place the fish on top, and cover with the remaining onion and orange.

3 Mix the remaining marinade ingredients and pour over the fish. Cover and stand for 4 hours, occasionally spooning the marinade over the top.

4 Preheat the oven to 180°C/350°F/Gas 4. Fold up the foil over the fish and seal loosely. Bake for 15 minutes per 450g/1lb, plus 15 minutes over. Serve with the juices.

Summer Herb Marinade for Salmon

MAKE THE BEST USE of summer herbs in this marinade, which can also be used with veal, chicken, pork or lamb.

Serves 4

INGREDIENTS

4 salmon steaks or fillets, about 175g/6oz each

For the herb marinade

large handful of fresh herb sprigs, e.g. chervil, thyme, parsley, sage, chives, rosemary, oregano
90ml/6 tbsp olive oil
45ml/3 tbsp tarragon vinegar
1 garlic clove, crushed
2 spring onions, chopped
salt and ground black pepper

1 Discard any coarse stalks or damaged leaves from the herbs, then chop them very finely.

2 Add the chopped herbs to the remaining marinade ingredients in a large bowl. Stir to mix thoroughly.

3 Place the salmon in the bowl and spoon the marinade over. Cover and leave to marinate in a cool place for 4–6 hours.

4 Drain the fish when you are ready to cook it on the barbecue. Use the marinade to baste the fish occasionally during cooking.

COOK'S TIP

Keep the discarded herb stalks to throw on to the barbecue coals when you cook, to add an extra dimension to the flavour.

Spicy Yogurt Marinade for Chicken

PLAN THIS DISH WELL in advance; the extra-long marinating time is necessary to develop a really mellow spicy flavour.

Serves 6

INGREDIENTS

6 chicken pieces
juice of 1 lemon
5ml/1 tsp salt
fresh mint, lemon and lime, to garnish

For the yogurt marinade

5ml/1 tsp coriander seeds
10ml/2 tsp cumin seeds
6 cloves
2 bay leaves
1 onion, quartered
2 garlic cloves
5cm/2in piece fresh root ginger, peeled and roughly chopped
2.5ml/½ tsp chilli powder
5ml/1 tsp turmeric
150ml/¼ pint/⅔ cup natural yogurt

1 Skin the chicken joints and make deep slashes in the fleshiest parts with a sharp knife. Sprinkle the lemon juice and salt over, and rub in.

2 Make the marinade. Spread the coriander and cumin seeds, cloves and bay leaves in the bottom of a large frying pan and dry-fry over a moderate heat until the bay leaves are crispy.

3 Allow the spice mixture to cool, then grind it coarsely in a mortar and pestle.

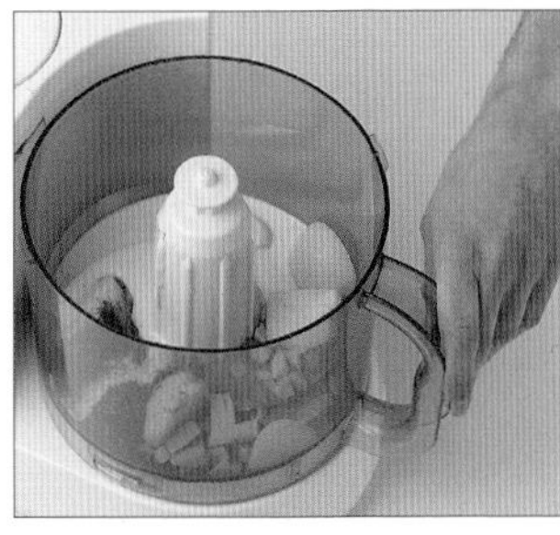

4 Finely mince the onion, garlic and ginger in a food processor or blender with the ground spices, chilli, turmeric and yogurt. Strain in the lemon juice from the chicken.

5 Arrange the chicken in a single layer in a roasting tin. Pour the marinade over, then cover and chill for 24–36 hours, turning the chicken pieces occasionally.

6 Preheat the oven to 200°C/400°F/Gas 6. Cook the chicken for 45 minutes, or until the juices run clear when the meat is pierced. Serve hot or cold, garnished with fresh mint and slices of lemon or lime.

VARIATION

This marinade will also work well brushed over skewers of lamb or pork fillet prior to grilling or barbecuing.

Lavender Balsamic Marinade for Lamb

LAVENDER IS AN UNUSUAL flavour to use with meat, but its heady, summery scent works well with barbecued lamb. Use the flower heads as garnish.

Serves 4

INGREDIENTS

4 racks of lamb, with 3–4 cutlets each

For the balsamic marinade

1 shallot, finely chopped
45ml/3 tbsp chopped fresh lavender
15ml/1 tbsp balsamic vinegar
30ml/2 tbsp olive oil
15ml/1 tbsp lemon juice
handful of lavender sprigs
salt and ground black pepper

1 Place the racks of lamb in a large mixing bowl or wide dish and sprinkle the chopped shallot over.

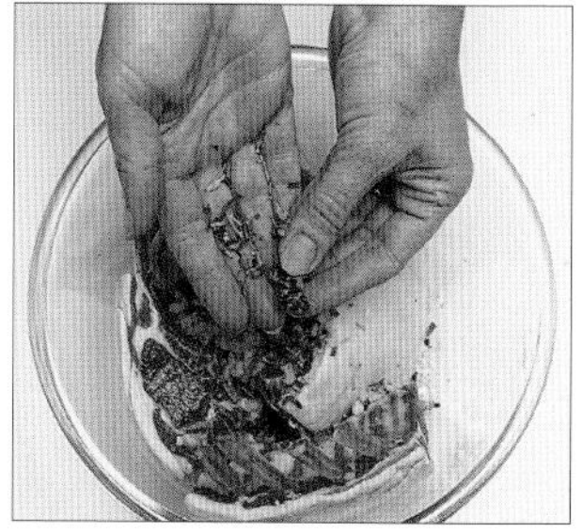

2 Sprinkle the chopped fresh lavender over the lamb in the bowl.

3 Beat together the vinegar, olive oil and lemon juice and pour them over the lamb. Season well with salt and ground black pepper and then turn the meat to coat evenly.

4 Scatter a few lavender sprigs over the grill or on the coals of a medium-hot barbecue. Cook the lamb for 15–20 minutes, turning once and basting with any remaining marinade, until golden brown on the outside and still slightly pink in the centre. Just before serving, garnish with lavender flower heads.

Red Wine and Juniper Marinade for Lamb

JUNIPER BERRIES HAVE A pungent flavour which is ideal to flavour lamb.

Serves 4–6

INGREDIENTS

675g/1½lb boned leg of lamb, trimmed and cut into 2.5cm/1in cubes
2 carrots, cut into batons
225g/8oz baby onions or shallots
115g/4oz/1½ cups button mushrooms
30ml/2 tbsp vegetable oil
150ml/¼ pint/⅔ cup stock
30ml/2 tbsp beurre manié
salt and ground black pepper

For the red wine and juniper marinade
4 rosemary sprigs
8 dried juniper berries, lightly crushed
8 black peppercorns, lightly crushed
300ml/½ pint/1¼ cups red wine

1 Place the meat in a bowl, add the vegetables, rosemary, berries and peppercorns, then pour over the wine. Cover and leave in a cool place for 4–5 hours, stirring once or twice during this time.

2 Remove the lamb and vegetables with a slotted spoon and set aside. Strain the marinade into a jug.

3 Preheat the oven to 160°C/325°F/Gas 3. Heat the oil in a pan and fry the meat and vegetables in batches until lightly browned. Transfer to a casserole and pour over the reserved marinade and stock. Cover and cook in the oven for 2 hours.

4 Twenty minutes before the end of cooking, stir in the beurre manié, then cover and return to the oven. Season to taste before serving.

COOK'S TIP

Beurre manié is made of equal parts of butter and flour blended together. It is used as a thickening agent and should be added a small piece at a time.

Lemon and Rosemary Marinade for Lamb

MARINATE THE leg of lamb overnight in the fridge so that the flavours have plenty of time to penetrate the meat fully.

Serves 6

INGREDIENTS

1.3–1.6kg/3–3½lb leg of lamb
2 garlic cloves, sliced
15ml/1 tbsp cornflour

For the lemon and rosemary marinade
1 lemon, sliced
6 rosemary sprigs
4 lemon thyme sprigs
300ml/½ pint/1¼ cups dry white wine
60ml/4 tbsp olive oil
salt and ground black pepper

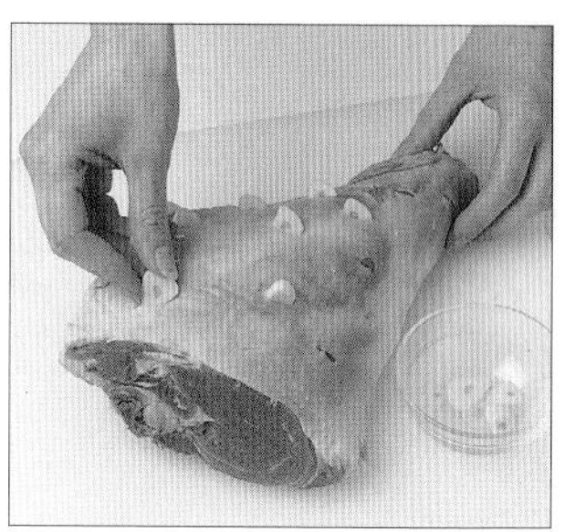

1 Make small cuts over the lamb surface. Insert a garlic piece in each.

2 Place the lamb in a tin, with the lemon slices and herbs scattered over it.

3 Mix the wine, oil and seasoning and pour over the lamb. Cover and leave in a cool place for 4–6 hours, turning occasionally.

4 Preheat the oven to 180°C/350°F/Gas 4, then roast the lamb for 25 minutes per 450g/1lb plus another 25 minutes. Baste with the marinade.

VARIATION

You can also use lemon and rosemary marinade for chicken pieces, but you must roast the meat without the marinade or it will become tough. Use the marinade for making into gravy when the chicken is cooked.

5 When the lamb is cooked, transfer to a warmed plate to rest. Drain the excess fat from the pan. Blend the cornflour with a little cold water and stir into the juices. Stir over a moderate heat for 2–3 minutes, then adjust the seasoning.

Chinese Sesame Marinade for Beef Strips

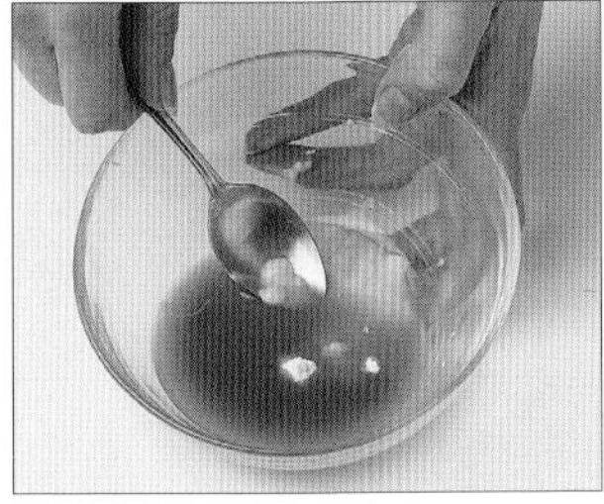

1 To make the marinade, blend the cornflour with the rice wine or sherry. Add the other marinade ingredients. Trim the steak and cut into thin strips about 1 x 5cm/½ x 2in. Stir into the marinade, cover and leave in a cool place for 3–4 hours.

2 Place the sesame seeds in a large frying pan or wok. Cook dry over a moderate heat, shaking the pan until the seeds are golden. Set aside.

TOASTED SESAME SEEDS BRING their distinctive smoky aroma to this Oriental marinade.

Serves 4

INGREDIENTS

450g/1lb rump steak
30ml/2 tbsp sesame seeds
15ml/1 tbsp sesame oil
30ml/2 tbsp vegetable oil
115g/4oz/1½ cups small mushrooms, quartered
1 large green pepper, seeded and diced
4 spring onions, chopped diagonally

For the Chinese sesame marinade
10ml/2 tsp cornflour
30ml/2 tbsp rice wine or sherry
15ml/1 tbsp lemon juice
15ml/1 tbsp soy sauce
few drops Tabasco sauce
2.5cm/1in piece fresh root ginger, peeled and grated
1 garlic clove, crushed

VARIATION

This marinade would also be good with lean pork fillet or chicken breast.

3 Heat the oils in the frying pan. Drain the beef, reserving the marinade, and brown a few pieces at a time. Remove with a slotted spoon.

4 Add the mushrooms and pepper and fry for 2–3 minutes, stirring continuously. Add the spring onions and cook for a further minute.

5 Add the beef and reserved marinade, and stir over a moderate heat for 2 minutes, or until evenly coated with the glaze. Sprinkle with the toasted sesame seeds, and serve.

Winter-spiced Ale Marinade for Beef

THIS MARINADE can also be used in a casserole of beef or lamb pieces. It will imbue the meat with a lovely malty flavour.

Serves 6

INGREDIENTS

1.3kg/3lb top rump beef

For the winter-spiced ale marinade

1 onion, sliced
2 carrots, sliced
2 celery sticks, sliced
2–3 parsley stalks, lightly crushed
large fresh thyme sprig
2 bay leaves
6 cloves, lightly crushed
1 cinnamon stick
8 black peppercorns
300ml/½ pint/1¼ cups brown ale
45ml/3 tbsp vegetable oil
30ml/2 tbsp beurre manié
salt and ground black pepper

1 Put the meat in a polythene bag placed inside a large, deep bowl. Add the vegetables, herbs and spices, then pour the ale over. Seal the bag and leave in a cool place for 5–6 hours.

2 Remove the beef and set aside. Strain the marinade into a bowl, reserving the marinade.

3 Heat the oil in a flameproof casserole. Fry the vegetables until lightly browned, then remove with a slotted spoon and set aside. Brown the beef all over in the remaining oil.

4 Preheat the oven to 160°C/325°F/Gas 3.

5 Return the vegetables to the casserole and pour the reserved marinade over the beef.

6 Cover the casserole and cook in the oven for 2½ hours. Turn the beef two or three times in the marinade during cooking.

7 To serve, remove the beef and slice neatly. Arrange on a plate with the vegetables. Gradually stir the beurre manié into the marinade and cook until thickened. Adjust the seasoning.

COOK'S TIP

A rich, dark brown ale has the ideal flavour for this recipe, but the choice depends on your own taste.

Sauces for Sweet Dishes

Hot and cold sweet sauces can transform a simple scoop of ice cream or a piece of fruit into a complete dessert. A good range of sweet sauces can increase your range of desserts three or four times over. Whether it's a tangy fruit coulis, a rich chocolate sauce, foaming sabayon or creamy custard, you can mix and match your favourite puddings and desserts with sauces to create a new dish every time.

Try a generous drizzle of Chocolate Sauce over profiteroles for a perfectly indulgent treat, then next time spoon it over your favourite vanilla ice cream. Or, for a lighter, less calorie-laden treat, how about Maple Yogurt Sauce with Poached Pears, then perhaps serve the Maple Yogurt Sauce with fresh strawberries for another occasion?

It's worth making the most of fruits in season to make deliciously fresh fruit coulis, to use in creative combinations at any time of year. Grilled pineapple is irresistible with a luscious spoonful of Papaya Sauce, or try Passion Fruit Coulis spooned on to scoops of frozen yogurt.

For a more traditional partnership, try runny Toffee Sauce poured on to Hot Date Puddings or old-fashioned Castle Puddings with Real Custard.

Papaya Dip with Fresh Fruit

SWEET AND SMOOTH PAPAYA teams up well with crème fraîche to make a luscious, tropical sweet dip which is very good with sweet biscuits or fresh fruit for dipping. If fresh coconut is not available, buy coconut strands and lightly toast in a hot oven until golden.

Serves 6

INGREDIENTS

2 ripe papayas
200ml/7fl oz/scant 1 cup crème fraîche
1 piece stem ginger
fresh coconut, to decorate
papaya or other fresh fruit, to serve

1 Halve the papayas lengthways, then scoop out and discard the seeds.

2 Scoop out the flesh and process it until smooth in a food processor or blender.

3 Stir in the crème fraîche and process until well blended. Finely chop the stem ginger and stir it in, then chill until ready to serve.

4 Pierce a hole in the "eye" of the coconut and drain off the liquid. Put the coconut in a polythene bag. Hold it securely in one hand and hit it sharply with a hammer.

5 Remove the shell from a piece of coconut, then snap the nut into pieces no wider than 2.5cm/1in.

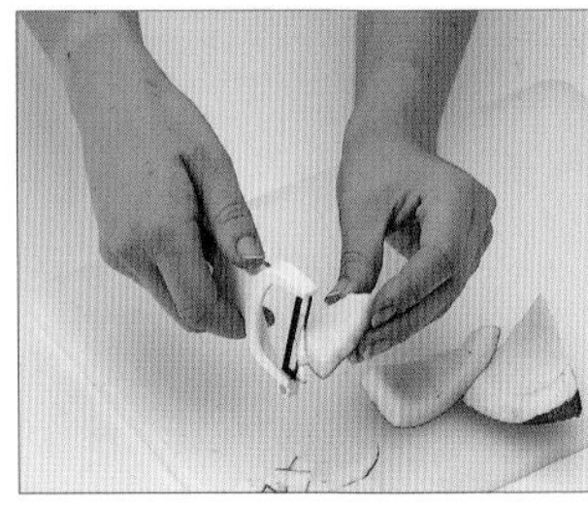

6 Use a swivel-bladed vegetable peeler to shave off 2cm/¾in lengths of coconut. Scatter these over the dip. Serve with pieces of extra papaya or other fresh fruit.

Malted Chocolate and Banana Dip with Fresh Fruit

CHOCOLATE AND BANANA combine irresistibly in this rich dip, served with fresh fruit in season. For a creamier dip, stir in some lightly whipped cream just before serving.

Serves 4

INGREDIENTS

50g/2oz plain chocolate
2 large ripe bananas
15ml/1 tbsp malt extract
mixed fresh fruit, such as strawberries, peaches and kiwi fruit, halved or sliced, to serve

1 Break the chocolate into pieces and place in a small, heatproof bowl. Stand the bowl over a pan of gently simmering water and stir the chocolate occasionally until it melts. Allow to cool slightly.

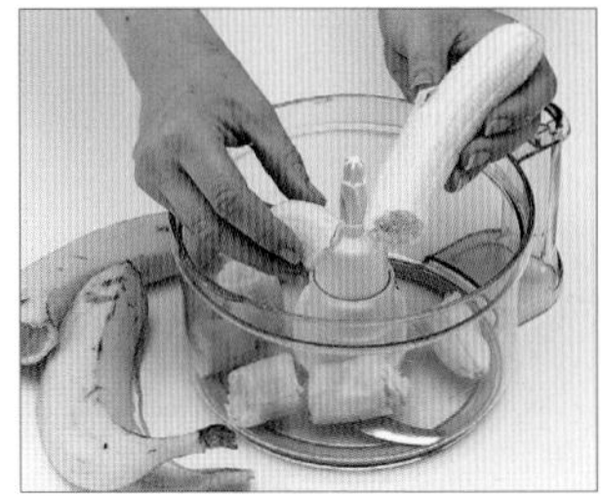

2 Break the bananas into pieces and process in a food processor or blender until finely chopped.

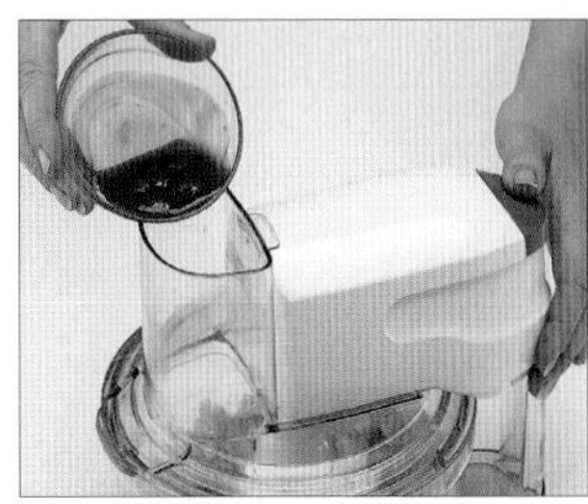

3 With the motor running, pour in the malt extract, and continue processing the mixture until it is thick and frothy.

4 Drizzle in the chocolate in a steady stream and process until well blended. Serve immediately, with the prepared fruit alongside.

COOK'S TIP

This smooth dip can be prepared in advance and chilled.

Passion Fruit Coulis with Yogurt Sundaes

FROZEN YOGURT makes a refreshing change to ice cream. Here, it is partnered with a delicious fresh fruit coulis that is simple to make. Fresh summer strawberries are unlikely to need sweetening, but some varieties may need a little sugar.

Serves 4

INGREDIENTS

175g/6oz/1½ cups strawberries, hulled and halved
2 ripe peaches, stoned and chopped
8 scoops (about 350g/12 oz) vanilla or strawberry frozen yogurt

For the passion fruit coulis

175g/6oz/1½ cups strawberries, hulled and halved
1 passion fruit
10ml/2 tsp icing sugar (optional)

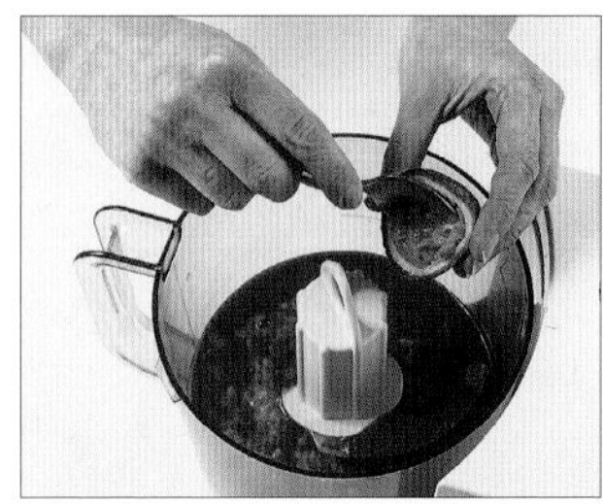

1 To make the coulis, purée the strawberries. Scoop out the passion fruit pulp and add it to the coulis. Sweeten with icing sugar if necessary.

2 Spoon half the remaining strawberries and half the chopped peaches into four tall sundae glasses.

3 Add a scoop of frozen yogurt. Set aside a few choice pieces of fruit for decoration, and use the rest to make a further layer on the top of each sundae. Top each with a final scoop of frozen yogurt.

4 Pour the passion fruit coulis over, and decorate the sundaes with the reserved strawberries and pieces of peach. Serve immediately.

Hazelnut Dip with Fruit Fondue

FRESH FRUIT IS ALWAYS a good choice for a colourful, simple dessert, and this recipe makes it complete, with a delicious sauce for dipping. Any fruit which can be served raw can be used for this dish. Try to use fruits in a range of different colours for an attractive presentation.

Serves 2

INGREDIENTS

selection of fresh fruits, such as satsumas, kiwi fruit, grapes, physalis and whole strawberries

For the hazelnut dip

50g/2oz/¼ cup soft cheese
150ml/¼ pint/⅔ cup hazelnut yogurt
5ml/1 tsp vanilla essence
5ml/1 tsp caster sugar
50g/2oz/⅓ cup shelled hazelnuts, chopped

1 First prepare the fruits. Peel and segment the satsumas. Then peel the kiwi fruit and cut into wedges. Wash the grapes and peel back the papery casing on the physalis.

2 To make the dip, beat the soft cheese with the hazelnut yogurt, vanilla essence and sugar in a bowl. Stir in three-quarters of the hazelnuts.

3 Spoon into a glass serving dish set on a platter or into small pots on individual plates and scatter the remaining hazelnuts on top. Arrange the prepared fruits around the dip and serve immediately.

Lemon and Lime Sauce with Pancakes

THIS IS A TANGY, refreshing sauce and is a perfect foil for the pancakes.

Serves 4

INGREDIENTS

90g/3½oz/scant 1 cup plain flour
pinch of salt
1 egg
300ml/½ pint/1¼ cups milk
vegetable oil, for frying
lemon balm or mint, to decorate

For the lemon and lime sauce

1 lemon
2 limes
50g/2oz/¼ cup caster sugar
25ml/1½ tbsp arrowroot
300ml/½ pint/1¼ cups water

1 First, make the sauce. Using a citrus zester, peel the rinds thinly from the lemon and limes taking care not to cut into the pith. Squeeze the juice from the fruit. Place the rind in a pan, cover with water and bring to the boil.

2 Drain through a sieve and reserve the rind.

3 In a small bowl, mix a little sugar with the arrowroot. Blend in enough water to give a smooth paste. Heat the remaining water, pour in the arrowroot mixture, and stir continuously until the sauce boils and thickens. Stir in the remaining sugar, citrus juice and reserved rind. Keep the sauce hot while you make the pancakes.

4 Sift the dry ingredients into a bowl and make a well in the centre. Add the egg and beat in with a wooden spoon. Beat in the milk, drawing in the flour to make a smooth batter.

5 Heat a little oil in a large, heavy-based frying pan. When hot, pour in a thin layer of batter and cook for 1–2 minutes, or until set. Toss the pancake and cook the other side until golden brown. Transfer the pancake to a plate and keep it warm while you make the rest of the pancakes.

6 Serve with the hot sauce and decorate with lemon balm or mint.

Butterscotch Sauce with Waffles

THIS IS A DELICIOUSLY sweet sauce which will be loved by everyone.

Serves 4–6

INGREDIENTS

1 pack ready-made waffles
vanilla ice cream, to serve

For the butterscotch sauce

75g/3oz/6 tbsp butter
175g/6oz/¾ cup dark muscovado sugar
175ml/6fl oz/¾ cup evaporated milk
50g/2oz/⅓ cup hazelnuts

1 Warm the waffles in a preheated oven, according to the packet instructions, while you make the butterscotch sauce.

2 Melt the butter and sugar in a heavy-based pan, bring to the boil and boil for 2 minutes. Cool for 5 minutes.

3 Heat the evaporated milk to just below boiling point, then gradually stir into the sugar mixture. Cook over a low heat for 2 minutes, stirring the sauce frequently.

4 Spread the hazelnuts on a baking sheet and toast under a hot grill until golden brown. Tip on to a clean dish towel and rub briskly to remove the skins.

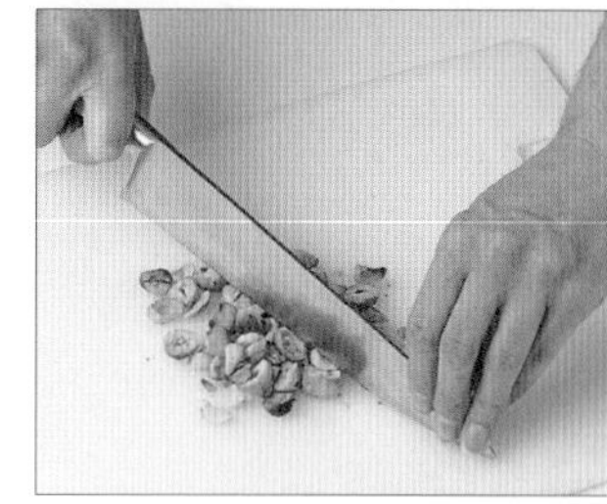

5 Chop the nuts roughly and stir into the sauce. Serve the sauce hot, poured over scoops of vanilla ice cream and the warm waffles.

VARIATION

Substitute any nut for the hazelnuts. Pecans, for example, add a luxurious flavour. You could also add plump, juicy raisins and a dash of rum instead of the nuts.

Maple and Cointreau Syrup with Oranges

THE MAPLE SYRUP MAKES this one of the most delicious ways to eat an orange. For an alcohol-free version, simply omit the Cointreau or Grand Marnier.

Serves 4

INGREDIENTS

melted butter, for brushing
4 medium oranges
crème fraîche or fromage frais, to serve

For the maple and Cointreau syrup
30ml/2 tbsp maple syrup
30ml/2 tbsp Cointreau or Grand Marnier liqueur
20ml/4 tsp butter

1 Preheat the oven to 200°C/400°F/ Gas 6. Cut four double-thickness squares of baking foil, large enough to wrap each of the oranges. Brush the centre of each square of foil with plenty of melted butter.

2 Remove some shreds of orange rind, to decorate. Blanch these, dry them and set them aside.

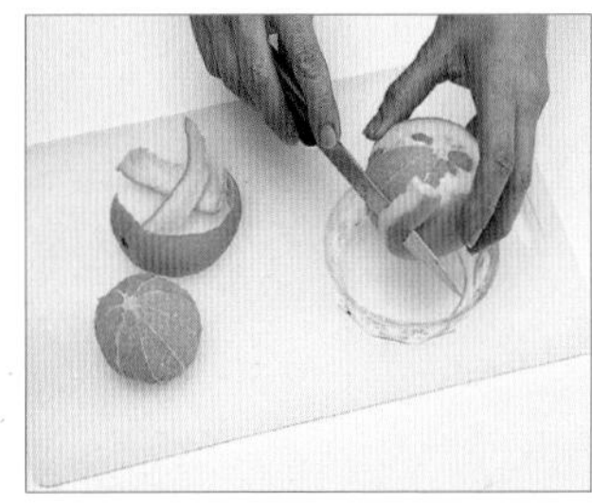

3 Peel all of the oranges, removing all the white pith and catching the juice in a bowl.

4 Slice each of the oranges crossways into thick slices. Reassemble the slices and place each stack on a square of double thickness baking foil.

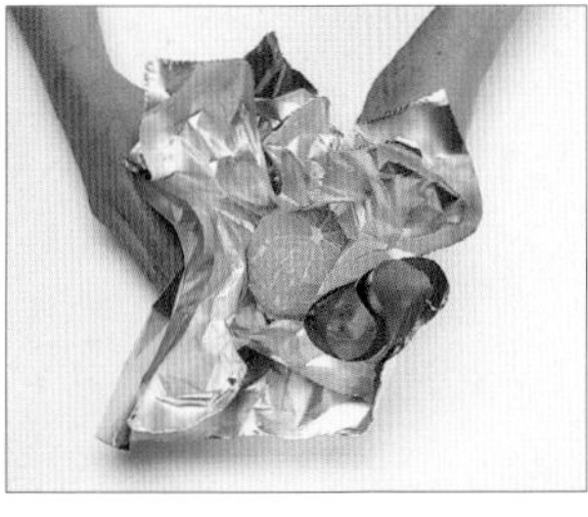

5 Tuck the baking foil up securely around the reassembled oranges to keep them in shape, leaving the foil parcels open at the top.

6 To make the syrup, mix together the reserved orange juice, maple syrup and liqueur and spoon the mixture over the oranges.

7 Add a knob of butter to each parcel and close the foil at the top to seal in the juices. Place the parcels in the oven for 10–12 minutes, or until hot. (The parcels can also be cooked on a hot barbecue, if liked.) Serve with crème fraîche or fromage frais, topped with the reserved shreds of orange rind.

Hot Plum Sauce with Floating Islands

THE PLUM SAUCE CAN be made in advance, then reheated just before you cook the meringues. This makes an unusual, and healthy pudding that is simpler to make than it looks.

Serves 4

INGREDIENTS

2 egg whites
30ml/2 tbsp concentrated apple juice syrup
freshly grated nutmeg

For the hot plum sauce

450g/1lb red plums
300ml/½ pint/1¼ cups apple juice

1 To make the plum sauce, halve the plums and remove the stones. Place them in a wide saucepan, with the apple juice.

2 Bring to the boil and then cover with a lid and leave to simmer gently for 15-20 minutes, or until the plums are tender.

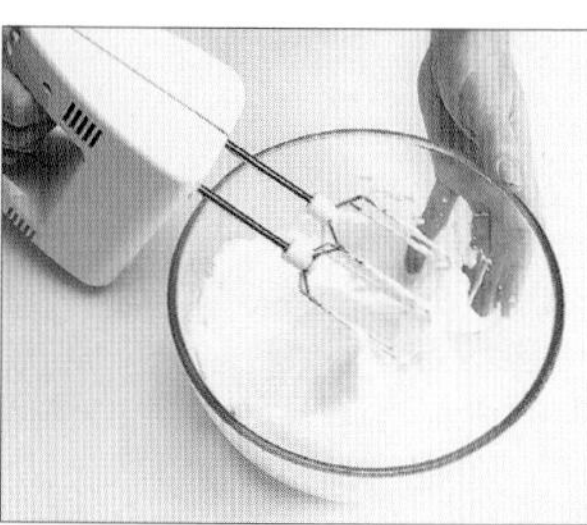

3 Meanwhile, place the egg whites in a clean, dry bowl and whisk them until they hold soft peaks.

4 Gradually whisk in the apple juice syrup, whisking until the meringue holds fairly firm peaks.

5 Using a tablespoon, scoop the meringue mixture into the gently simmering plum sauce. You may need to cook the "islands" in two batches.

6 Cover and allow to simmer gently for 2–3 minutes, or until the meringues are just set.

7 Serve the pudding straight away, sprinkled with a little freshly grated nutmeg.

Real Custard with Castle Puddings

THIS TRADITIONAL PUDDING is served with one of the most traditional sweet sauces – a really creamy vanilla custard.

Serves 4

INGREDIENTS

about 45ml/3 tbsp berry jam
115g/4oz/½ cup butter
115g/4oz/generous ½ cup caster sugar
2 eggs, beaten
few drops of vanilla essence
130g/4½oz/generous 1 cup self-raising flour

For the real custard
4 eggs
25–30ml/1½–2 tbsp sugar
450ml/¾ pint/scant 2 cups milk
few drops of vanilla essence

1 Preheat the oven to 180°C/350°F/Gas 4. Butter four dariole moulds. Put about 10ml/2 tsp jam in the base of each mould.

2 Beat the butter and sugar together until light and fluffy, then gradually beat in the eggs, beating well after each addition and adding the vanilla essence towards the end.

3 Lightly fold in the flour, then divide the mixture among the moulds.

4 Bake the puddings in the oven for about 20 minutes until well risen and a light golden colour.

5 Meanwhile, make the custard. Whisk the eggs and sugar together. Bring the milk to the boil in a heavy saucepan, preferably non-stick, then slowly pour on to the sweetened egg mixture, stirring constantly.

6 Return the milk and egg mixture to the pan and heat very gently, stirring, until the mixture thickens enough to coat the back of a spoon; do not allow to boil. Stir in the vanilla essence. Cover the pan and remove from the heat.

7 Remove the moulds from the oven, leave to stand for a few minutes, then turn the puddings on to warmed plates and serve with the hot custard.

COOK'S TIPS

- *If you prefer, instead of baking the puddings, you can cover and steam them for 30–40 minutes.*
- *If you do not have dariole moulds, use ramekin dishes.*
- *Make sure you buy real vanilla essence and not the artificial flavouring. You will only need a drop or two.*

Toffee Sauce with Hot Date Puddings

THIS TOFFEE SAUCE IS A great standby for hot or cold desserts. It is equally delicious served with poached apple or pear slices, spooned over ice cream or drizzled over a hot steamed pudding.

Serves 6

INGREDIENTS

50g/2oz/¼ cup butter, softened
75g/3oz/6 tbsp light muscovado sugar
2 eggs, beaten
115g/4oz/1 cup self-raising flour
2.5ml/½ tsp bicarbonate of soda
175g/6oz/generous 1 cup fresh dates, peeled, stoned and chopped
75ml/5 tbsp boiling water
10ml/2 tsp coffee and chicory essence

For the toffee sauce

75g/3oz/6 tbsp light muscovado sugar
50g/2oz/¼ cup butter
60ml/4 tbsp double cream
30ml/2 tbsp brandy

1 Preheat the oven to 180°C/350°F/Gas 4. Place a baking sheet in the oven to heat up. Grease six individual pudding moulds or tins.

2 Cream the butter and sugar in a large mixing bowl until pale and fluffy. Gradually add the beaten eggs a little at a time, beating well after each addition.

3 Sift the flour and bicarbonate of soda together and fold into the creamed mixture.

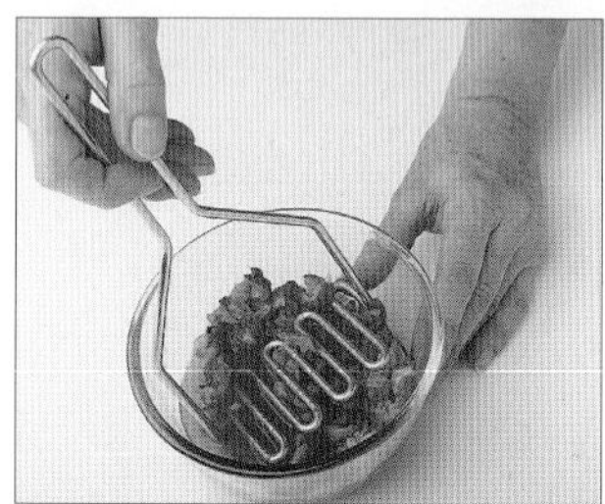

4 Put the dates in a heatproof bowl, pour over the boiling water and mash with a potato masher. Add the coffee and chicory essence, then stir the paste into the creamed mixture.

COOK'S TIP

It is preferable to peel the dates as the skins can be rather tough: simply squeeze them between your thumb and forefinger and the skins will pop off.

5 Spoon the mixture into the prepared moulds or tins. Place on the hot baking sheet and bake for 20 minutes.

6 To make the toffee sauce, put all the ingredients in a pan and heat gently, stirring until smooth.

7 Increase the heat and boil for 1 minute. Turn the warm puddings out on to individual dessert plates. Spoon a generous amount of sauce over each and serve at once.

Banana Sauce with Chocolate Cinnamon Cake

THIS CREAMY BANANA SAUCE makes a simple chocolate cake into a really luxurious dessert that is suitable for any special occasion.

Serves 6

INGREDIENTS

90g/3½oz/7 tbsp unsalted butter, at room temperature, plus extra for greasing
115g/4oz plain chocolate, finely chopped
15ml/1 tbsp instant coffee powder
5 eggs, separated
200g/7oz/1 cup granulated sugar
115g/4oz/1 cup plain flour
10ml/2 tsp ground cinnamon

For the banana sauce
4 ripe bananas
50g/2oz/¼ cup light muscovado sugar
15ml/1 tbsp fresh lemon juice
175ml/6fl oz/¾ cup whipping cream
15ml/1 tbsp rum (optional)

1 Preheat the oven to 180°C/350°F/ Gas 4. Grease a 20cm/8in round cake tin.

2 Combine the chocolate and butter in a heatproof bowl set over hot water or in the top of a double boiler. Stir until melted. Remove from the heat and stir in the coffee. Set aside.

3 Beat the egg yolks together with the granulated sugar until thick and lemon-coloured. Add the chocolate mixture and beat on low speed just to blend evenly.

4 Sift together the flour and ground cinnamon into a bowl. In another bowl, beat the egg whites until they hold stiff peaks.

5 Fold a dollop of whites into the chocolate mixture to lighten it. Fold in the remaining whites in three batches, alternating with the sifted flour.

6 Pour the cake mixture into the prepared tin.

7 Bake the cake for 40–50 minutes, or until a skewer inserted in the centre comes out clean. Turn out the cake on to a wire rack.

8 Meanwhile, make the sauce. Preheat the grill. Slice the bananas into a shallow, heatproof dish. Add the muscovado sugar and lemon juice and stir to blend. Place under the grill and cook, stirring occasionally, for about 8 minutes, or until the sugar is caramelized and bubbling.

9 Transfer the bananas to a bowl and mash with a fork until almost smooth. Stir in the cream and rum, if using. Cut the chocolate cake into slices and serve it warm, with the banana sauce.

VARIATION

For a special occasion, top the cake slices with a scoop of ice cream (rum and raisin, chocolate or vanilla) before adding the sauce. With this addition, the dessert will serve at least 8.

Berry Sauce with Baked Ricotta Cakes

THE FLAVOUR OF THIS fragrant fruity sauce contrasts well with these honey and vanilla-flavoured desserts.

Serves 4

INGREDIENTS

250g/9oz/generous 1 cup ricotta cheese
2 egg whites, beaten
about 60ml/4 tbsp clear honey
few drops of vanilla essence
fresh mint leaves, to decorate (optional)

For the red berry sauce

450g/1lb/4 cups mixed fresh or frozen fruit, such as strawberries, raspberries, blackberries and cherries

COOK'S TIPS

- *The sauce can be made a day ahead. Chill until ready to use.*
- *Frozen fruit doesn't need extra water, as there will be ice crystals clinging to the berries.*

1 Preheat the oven to 180°C/350°F/ Gas 4.

2 Place the ricotta cheese in a bowl and break it up with a wooden spoon. Add the beaten egg whites, honey and vanilla essence and mix thoroughly until the mixture is smooth and well combined.

3 Lightly grease four ramekins. Spoon the ricotta mixture into the prepared ramekins and level the tops. Bake for 20 minutes or until the ricotta cakes are risen and golden.

4 Meanwhile, make the berry sauce. Reserve about a quarter of the fruit for decoration. Place the rest of the fruit in a saucepan, with a little water if the fruit is fresh, and heat gently until softened. Leave to cool slightly, remove any cherry stones, if using cherries.

5 Press the fruit through a sieve, then taste and sweeten with honey if it is too tart. Serve the sauce, warm or cold, with the ricotta cakes. Decorate with the reserved berries and mint leaves, if using.

Calvados and Chocolate Sauce with Iced Pear Terrine

THIS RICH CHOCOLATE SAUCE would complement vanilla ice cream for a simpler dessert.

Serves 8

INGREDIENTS

1.3–1.6kg/3–3½lb ripe William's pears
juice of 1 lemon
115g/4oz/generous ½ cup caster sugar
10 whole cloves
julienne strips of orange rind, to decorate

For the Calvados and chocolate sauce
200g/7oz plain chocolate
60ml/4 tbsp hot strong black coffee
200ml/7fl oz/scant 1 cup double cream
30ml/2 tbsp Calvados or brandy

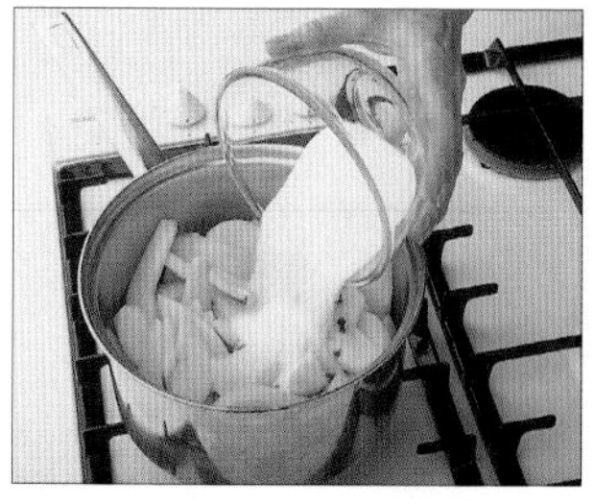

1 Peel, core and slice the pears. Place in a pan with the lemon juice, sugar, cloves and 90ml/6 tbsp water. Cover and simmer for 10 minutes. Remove the cloves. Allow to cool.

2 Process the pears with their juice and pour the purée into a freezer-proof bowl. Cover and freeze until firm.

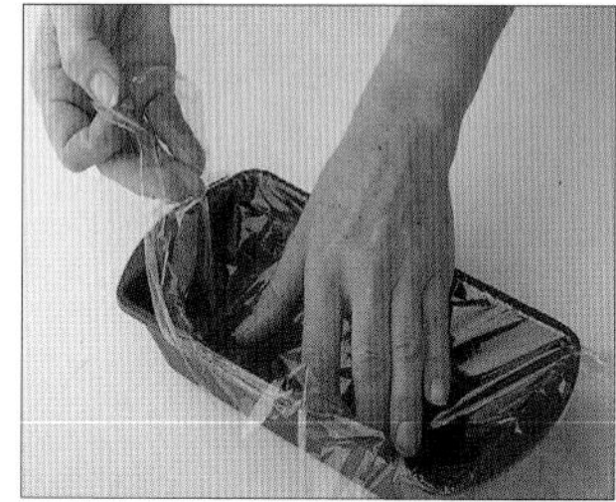

3 Line a 900g/2lb loaf tin with clear film. Allow the film to overhang the sides of the tin. Remove the frozen pear purée from the freezer and spoon it into a food processor. Process until smooth. Pour into the prepared tin, cover and freeze until firm.

4 To make the sauce, break the chocolate into a large, heatproof bowl. Place the bowl over a saucepan of hot water and allow to melt.

5 Stir the coffee into the melted chocolate until smooth. Gradually stir in the cream and then the Calvados or brandy. Set aside.

6 About 20 minutes before serving, remove the tin from the freezer. Invert the terrine on to a plate, lift off the clear film and place the terrine in the fridge to soften slightly. Warm the sauce over hot water.

7 Place a slice of terrine on to each dessert plate and spoon over some of the sauce. Decorate with julienne strips of orange rind and serve at once.

COOK'S TIP

This is a good dish to prepare in advance for a dinner party, as the terrine will store successfully for a month in the freezer, but remember to remove it in time to soften slightly before serving.

Mexican Hot Fudge Sauce with Sundaes

DEFINITELY NOT ONE FOR dieters, but best kept for those special, indulgent days!

Serves 4

INGREDIENTS

600ml/1 pint/2½ cups vanilla ice cream
600ml/1 pint/2½ cups coffee ice cream
2 large ripe bananas, sliced
whipped cream
toasted sliced almonds

For the hot fudge sauce

60ml/4 tbsp light muscovado sugar
115g/4oz/⅓ cup golden syrup
45ml/3 tbsp strong black coffee
5ml/1 tsp ground cinnamon
150g/5oz plain dark chocolate, broken up
75ml/5 tbsp whipping cream
45ml/3 tbsp coffee liqueur (optional)

1 For the sauce, combine the sugar, golden syrup, coffee and cinnamon in a heavy saucepan. Bring to the boil. Boil the mixture, stirring constantly, for about 5 minutes.

COOK'S TIP

Use a good quality, plain dark chocolate with at least 70% cocoa solids.

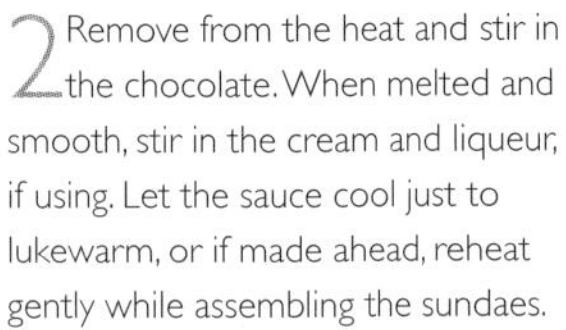

2 Remove from the heat and stir in the chocolate. When melted and smooth, stir in the cream and liqueur, if using. Let the sauce cool just to lukewarm, or if made ahead, reheat gently while assembling the sundaes.

3 Using an ice-cream scoop, fill the sundae dishes with 1 scoop each of vanilla and coffee ice cream.

4 Arrange the bananas on the top of each dish. Pour the warm sauce over the bananas.

5 Top each sundae with a generous rosette of whipped cream. Top with the toasted almonds and serve immediately.

Sabayon Sauce

THIS FROTHY SAUCE is very versatile and can be served alone with light dessert biscuits or hot over cake, fruit or even ice cream. Never let the sauce stand before serving, as it will collapse.

Serves 4–6

INGREDIENTS

1 egg
2 egg yolks
75g/3oz/scant ½ cup caster sugar
150ml/¼ pint/⅔ cup Marsala or other sweet white wine
finely grated rind and juice of 1 lemon
dessert biscuits, to serve

1 Put the egg, yolks and sugar into a medium bowl and whisk until they are pale and thick.

2 Stand the bowl over a saucepan of hot, but not boiling, water. Gradually add the Marsala or white wine and lemon juice, a little at a time, whisking vigorously.

3 Continue whisking until it is thick enough to leave a trail.

COOK'S TIP

A generous pinch of arrowroot whisked together with the egg yolks and sugar will prevent the sauce collapsing too quickly.

4 To serve the sabayon cold, place it over a bowl of iced water and continue whisking until chilled. Add the finely grated lemon rind and stir in. Pour into small glasses and serve at once, with the dessert biscuits.

Chocolate Sauce with Profiteroles

A REAL TREAT IF you're not counting calories, this sauce is also good with scoops of vanilla ice cream.

Serves 6

INGREDIENTS

65g/2½oz/9 tbsp plain flour
50g/2oz/¼ cup butter
150ml/¼ pint/⅔ cup water
2 eggs, lightly beaten
150ml/¼ pint/⅔ cup whipping cream, whipped

For the chocolate sauce

150ml/¼ pint/⅔ cup double cream
50g/2oz/¼ cup butter
50g/2oz/¼ cup vanilla sugar
175g/6oz plain chocolate
30ml/2 tbsp brandy

VARIATION

White chocolate and orange sauce

40g/1½oz/3 tbsp caster sugar, to replace vanilla sugar
finely grated rind of 1 orange
175g/6oz white chocolate, to replace plain chocolate
30ml/2 tbsp orange liqueur, to replace brandy

1 Make the chocolate sauce. Heat the cream with the butter and vanilla sugar in a bowl over a saucepan of hot, water. Stir until smooth, then cool.

2 Break the chocolate into the cream. Stir until it is melted and thoroughly combined.

3 Stir in the brandy a little at a time, then leave the sauce to cool to room temperature.

4 For the white chocolate and orange sauce, heat the cream and butter with the caster sugar and orange rind in the top of a double boiler, until dissolved. Use the white chocolate instead of plain chocolate in step 2, and orange liqueur instead of the brandy in step 3.

5 To make the profiteroles, preheat the oven to 200°C/400°F/Gas 6. Sift the flour on to a plate. Melt the butter and water in a saucepan and bring to the boil.

6 Remove the saucepan from the heat and tip the flour in all at once. Beat with a wooden spoon until smooth. Cool for 1–2 minutes then gradually beat in enough egg to give a piping consistency. Beat well until glossy. Pipe small balls of the mixture on to dampened baking sheets.

7 Bake in the oven for 15–20 minutes, or until crisp. Make a slit in the sides and cool on a wire rack.

8 Fill a piping bag with cream and pipe some into each profiterole. Pile on to a plate, topped with a little sauce. Serve the remaining chocolate sauce separately.

Papaya Sauce with Grilled Pineapple

TRY THE PAPAYA SAUCE with savoury dishes, too. It tastes great with grilled chicken and game birds as well as pork and lamb.

Serves 6

INGREDIENTS

1 sweet pineapple
melted butter, for greasing and brushing
2 pieces drained stem ginger in syrup, cut into fine matchsticks
30ml/2 tbsp demerara sugar
pinch of ground cinnamon
30ml/2 tbsp stem ginger syrup
fresh mint sprigs, to decorate

For the papaya sauce
1 ripe papaya, peeled and seeded
175ml/6fl oz/¾ cup apple juice

1 Peel the pineapple and take spiral slices off the outside to remove the eyes. Cut it crossways into six slices, each 2.5cm/1in thick.

2 Line a baking sheet with a sheet of foil, rolling up the sides to make a rim. Grease the foil with melted butter. Preheat the grill.

VARIATION

If you like, substitute half apple juice and half papaya nectar for the apple juice in the sauce.

3 Arrange the pineapple slices on the baking sheet. Brush with butter, then top with the ginger matchsticks, sugar and cinnamon. Drizzle over the stem ginger syrup. Grill for 5–7 minutes, or until the slices are lightly charred.

4 Cut a few slices from the papaya and set aside, then purée the rest together with the apple juice in a food processor or blender.

5 Press the purée through a sieve placed over a bowl, then stir in any juices from cooking the pineapple.

6 Serve the pineapple slices with a little sauce drizzled around each plate. Decorate with the reserved papaya slices and the mint sprigs.

Nectarine Sauce with Latticed Peaches

MAKE THIS IN SUMMER when the fruits are in season, and enjoy the fresh flavour.

Serves 6

INGREDIENTS

For the pastry

115g/4oz/1 cup plain flour
45ml/3 tbsp butter or sunflower margarine
45ml/3 tbsp natural yogurt
30ml/2 tbsp orange juice
milk, for brushing

For the filling

3 ripe peaches or nectarines
45ml/3 tbsp ground almonds
30ml/2 tbsp low-fat natural yogurt
finely grated rind of 1 small orange
1.5ml/¼ tsp natural almond essence

For the nectarine sauce

1 ripe nectarine or peach
45ml/3 tbsp orange juice

1 For the pastry, sift the flour into a bowl and, using your fingertips, rub in the butter or margarine. Stir in the yogurt and orange juice to bind the mixture to a firm dough.

2 Roll out about half the pastry thinly, and use a biscuit cutter to stamp out rounds of about 7.5cm/3in in diameter, or slightly larger than the circumference of the peaches. Place on a lightly greased baking sheet.

3 Skin the peaches or nectarines, halve them and remove the stones.

4 Mix together the almonds, yogurt, orange rind and almond essence. Spoon into each peach half and place, cut side down, on to the pastry rounds.

5 Roll out the remaining pastry thinly and cut into thin strips. Arrange the strips over the peaches to form a lattice, brushing with milk to secure firmly. Trim off the ends neatly.

6 Chill in the fridge for 30 minutes. Preheat the oven to 200°C/400°F/Gas 6. Brush the tarts with milk, and bake for 15–18 minutes.

7 For the sauce, skin the nectarine or peach and remove the stone. Purée it in a food processor, with the orange juice. Serve the peaches hot, with the sauce spooned around.

COOK'S TIP

To peel peaches, blanch them in boiling water for about 30 seconds then place in iced water. The skins will slip off.

Lime and Cardamom Sauce with Bananas

THE WARM SPICY-SWEET FLAVOUR of cardamom is offset by the tang of lime in this unusual sauce.

Serves 4

INGREDIENTS

6 small bananas
25g/1oz/2 tbsp butter
vanilla ice cream, to serve

For the lime and cardamom sauce
25g/1oz/2 tbsp butter
seeds from 4 cardamom pods, crushed
50g/2oz/½ cup flaked almonds
thinly pared rind and juice of 2 limes
50g/2oz/¼ cup light muscovado sugar
30ml/2 tbsp dark rum

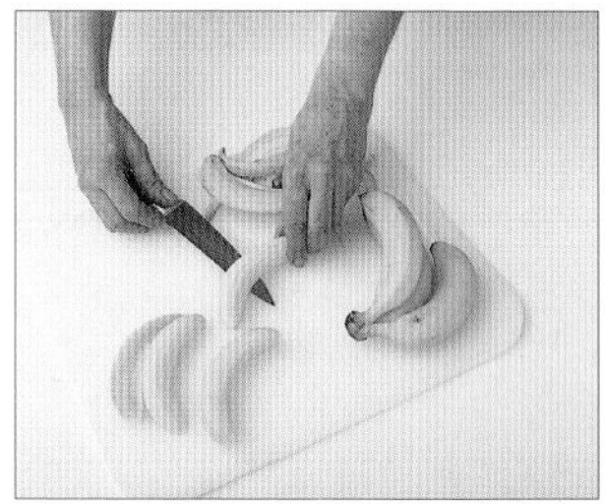

1 Peel the bananas and cut them in half lengthways. Heat the butter in a large frying pan. Add half the bananas, and cook until the undersides are golden. Turn carefully, using a fish slice.

2 As they cook, transfer the bananas to a heatproof serving dish. Cook the remaining bananas in the same way.

VARIATION

If you prefer not to use alcohol in your cooking, replace the rum with orange juice or even pineapple juice.

3 To make the lime and cardamom sauce melt the butter, then add the cardamom seeds and almonds. Cook, stirring, until golden.

4 Stir in the lime rind and juice, then the sugar. Cook, stirring, until the mixture is smooth, bubbling and slightly reduced. Stir in the rum.

5 Pour the sauce over the bananas and serve immediately, with vanilla ice cream.

COOK'S TIP

Crush the cardamom seeds in a mortar and pestle just before using, to retain their essential flavour.

Maple Yogurt Sauce with Poached Pears

THE SWEET-SOUR TASTE OF the maple syrup and yogurt will partner most poached fruit but is especially good with pears. Choose a firm but ripe pear such as Conference.

Serves 4

INGREDIENTS

4 firm dessert pears
15ml/1 tbsp lemon juice
250ml/8fl oz/1 cup sweet white wine or cider
thinly pared rind of 1 lemon
1 cinnamon stick

For the maple yogurt sauce

pear cooking liquid
30ml/2 tbsp maple syrup
2.5ml/½ tsp arrowroot
150g/5oz/⅔ cup Greek yogurt

1 Thinly peel the pears, leaving them whole and with stalks. Brush them with lemon juice, to prevent them from browning. Use a potato peeler or small knife to scoop out the core from the base of each pear.

2 Place the pears in a wide, heavy saucepan and pour the wine or cider over, with enough cold water almost to cover the pears.

3 Add the lemon rind and cinnamon stick and bring to the boil. Reduce the heat, cover the pan and simmer gently for 30–40 minutes, or until the pears are tender. Turn the pears occasionally so that they cook evenly. Lift out the pears carefully, draining them.

4 To make the sauce, bring the liquid to the boil and boil uncovered to reduce it to about 105ml/7 tbsp. Strain and add the maple syrup. Blend a little with the arrowroot. Return to the pan and cook, stirring, until thick. Cool.

5 Slice each cored pear about three-quarters of the way through, leaving the slices attached at the stem end. Fan out on a serving plate.

6 Stir 30ml/2 tbsp of the cooled syrup into the yogurt and spoon it around the pears. Drizzle with the remaining syrup and serve immediately.

VARIATION

If you want to make this sauce for another dessert, substitute fruit juice for the pear cooking liquid in step 4.

Strawberry Sauce with Lemon Hearts

This speedy sweet sauce makes a delicious accompaniment for these delicate lemon and cheese hearts.

Serves 4

INGREDIENTS

175g/6oz/¾ cup ricotta cheese
150ml/¼ pint/⅔ cup natural yogurt
15ml/1 tbsp sugar
finely grated rind of ½ lemon
30ml/2 tbsp lemon juice
10ml/2 tsp powdered gelatine
2 egg whites
oil, for greasing

For the strawberry sauce
225g/8oz/2 cups fresh or frozen and thawed strawberries, plus extra to decorate
15ml/1 tbsp lemon juice

1 Beat the ricotta until smooth. Stir in the yogurt, sugar and lemon rind.

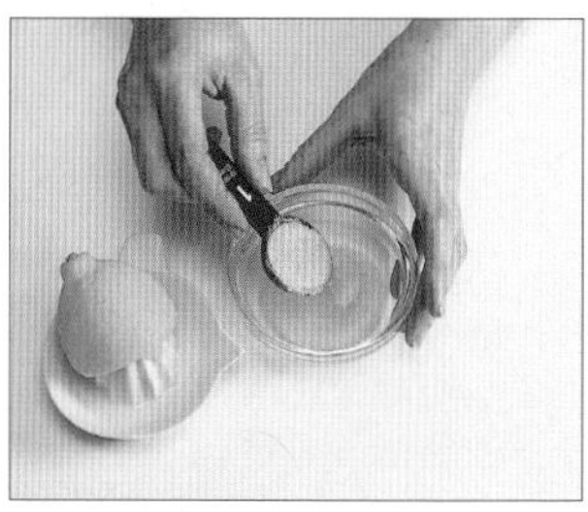

2 Place the lemon juice in a small bowl and sprinkle the gelatine over it. Place the bowl over a pan of hot water and stir the mixture to dissolve the gelatine completely.

3 Beat the egg whites until they form soft peaks. Quickly stir the gelatine into the ricotta cheese mixture, mixing it in evenly, then immediately fold in the beaten egg whites.

4 Spoon the mixture into four lightly oiled, individual heart-shaped moulds and chill the moulds until set.

5 To make the sauce, place the strawberries and lemon juice in a food processor and process until smooth. Pour on to plates and top with turned-out hearts. Decorate with the extra strawberries.

VARIATION

Add a dash of Cointreau or Grand Marnier liqueur to the strawberry sauce.

Raspberry Sauce with Baked Peaches

PEACHES AND RASPBERRIES are classic partners – a combination that's hard to beat for a sophisticated summer dessert. Fresh nectarines can also be used instead of peaches. Try this sauce with a cool slice of melon for a summer starter.

Serves 6

INGREDIENTS

45ml/3 tbsp unsalted butter, at room temperature
50g/2oz/¼ cup caster sugar
1 egg, beaten
50g/2oz/½ cup ground almonds
6 ripe peaches

For the raspberry sauce

175g/6oz/1 cup raspberries
15ml/1 tbsp icing sugar
15ml/1 tbsp fruit-flavoured brandy (optional)

1 Preheat the oven to 180°C/350°F/Gas 4. Beat the butter with the sugar until soft and fluffy. Beat in the egg. Add the ground almonds and beat just to blend well together.

2 Halve the peaches and remove the stones. With a spoon, scrape out some of the flesh from each peach half, slightly enlarging the hollow left by the stone. Reserve the excess peach flesh to use in the sauce.

3 Place the peach halves on a baking sheet (secure with crumpled foil to keep them steady). Fill the hollow in each peach half with the butter and almond mixture.

4 Bake for about 30 minutes, or until the almond filling is puffed and golden and the peaches are very tender.

5 For the sauce, combine all the ingredients in a food processor or blender. Add the reserved peach flesh. Process until smooth. Press through a strainer set over a bowl to remove fibres and seeds.

6 Let the peaches cool. Place two halves on each plate and spoon the sauce over. Serve immediately.

Index

Acknowledgements

Thanks to the following photographers:
Karl Adamson, Edward Allwright, David Armstrong, Steve Baxter, James Duncan, John Freeman, Michelle Garrett, John Heseltine, Amanda Heywood, Janine Hosegood, Don Last, Michael Michaels, Patrick McLeavy, Thomas Odulate, Debbie Patterson, Juliet Piddington and William Lingwood.

Recipes by: Alex Barker, Angela Boggiano, Carla Capalbo, Jacqueline Clark, Carole Clements, Roz Denny, Nicola Diggins, Tessa Evelegh, Joanna Farrow, Christine France, Silvana Franco, Shirley Gill, Nicola Graimes, Juliet Harbutt, Christine Ingram, Peter Jordan, Soheila Kimberley, Ruby Le Bois, Lesley Macklay, Sue Maggs, Maggie Mayhew, Sallie Morries, Janice Murfitt, Maggie Pannell, Louise Pickford, Katherine Richmond, Laura Washburn, Steven Wheeler, Kate Whiteman and Jeni Wright.

NOTES

NOTES

Notes

Notes

Notes

Notes

Notes

NOTES